Jewelrymaking through History

Recent Titles in
Handicrafts through World History

Needlework through History: An Encyclopedia
Catherine Leslie

JEWELRYMAKING THROUGH HISTORY

An Encyclopedia

Rayner W. Hesse, Jr.

GREENWOOD PRESS

Westport, Connecticut • London

Library of Congress Cataloging-in-Publication Data

Hesse, Rayner W.

   Jewelrymaking through history : an encyclopedia / Rayner W. Hesse, Jr.

     p. cm. — (Handicrafts through world history, ISSN 1552–8952)

   Includes bibliographical references and index.

   ISBN-13: 978–0–313–33507–5 (alk. paper)

   ISBN-10: 0–313–33507–9 (alk. paper)

   1. Handicraft—Encyclopedias. 2. Handicraft—History. I. Title.

   TT9.H47   2007

   745.594'203—dc22   2007003658

British Library Cataloguing in Publication Data is available.

Library of Congress Catalog Card Number: 2007003658

ISBN-13: 978–0–313–33507–5

ISBN-10: 0–313–33507–9

ISSN: 1552–8952

First published in 2007

Greenwood Press, 88 Post Road West, Westport, CT 06881

An imprint of Greenwood Publishing Group, Inc.

www.greenwood.com

Printed in the United States of America

The paper used in this book complies with the
Permanent Paper Standard issued by the National
Information Standards Organization (Z39.48–1984).

10 9 8 7 6 5 4 3 2 1

Every reasonable effort has been made to trace the owners of copyright materials in this book,
but in some instances this has proven impossible. The author and publisher will be glad to
receive information leading to a more complete acknowledgments in subsequent printings of
the book and in the meantime extend their apologies for any omissions.

Contents

List of Entries

Acknowledgments

The writing of this book took place over a period of two years and was accomplished with the aid of friends and colleagues. Many thanks to Anthony Chiffolo for his help in proofreading and his willingness to take photos of the many jewelry items; and to Peter Smith, who seemed to have a sample of just about every item I needed to write about. Thanks also to Irene Schindler for her advice and to Debra Adams at Greenwood for her patience and help in bringing this volume to fruition.

The author and publisher gratefully acknowledge permission to reprint the following:

"Birthstones" epigraph by Mephistopheles. "Birthstones." http://www. oedilf.com

"Body Piercing," "Buttons," "Coins," and "Settings" epigraphs used by permission of Memory Lane: Antiques and Collectibles, Hartsdale, NY.

"Costume Jewelry" epigraph from *The Secret Life of Salvador Dalí*, chapter 4, used by permission of Dover Publications.

"Cuts" epigraph from *Death of a Salesman* by Arthur Miller, copyright 1949, renewed © 1977 by Arthur Miller. Used by permission of Viking Penguin, a division of Penguin Group (USA) Inc.

"Grading (Diamonds)" epigraph used by permission of The Diamond Registry Inc. at www.DiamondRegistry.com

"Hallmark" definition by permission. From the Merriam-Webster Online Dictionary © 2006 by Merriam-Webster Inc. (www.Merriam-Webster.com)

Eric Hatch quote in "Hatpins" courtesy of Harold Ober Associates.

"Karats" epigraph by Victor Kandampully. "Carat." http://www.oedilf.com

Quote in "Necessaries" entry from "Fabergé's Labor of Love: A Case of Cherchez la Femme," by Constance Bond. Used by permission of the author.

"Plastics" epigraph used by permission of Wilson Arts International of Temple, TX, courtesy of Grace Jeffers, decorative arts historian.

"Rings" epigraph used by permission of the Liberace Foundation of the Performing and Creative Arts. The mission of the Liberace Foundation is to help talented students pursue careers in the performing and creative arts through scholarship assistance.

"Souvenir" definition copyright © 2006 by Houghton Mifflin Company. Adapted and reproduced by permission from *The American Heritage Dictionary of the English Language, Fourth Edition.*

"Wood Jewelry" epigraph used by permission of author, Wayne P. Armstrong, from his site at http://waynesword.palomar.edu/ww0901.htm

Scriptures marked as "(CEV)" are taken from the Contemporary English Version. Copyright © 1995 by American Bible Society.

Scriptures marked as "(NKJV)" are taken from the New King James Version. Copyright © 1982 by Thomas Nelson, Inc.

Abbreviations

B.C.E.	Before the Common Era (known in some texts as B.C.)
C.E.	Common Era (known in some texts as A.D.)
CFW	Cultured freshwater pearls
Ct.	Carat (used in weighing gemstones)
Kt.	Karat (used with gold)
LGBTQ	Lesbian/Gay/Bisexual/Transgendered/Questioning
M.O.P.	Mother-of-pearl
TCW	Total carat weight

Introduction

Though it was not clear at first, two years into the writing of this book it became apparent that to attempt to write a history of jewelrymaking and jewelrycrafting throughout history was more than a daunting task: It was, in short, a near-impossible challenge. At first it seemed as though the history of jewelry could be confined to the last 5,000 years or so, and to be sure, a good part of what we know about body adornment and fashion falls within these parameters. But astoundingly, it seems that our human ancestors have been fascinated with stringing shells and seeds and other parts of nature to decorate the body going back as far as 100,000 years! One hundred thousand years of jewelrymaking? That was not the book I set out to write.

With this new challenge came good news and bad news. The good news is that a major portion of jewelry history, about 90,000 years or so, has only begun to be discussed among paleontologists, botanists, and other interested parties in the past few years. Hence, the writer cannot worry about constructing a complete history of what has yet to be uncovered and explored. However, the bad news is that these new discoveries obliterate the assumptions and fact-finding, not to mention the starting points, of most jewelry histories written in the past 50 years. In other words, it was most difficult to find texts on jewelrycrafting that were up-to-date and that considered alternate theories of jewelry origins.

A point in fact: A history of jewelry throughout the millennia should seek to adopt a worldwide view on the crafting abilities and interests of all peoples. Sadly, most current texts examine jewelry's rich history through an almost completely Eurocentric lens, ignoring the contributions of natives from other continents, particularly Asia, Africa, South America, and Australia. To learn what was happening in these parts of the world required in-depth research on many Web sites and in several languages. It was nearly impossible to locate survey histories of jewelrycrafting that did not begin in ancient Rome, Egypt, Greece, or some portion of the Middle East. Yet the peoples of China, Japan, and India, the aborigines of Australia, most African tribes, and all the Native American peoples have a rich jewelry heritage. Though it is only a start, it is my hope that through this volume some light has been shed on the crafting abilities of these nations and peoples as well.

Of course, having just offered a critique, I am only too aware of the difficulty of any book to be comprehensive, and there are choices and pathways that take the writer on some journeys while at the same moment ignoring other trips that the reader might find helpful. For my part, I would have liked to have spent more time in the Middle Ages, an era where I believe that the greatest appreciation of jewelry as adornment versus fashion began to be worked out. I suspect also that the ancient Etruscans had a greater appreciation of costume and self-presentation than is generally credited to them; in a Europe long dominated by Greco-Roman influences, it can be difficult to project one's own voice.

There are a few personalities who stand out in all of this history, names that transcend eras and styles, trends and the fickleness of politics and fashion. King Louis XVI of France and his beleaguered wife, Marie Antoinette; Queen Victoria and Queen Elizabeth I of England; Peter Carl Fabergé, René Lalique, Louis Comfort Tiffany, and the House of Cartier; Hattie Carnegie and Coco Chanel; King Tut and Napoleon Bonaparte show up time and again, which causes one to appreciate not only raw talent, but the effect of the political process on how the making of jewelry came to be such an important craft over these many years.

Jewelrymaking through History is set up as a reader's and researcher's glossary, a kind of A–Z reference book, with short entries about the craft of jewelrymaking. Wherever available, books and other texts in print that spoke of the cultural history of specific eras and peoples, as well as crafting (jewelrymaking in particular) were used as source materials for this book. However, much of the information regarding the latest tools, techniques, availability of materials, and new trends was simply not to be found in current jewelry books in print; therefore, reliable and well-established Internet sources were also used in a manner that hopefully encourages the reader to check out the wealth of jewelrymaking knowledge that is available at one's fingertips. A timeline has been provided to give a sense of some of the major (and minor) contributions of jewelry and jewelrymaking in our history. Information regarding crafting prior to the seventeenth century[1] is worked into each relevant entry (for instance, what was happening in ancient Greece, or among the Vikings, or in Renaissance Europe).

The 63 categories chosen as entries include a look at most precious metals used in jewelrymaking; major jewelry trends from the Georgian era through the Retro period of the twentieth century; gemstones and jewelry markings/terminology; a head-to-foot look at body adornment, from toe rings to hair adornments; jewelrymaking materials; and finally, miscellaneous categories that seemed both relevant, interesting, and fun. Many of these entries are further subdivided when a more detailed explanation was merited. Each entry also contains either a quote about jewelry, to help provide a literary context, or an information box that sets forth at a glance the most pertinent details regarding the entry. At the end of each entry, the reader will find a "Did You Know?" that highlights some aspect of the history of jewelrycrafting and/or provides entertaining trivia about jewelry in general. There are also a wide variety of pictures and illustrations that further illuminate the text.

NOTE

1. There are a few exceptions: It seemed convenient to combine Gothic and Neo-Gothic jewelry into one category; and the entry on Celtic jewelry covers a wide time span. However, among younger jewelry afficionados today, both of these categories appear to have a broad interest and so have been given separate entries in the book.

Timeline

Most dates are approximations. The more culturally inclusive terms B.C.E. (Before the Common Era) and C.E. (Common Era) are used in place of the traditional B.C. and A.D.

B.C.E.

98,000	In Africa, first beads are strung for wearing, made out of shells, carved pieces of animal bone, minute stones, and seeds.
18,000	In China, necklaces made of ostrich eggshells are polished, drilled, and strung on sinew for wearing.
8700	Some of the first copper jewelry is made in the ancient Middle East.
5000	Cameos of great artistry are first made in ancient Greece.
4000	Mother-of-pearl is used in Egypt as decoration on jewelry and furniture items.
3500	Nickel is first used in the countries of the Middle East.
3100	First Egyptian dynasty comes to power.
3000	Ötzi the Iceman dies in Austria; his frozen body is discovered 5,000 years later and shows evidence of ear piercing with earplugs, the earliest recorded body piercing.
	Celtic tribes make jewelry of stone as body adornments.
	Glass-type glaze is first used on vessels and jewelry.
	Thread, textiles, and thimbles come into common usage.
	Egyptians wear rings with scarabs attached as amulets or signets.
2500	China begins to refine silver for use in jewelry and other products.
2000	Anklets are first worn by Persian women.
	Buttons are first used in Southeast Asia's Indus Valley.

1900	Assyrian empire comes of age, lasts until 627.
1552	The Egyptian Eber Papyrus extols the healing properties of wearing copper.
1333	Beginning of reign of King Tut of Egypt.
1200	Gold containing traces of platinum is first imported into Egypt from neighboring Nubia.
1000	China uses brass to make pierced coinage, which is worn around the neck or on the wrist for easy transport.
	In the Americas, the Incas begin to use platinum in their jewelry and adornments.
700	Theban high-priestess Shepenupet dies and is buried in a sarcophagus that features gold and platinum hieroglyphics.
650	Middle-Eastern kingdom of Lydia mints some of the first-known coinage, made of gold and silver.
600	Native Americans learn to mine local deposits of copper.
333	Snake and gemstone rings are popular among the Greeks.
300	Jade necklaces are worn by the Yelang people of southwestern China; men and women of the Mauryan and Sunga eras of India's history wear necklaces as part of daily costume.
200	The necktie appears on the fashion scene in ancient Rome and pre-Common Era China.
30	Invention of the blow-pipe revolutionizes glassmaking.
C.E.	
30	Ancient Greek, Roman, and Egyptian civilizations express themselves with uniquely identifiable jewelry creations; however, the wearing of jewelry is mostly confined to the wealthy and upper classes.
680	Sixth Ecumenical Council rules that all representations of Christ must include the entire corpus; from then on crucifixes are worn in place of plain crosses.
1074	First recorded use of pewter in Western history.
1160	Crosses first appear at the end of rosary beads.
1200	Buttons and buttonholes are used together for first time.
1270	Venetian glassmaking industry is moved to the island of Murano, establishing it as one of the primary sites for glass production in the world.
1300	Modern diamond trade establishes itself in Vienna, and from there expands to the Benelux countries.
1350	Gothic era of jewelrycrafting begins; continues to the sixteenth century in Europe.

1363	Statute of England's Edward III forbids "craftsmen and yeoman (and their wives and children) to wear gold or silver jewelry"; also denies knights "the right to wear rings and brooches made of gold or studded with precious stones".
1368	Start of the Ming dynasty in China; height of folding fan fashion in China.
1477	Diamond wedding rings come into fashion in Europe.
1500	The Spanish "discover" silver in the Americas.
1510	Nürnberg locksmith Peter Henlein invents the prototype for the first watch.
1538	Table diamond cut introduced in Europe, succeeding the point cut, one of the earliest known diamond cuts.
1660	The Grand Tour is initiated in Europe for the wealthy and upper class as a kind of finishing school; many travelers bring home souvenir pieces, particularly jewelry, from places visited.
1700	Christopher Pinchbeck, a London clockmaker, alloys copper and zinc in a way that resembles gold; the new element is named for him.
1714	Beginning of the Georgian era in jewelrycrafting, which lasts until the start of the Victorian era in 1837.
1720	The *étui* is in fashion in Europe to carry all one's "necessaries".
1726	Diamonds are discovered in Brazil.
1728	English factoryowner Matthew Boulton is born; goes on to be the major purveyor of cut steel in his day.
1741	English chemist Charles Wood independently isolates platinum in the laboratory.
1746	German chemist Andreas Marggraf is credited with the "discovery" of zinc.
1751	Swedish chemist Axel Fredrik Cronstedt "discovers" nickel.
	Swedish chemist Theophil Scheffer designates platinum a "precious metal".
1759	Enoch Noyes and William Cleland launch an entire cottage industry of combmaking in Massachusetts, using cattle horn.
1770	Swiss watchmaker Abraham-Louis Perrelet invents the self-winding watch.
1783	José and Fausto Elhuyar of Spain "discover" tungsten.
1789	French Revolution takes place; King Louis XVI and his bride, Marie Antoinette, are executed; major fashion trends change with her death.
1791	Titanium "discovered" by (The Rev.) George William Gregor at Creed in Cornwall, England.

1795	Marc-Étienne Janety, jeweler to the late King of France, Louis XVI, returns home to create the prototype from platinum for standard metric kilogram.
1796	Berlin Iron Work jewelry comes to market, but is so fine and difficult to produce that it disappears by 1850.
1798	"18k" first used to mark gold in England.
1800	J. F. Voigtlander introduces the monocle in England.
1802	Abel Porter opens the first buttonmaking company in the United States; first shank button is used on clothing.
1803	English chemist W. H. Wollaston "discovers" palladium in London and finds a way to make platinum malleable for wider usage.
1804	Wollaston "discovers" rhodium.
1805	Napoleon founds a school of stonecarving in France to promote the production of cameos; Pope Leo XII sponsors a school for cameo engraving in Rome.
	Luigi V. Brugnatelli invents the process of electroplating silver and other metals.
1812	Mohs scale of mineral hardness is established by German mineralogist Frederich Mohs.
1817	German chemist Friedrich Strohmeyer is credited with the "discovery" of cadmium.
1825	Danish physicist and chemist Hans Christian Ørsted "discovers" aluminum.
1827	Hannah Lord Montague of Troy, New York, invents removable shirt collars; the collar button industry is born.
1837	Queen Victoria of England comes to the throne, which is the start of the Victorian era in jewelrycrafting.
1838	Bon Marché, the first department store, opens in Paris.
1840	Discovery of ruins at ancient Nineveh launches the Assyrian Revival Movement in jewelrycrafting.
	First porcelain button made for U.S. garment market.
	Gold and silver electroplating begins.
1848	Gold is "discovered" in California, igniting a major gold rush; gold is then "discovered" a year later in Alaska, meaning more prospectors head to the West and Northwest to try their hand at panning.
1849	Opals are "discovered" in Australia.
	U.S. inventor Walter Hunt creates the safety pin.
1850	Waltham Watch Company begins to mass-produce watches in the United States, followed by Elgin in 1864 and Hamilton in 1892.
1851	The Great Exhibition of London opens, showcasing new jewelry incorporating Assyrian designs.

1853	Navajo/Black Sheep artisan Atsidi Sani crafts his first silver jewelry pieces and then begins to teach other Native American peoples the jewelrymaking trade.
1854	"9k," "12k," "15k" marked on English gold pieces for the first time due to Stamp Act.
1855	Henry Bessemer of Sheffield, England, develops the method to mass-produce steel.
1859	Silver is "discovered" at the Comstock Lode in Virginia City, Nevada, setting off a large-scale silver rush.
1860	René Lalique, said to be the inventor of costume jewelry, is born.
1867	Diamonds are "discovered" in South Africa.
1869	Celluloid is invented by U.S. chemist John Wesley Hyatt as a substitute for ivory in billiard balls.
1870	Arts and Crafts Movement is born in England, continues to 1900.
	Plain gold bangle bracelets come into fashion.
	Multicolored gold is developed.
1875	Art Nouveau era is born, continues to 1919.
1886	Tiffany and Company introduces its own version of the popular claw setting for diamonds (using six prongs); it is henceforth called the "Tiffany setting".
1893	First cultured pearls developed in Japan; Kokichi Mikimoto gets patent in 1914 and begins to mass-produce cultured pearls.
1895	Daniel Swarovski sets up a factory in Austria specializing in the industrial production of cut crystal jewelry stones.
1899	The House of Cartier opens stores in international venues.
1901	King Edward VII comes to the English throne; Edwardian era of jewelrycrafting emerges, lasts until 1914.
1904	Frederick Carder of Steuben Glass creates new kinds of art glass, which are incorporated into glass beadmaking.
	Louis Cartier makes the first men's wristwatch.
1905	Moissanite is discovered in a meteorite at Diablo Canyon in Arizona.
	Cullinan diamond found in South Africa; this largest gem-quality diamond ever found weighed in at 3,106.75 carats.
	Charles Horner begins to mass-produce brooches and other jewelry, as well as thimbles, at his factory in Halifax, England.
1907	Belgian scientist Leo Baekeland invents Bakelite, a new kind of "plastic," as a substitute for the highly flammable celluloid.
1910	Art Deco period begins; lasts until 1939; post-Deco period until late 1950s.
1912	Jewelers of America Association adopts official birthstone list.

1914	International Committee on Weights and Measures sets metric standard of one-fifth of a gram = one carat for diamonds and other precious gemstones.
1917	All U.S. soldiers are issued aluminum dog tags for easy identification in case of death on the battlefield.
1919	Marcel Tolkowsky develops a mathematical schema to achieve the perfect cut for any diamond design, revolutionizing the diamond trade.
1920	Aigrettes become popular as a hair ornament among the flapper crowd.
	Fashion designer Jean Patou invents the modern silk necktie.
1922	Explorer and archaeologist Howard Carter unearths King Tutankhamen's tomb in Egypt.
1937	German mineralogists M. V. Stackelberg and K. Chudoba "discover" cubic zirconias (cz's), though their use as a diamond substitute does not come about until 1976.
	DuPont Chemical Company invents lucite, a lightweight, transparent, thermoplastic resin.
1938	Museum of North Arizona initiates a program to produce jewelry that would be understood as exclusively and expressly "Hopi" (Native American).
1939	Copper jewelrysmith Frank Rebajes exhibits his line of jewelry at the World's Fair in New York and later goes on to open spectacular Fifth Avenue store featuring all his designs.
	Fashion house Volupté introduces the Scarlett O'Hara compact, which is an instant best seller.
	The 4Cs for grading diamonds are introduced to the diamond industry.
	Start of the era of Retro jewelry in the United States.
1946	Jewelrysmith Jerry Fells introduces Renoir line of copper jewelry to U.S. market; Matisse line follows in 1952.
1952	Captain A.W.F. Fuller donates a ninth-century Anglo-Saxon brooch from his personal collection to the British Museum (henceforth, the Fuller Brooch).
	Battery-powered watches enter the market.
1969	Seiko introduces the quartz watch to the general public.
1970	Prisoner of War (POW) bracelets are first sold to remind the public of families whose loved ones were missing in action or POWs during the Vietnam War.
	Electronic watches, most made in Asia, hit the marketplace.
1971	Extremely rare gold coral discovered in Hawaiian waters.

1980   Hypoallergenic jewelry comes to the marketplace.

1981   *The Copper Bracelet and Arthritis* makes the best seller list, and soon millions of copper bracelets flood the jewelry market.

1988   A large South African diamond is found, weighing 599 carats; it is cut into several stones, the largest of which is called the Centenary; weighing 273 carats, it is the largest, modern-cut, top-color, and flawless diamond in the world.

1995   Charles and Covard partner with Cree Laboratories to mass-produce moissanite.

1996   Tour de France champion Lance Armstrong is diagnosed with cancer; Nike markets synthetic silicone rubber bracelets to help raise cancer awareness; 50 million are sold in the next ten years.

1998   Moissanite, a diamond alternative, becomes commercially available.

2001   Following in the footsteps of other famous movie stars, soap actress Susan Lucci premieres her own line of fashion jewelry.

2005   A Greek hiker finds a Neolithic period solid gold pendant while hiking in the town of Ptolemaida, near Thessaloniki in Greece; measuring 1 1/2" by 1 1/2", it is over 6,500 years old.

2006   The largest diamond to be found in 13 years is unearthed in the tiny African kingdom of Lesotho; called the Lesotho Promise, it weighed in at 603 carats and was immediately sold for US$12 million.

Former Philippine First Lady Imelda Marcos launches a jewelry line bearing her name; pop singer Mariah Carey, *American Idol* judge Paula Abdul, and socialite Paris Hilton crowd the celebrity jewelry designer market with their new lines of fashion jewels.

The Encyclopedia

Amulets

Forget! The lady with the Amulet
Forget she wore it at her Heart. . . .
(Emily Dickinson [1830–1886], "Forget! The Lady with the Amulet")

Jewelrymakers and craftspeople of all centuries have been dutifully employed by nearly every culture in the making and production of amulets (from the old Latin term *amoletum*, "means of defense"). From the beginnings of human understanding and reasoning, it would appear that we as a species have sought ways to protect ourselves and have therefore appropriated a variety of objects to keep us safe from trouble and adversity, to cure our ills, and to ward off all types of bodily and spiritual harm.

Every ancient culture, it would seem, had its own version of the amulet: In some places, amulets were bits of dust from sandy tombs, carried in small sacks; often an amulet was a piece of paper upon which were written the words or symbols of a holy book that contained magical names and numbers. Most times an amulet was fashioned into something wearable, usually around the neck, so that it was close to the heart. Hence we begin to understand how important jewelry was to the wearer, and the role of the jewelrycrafter as both medicine man, healer, and shaper of cultural expressions. To wear an amulet was not merely a fashion statement (though it might be disguised as one); having an amulet in one's pocket or around one's neck was a matter of life and death and the difference between a good life and a life filled with pain and despair.

For the ancient Egyptians, Assyrians, Babylonians, and Hebrews, great importance was placed on the use of amulets. In ancient Egypt, charms worn in the shape of frogs assured fertility; ankhs represented resurrection and eternal life; and the *udjat,* or all-seeing eye of the god Horus, was ubiquitous in collars, pendants, and bracelets. And of course the scarab beetle, with its magical abilities

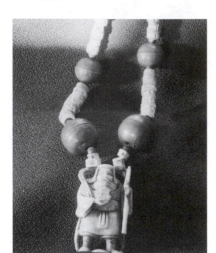

A *netsuke* (Japanese, nineteenth century) used as an amulet. Copyright © 2007 by Anthony F. Chiffolo.

against bad spells and omens and its promise of bodily resurrection from the dead, was in great demand, readily fashioned for any person of means. In Assyria and Babylonia, cylinder seals embedded with semiprecious and precious stones were common; each stone, with its brilliant cuts and colors, had its own special powers. Amulets shaped as animals were popular, too. In the home of a great warrior, king, or soldier, it would not have been uncommon to encounter pendants, belts, or armbands decorated with a ram (virility) or a bull (great strength). The Hebrew people wore jewelry fashioned in the shape of crescent moons or small bells, often attached to scarves, waistbands, or the hems of clothing, keeping them safe from the "evil eye." In some African countries, necklaces and bracelets with many charms shaped like animals or mythical figures were encountered by Western missionaries, who named them fetishes; these too were worn for protection.

Perhaps the two most common symbols in all periods of history that have been made into amulets have been those that represented the human eye (see above) and male genitalia (phallic symbols). Jewelers have crafted many pieces in the shape of horns or fingers/hands, all of which are merely a euphemism for the penis. It was thought that to stand up to the evil eye, one had to exude an incredible amount of testosterone, and men were taking all the help they could get!

In the Christian era, it has been very common to wear figurines shaped in the likeness of the saints. For many years, the Church has chastised believers who walk a fine line between emulation and idol worship. Wearing a cross or some relic of a saint was "in the mind of the Church, in no wise thought to have any latent power or divinity in them, or to be calculated to assure, as of themselves, to their possessors, protection against harm or success in undertakings."[1] But the traditions surrounding the wearing of medals or "Christian jewelry" as a talisman against evil are too deeply rooted in the belief system of millions of the

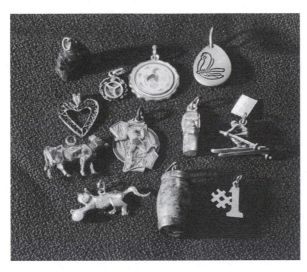

Charms are a very common and popular type of amulet or talisman. Copyright © 2007 by Anthony F. Chiffolo.

faithful. Regardless of what the Church says (or has said), believers continue to wear crosses, pictures of Jesus and the Virgin Mary, and images of the saints as amulets to protect both themselves and their mortal souls.

During the Middle Ages, jewelrymakers were busy creating pentacles as amulets to attract money and love and to protect against envy, misfortune, and other bad events. With the arrival in Europe of the Great Plague and the horrible Spanish Inquisition (designed to root out witches and non-Christian believers), a whole new amuletic industry was launched. Wearing a cross or carrying religious articles was proof of one's loyalty, not only to the Church, but to the nation as well (as there was no separation of religion and the state). Today, in defiance of long-standing persecutions, witches and some groups connected to demonolatry wear the pentagram star in a downward position as a means of communicating with demons and showing friendship towards them.

In modern times, it is not unusual to see amulets in all forms of jewelry, made in every shape, size, and material. Rabbit feet, coral, bamboo, horseshoes, four-leaf clovers, runes, bells, St. Christopher medals—all are longstanding recipes and remedies for what ails us, or could hurt us, or could bring us good luck or fortune. To this day, in any jewelry store one is sure to find an amulet to suit the need or occasion, just as generations of folks have for years.

☞ DID YOU KNOW?

Perhaps the most popular of all amulets are charms, tiny representative ornaments that are worn on bracelets, pendant necklaces, or earrings. The practice of wearing charms has its origins in prehistory, when men and women first used tiger claws, human hair, bones of dead animals, crocodile teeth, poison plant seeds, and so forth, as talismans or folk magic against certain of life's evils. Wearing an image or likeness was thought to be a particularly good form of magic. Charms and charm bracelets are extremely popular once again, but more as souvenirs of places visited (see **Souvenir Jewelry**) or remembrances of special occasions. One might ponder, therefore, what must have been going on in the life of Mrs. Charles Darrow, wife of the inventor of the board game *Monopoly*:[2] according to legend, the idea for the game pieces used in Monopoly came from a charm bracelet owned by Mrs. Darrow at the time.[3] Originally there were ten playing tokens: the flatiron, purse, lantern, car, thimble, shoe, top hat, rocking horse, battleship, and cannon. After World War II, the lantern, purse, and rocking horse were replaced by a Scottie dog, wheelbarrow, and horse and rider. Today, the line-up includes the Scottie, car, iron, old boot, horse and rider, wheelbarrow, top hat, thimble, cannon, battleship, a sack of money, and, in the Deluxe edition only, a train. That Mrs. Darrow—she sure did lead an interesting life!

NOTES

1. Delaney, Joseph F., "Use and Abuse of Amulets" in *Catholic Encyclopedia* on CD-Rom at http://www.newadvent.org/cathen/01443b.htm

2. Though it is said that Darrow did not invent the game, he did get rich from selling it to Parker Brothers. For an interesting discussion on just who did invent *Monopoly*, see the article by Mary Bellis titled "Monopoly Monopoly" at http://inventors.about.com/library/weekly/aa121997.htm

3. The official Hasbro story on the significance of the playing pieces disputes the legend. See "What's the significance of Monopoly game pieces?" at http://www.straightdope.com/mailbag/mmonopoly.html

Anklets

> Hail to that foot of the lusty beloved which hits the head of the lover, that foot which is adorned with red paste and jingling anklets is the banner of love and which is worthy of adoration by inclining one's head. (From the fifth-century drama *Padataditakam*)

An anklet is a bracelet often made of metal (silver, gold), leather or grass, beads or pearls, and is worn around the ankle. Anklets (or ankle bracelets) have been worn for centuries by both men and women, particularly unmarried women in India, and more recently, by fashion-conscious modern women in liberal-minded countries.[1] In some modern cultures, such as the United States, men also wear ankle bracelets, usually made of leather (very popular on the surfer and skateboarder scene).

The history of anklets traverses hundreds of centuries and all ancient cultures. Jewelry found in Persian archaeological digs indicates that women wore anklets as adornment as early as 2000 B.C.E. Anklets from the same area dating to 700 B.C.E. were discovered in the shape of ibex with curved horns. Anklets were common in the body adornment of ancient Egyptian men and women and among Celtic tribes in Northern Europe.

In the biblical era, some women, especially in the area near Magdala, were known for their extensive use of jewelry, particularly anklets, which were fashioned with little bells so as to make a sound when walking. Often anklets were linked from one foot to the other, obliging the wearer to move in slow, shuffling steps.[2]

In the Americas, native dancers (usually men) wore anklets as part of their dress for grass dances at powwows; these anklets were usually covered with colored yarn or angora along with sheep bells, which helped to accentuate the dance beat and movements.[3] This was especially true among the Shoshone and Bannock tribes. In like manner, native Hawaiians wear anklets made of whale bone, dog teeth, or woven grasses as part of their traditional costume when performing the hula.

In modern Africa, anklets play an important role in the social life of young women, as they have for millennia. Among the Moors of North Africa, the yearly salt festival known as *Cure Salee* is a time when young girls in celebration wrap their hair and ankles in brass. The anklets are called *jabo* and are worn to attract young men. Moorish women wear anklets until the birth of their first child.[4] The Mbole peoples of Southwestern Congo use anklets both as decoration and currency. Created from molten metal poured into a mud cast called a

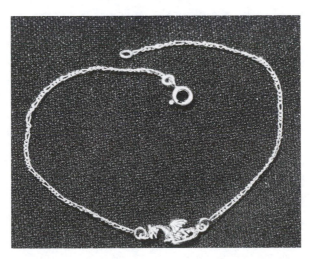

A modern-day silver anklet, carrying on a tradition going back more than 4,000 years. Copyright © 2007 by Anthony F. Chiffolo.

"puddle mold," they are fitted to the body as the metal cools. These anklets are highly prized all throughout the equatorial rainforest. The women of the Igbo tribe of Nigeria have long worn heavy brass anklets.

It is perhaps in India that anklets have had the longest consistent history of usage, where the ornamentation of a woman's whole body is an essential aspect of daily life and has great spiritual and social significance. Hundreds of years of Indian romantic history, as well as the arts, depict women who have given great care and attention to the beauty of their feet as an object of sensual and sexual desire to attract the opposite sex. Classical Indian dance is replete with movements that accentuate the foot; to further heighten the attention, anklets were worn, often with bells (called a *ghungroo*) or coins strung together, which were designed to direct the gaze of the viewer toward bewitching foot movements. In modern India, anklets are making a kind of comeback with women, who are now wearing them more as a fashion statement than in keeping with the older traditions for married women. These anklets sport a wide variety of colors and materials, including white metal, beads, ornaments, stones, and carved animals. Popular with many Indian women are elaborately carved and gold-plated *kundan* anklets.

☞   DID YOU KNOW?

File this under that category of a jewelry gift you wish you could return! Beginning in 2005, the U.S. Department of Homeland Security got into the jewelry business in a rather bizarre way by requiring that immigrants who are applying to remain in the country while they seek asylum wear an anklet to monitor their movements. While electronic anklets have long been a part of house-detention monitoring for convicted criminals, most new immigrants have never been convicted of any crime. So far the bracelets only come in one color and style, though accommodations have been made for size variations.[5]

NOTES

1. That is to say, liberal about what women wear and how they comport themselves in public.

2. Edersheim, Albert. "Sketches in Jewish Social Life" at http://www.godrules.net/library/edersheim/edersketch13b.htm

3. See Winder, Mimi. "What Is a Pow Wow?" at http://www.unh.edu/naca/history.html

4. Camera, Lucille. "The History and Aesthetics of African Jewelry" at http://www.yale.edu/ynhti/curriculum/units/1993/4/93.04.02.x.html

5. Source: National Public Radio.

Art Deco Jewelry

Period: 1910–1939

Birthplace: Paris, France

Origins: German Bauhaus school of design

Influences: Pharaonic Egypt, Asia, tribal Africa, Cubism, Futurism, machinery, and graphic design

Soon after the death of King Edward VII (1841–1910) of England, a new style in architecture, decorative art, fashion, furniture design, interior decoration, textiles, and jewelry began to take shape. It began as a modern reform of the Art Nouveau style, but it was simpler and more adaptable to mass production. Its crowning moment was the emphasis seen in nearly every presentation at the Exposition Internationale des Arts Decoratifs Industriels et Modernes, held in Paris in 1925. An innovative use of geometry and symmetry, a boldness of form and color, and the inclusion of new materials contributed greatly to its widespread appeal. Soon Art Deco, as it came to be known, was all the rage.

In jewelry design, the crafters of this new movement were greatly influenced by the works of the Edwardian and Art Nouveau periods, which preceded it and which continued to overlap it, both in form and substance. However, the flowing curves of Art Nouveau's classical and mythical themes were now about, replaced by straight lines or harsh geometric forms. Gone were the irises, orchids, and lilies; Art Deco jewelry was more about roses and camellias, baskets of flowers and fruit, now rendered in a kind of Cubist form. No more nouveau-style lions and sphinxes and horses with plumes; panthers, tigers, gazelles, cats, birds, and greyhounds, meant to convey a sense of speed and power, a characteristic of the Art Deco movement, became the new offerings at every fine jewelry counter. Jewelers of this period transformed the diamonds, crystals, and platinum of the Edwardian era into new and intricate forms and outlines. The once popular mine cut of gemstones was replaced by shapes never seen before—emerald cuts, pear shapes, marquises—all of which served to highlight the symmetrical nature of the jewelry and to convey elegance and sophistication. Pavé bracelets, called such because the stones set so closely together appeared to be "paved" into the metal, were popular among those who could afford diamonds and platinum ("white jewelry").

In many ways, the Art Deco movement was more of a reaction to previous design eras, so much so that it might be called a "reformation." In stark contrast to the works of the late nineteenth century and the early part of the twentieth, jewelrycrafters abandoned the pastels that were popular in Art Nouveau works and replaced them with vibrant greens, oranges, blues, and reds. Though many pins, bracelets, and rings of the Art Deco period stayed with the Edwardian

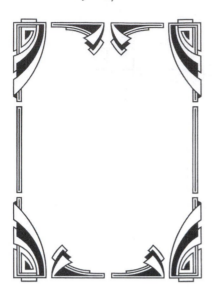

An Art Deco pin design. Note the triangular forms and heavy lines, a standard Deco motif. Courtesy of Dover Publications, Inc., NY.

black-and-white crystal-and-jet color scheme, rubies, sapphires, emeralds, turquoise, coral, and pearls came into vogue and were used extensively to create a splash. After all, this was the age of the flapper, jazz, Bakelite, women's suffrage, and modern machinery, and variety was the spice of life!

Deco jewelry was quite different from any fashion that had been seen or known previously. The "must-have" cameos and tiaras and crystal-drop earrings of the Victorian and Edwardian eras were edged out, replaced by long pendants, Bakelite bracelets, cocktail rings, and the double-clip brooch. Materials such as chrome, steel, wood, and glass were employed by jewelers and designers to create a new look that was both rigorous and clean-cut. Saks of New York displayed and purveyed this modern look in its Fifth Avenue store to gawking and bedazzled window shoppers. These "new" adornments were the creation of some of the finest and best-known designers on the scene in twentieth-century America: Hattie Carnegie (1889–1956), Nettie Rosenstein (1895–1980), Miriam Haskell (1899–1981), and Jonas and Sam Eisenberg.[1] Yet these brilliant jewelrycrafters were late to the movement in comparison to their counterparts in Europe who, though perhaps less well known, nevertheless were major contributors to the success of the Art Deco movement.

The Swiss-born designer Jean Dunand (1877–1942), best remembered for his hammered metal and lacquered pieces of furniture, created an equally stunning body of silver-lacquered, red and black jewelry in zigzags, openwork squares, and triangles. His compatriot, Paul Emile Brandt (b. 1879), created beautifully bejewelled geometric-design ladies' cocktail watches.

The French goldsmiths Jean Després (1889–1980), Jean Fouquet (b. 1899), and Gérard Sandoz (b. 1902) fashioned pieces that are highly sought after by Art Deco collectors. Other French jewelers, such as Raymond Templier

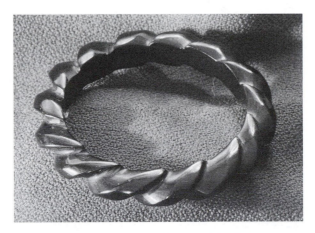

A Bakelite bracelet, circa 1930. Copyright © 2007 by Anthony
F. Chiffolo.

(1891–1968) and Louis Cartier (1875–1942), used diamonds and platinum
with deeply colored and dark stones (such as onyx and rubies), combining
them with jade and gold to create stunning works of art. René Lalique (1860–
1945) and Gabriel Argy-Rousseau (1885–1953) crafted glass pendants that
were superb expressions of Art Deco modernism. These Frenchmen introduced
the jewelry-buying public to animal, insect, and female motifs hanging on
silk cords with tasseled endings. Romain de Tirtoff, aka Erté (1892–1990),
presented highly stylized figures of jade and pearls in his hair jewelry. And
the female designers "Coco" Chanel (1883–1971) and Elsa Schiaparelli
(1890–1973) made their mark with designs meant to complement their clothing and perfume lines.

The Art Deco style was widely developed in other European countries as well, long
before its popularity in the United States. Alfredo Ravasco (1873–1958) in Italy and
Theodor Fahrner (d. 1919) in Germany were creating exquisite diamond-studded
geometric necklaces, bracelets, and earrings in the early 1900s.[2] British craftspersons, among them H. G. Murphy (1884–1939), Sybil Dunlop (1889–1968), and
Harold Stabler (1872–1945) earned solid reputations for their moderne creations, while retailers such as Asprey, Van Cleef & Arpels, and Mappin & Webb
sought out and sold the most creative designs of the period. In Denmark, Georg
Jensen (1866–1935) and his co-workers were largely responsible for what is considered among the best of Art Deco silver brooches ever made.

Inspired by Jensen, the American architect William Spratling (1900–1967)
took his talents to Mexico, where he founded a series of silver workshop factories in Taxco, called *talleres,* using indigenous designs to produce sterling rings,
bracelets, earrings, necklaces, and other finery. A key figure of the Art Deco
jewelry movement, Spratling's work is considered by many to be unparalleled in
its innovation and quality.

The onset of the Depression and the outbreak of World War II virtually ended the Art Deco movement. Fortunately, many fine examples of this prolific era in jewelrycrafting still exist and can be found at flea markets, church bazaars, or in grandma's treasure box today.

☞ DID YOU KNOW?

The plastic-like material Bakelite was invented by Dr. Leo Baekeland (1863–1944) of Belgium. Bakelite has an electric polymer structure that can only be molded once; it cannot be melted down and reconstituted or reformed into something else. However, since it could be molded into rather small components, it was an ideal substance for jewelrymaking. Bakelite was manufactured in nearly every primary and secondary color and was used to make rings, bracelets, pins, and other jewelry. Today, Bakelite pieces in good condition bring high prices among collectors.

NOTES

1. The Eisenberg Jewelry company was founded in Chicago in 1914 by Jonas Eisenberg.

2. According to *Theodor Fahrner Jewelry: Between Avante-Garde and Tradition* by Ulrike von Hase-Schmundt, Christianne Weber, and Ingeborg Becker (Lancaster, PA: Schiffer Publishing, 1991), the firm of Theodor Fahrner both led and was inspired by the major European art movements of Arts and Crafts, Art Nouveau, Art Deco, Art Moderne, and the contemporary periods; his workshops created fine jewelry from 1885–1979 that exemplified all these styles. Fahrner himself was most active in design work between 1899 and 1906.

Art Nouveau Jewelry

Period: 1875–1919[1]

Birthplace: Europe, primarily Paris and Brussels

Origins: London, at Liberty & Co., and Arthur Mackmurdo's (1851–1942) book *Wren's City Churches; Jugendstil* in Germany and the Netherlands; *Sezessionsstil* in Vienna; *World of Art* magazine in Russia; *Modernisme* in Barcelona

Influences: Arts and Crafts movement and Rococo style in Europe, Nature, Asian arts, symbolism, Japanese woodblock prints, Greek and Roman mythology, mystery, and fantasy

Art Nouveau, one of the most highly stylized and popular periods of jewelry-crafting, was born from the Arts and Crafts movement of art, primarily in Europe, during the latter part of the nineteenth century. Like the Edwardian and Art

Deco movements, which both followed it and overlapped it, Art Nouveau was a reaction, in many ways, to the strict rules of fashion dominated by Victorian sensibilities in England and "proper comportment" in Paris; it was also a rejection of the machine age and an attempt to reinstate a hands-on approach to production. The name "Art Nouveau" was derived from a shop in Paris known as Maison de l'Art Nouveau, at the time run by Samuel Bing (1838–1905), that featured objects following this approach to design.[2] Art Nouveau had its crowning moment at the Universal Exposition of 1900 in Paris, and by the time of the 1902 Turin Exposition in Italy, designers from nearly every country involved with the Art Nouveau movement were on hand to exhibit their works. By this time, Art Nouveau had firmly established that design was to be more highly considered than material—a revolutionary concept in its day, which promoted the view of jewelers as more than craftspersons: Indeed they were, at the very least, design artists in a trade worthy of the same respect afforded masters of the fine arts.

A piece of jewelry created during this era, therefore, can best be understood as a work of art in and of itself. Art Nouveau jewelers and craftspersons spent a great deal of time and were meticulous in their treatment of surface decoration for their creations, often utilizing nontraditional materials, such as bone, copper, shell, ivory, and glass. The focus of this era was on curves and waves and silhouettes, on extending the boundaries of line and form. It was during this époque that superb enameling techniques found their way into jewelrymaking: cloisonné, a process by which gold wire is shaped into small partitions into which the enamel is poured; plique-à-jour, a method that removes the metal backing from translucent enamel after kiln firing, creating the appearance of stained glass; *basse-taille,* a rather rare form of handicraft in which a transparent enamel covers the engraved design in the base metal; and champlevé, a format that fills the recesses cut out of the background metal with molten enamel.

Art Nouveau jewelry was, in many ways, the stuff of fantasy and myth. Jewelrycrafters of the late nineteenth century fashioned thousands upon thousands of unique pieces in the shape of orchids, poppies, lilies, irises, ferns, insects, snakes, dragonflies, birds, and butterflies. Water nymphs, angels, and Greek goddesses with flowing hair and drapery were ubiquitous. To add depth and a richness to their creations, jewelry designers introduced many newfangled notions into their works, such as the use of opals and semiprecious stones, cut glass, lava, ivory, marcasite, gold-filled and gold-plated items, mother-of-pearl, and textiles.

Because the Art Nouveau movement was extremely widespread, there were many work-production centers during this period. The jewelers of Paris and Brussels created and defined Art Nouveau in jewelry, and it was in these cities that it achieved the most renown.[3] Yet throughout the rest of Europe there were many adherents and followers of its groundbreaking style. Among the most well-known are René Lalique (1860–1945), Alphonse Mucha (1860–1939), Georges Fouquet (1862–1957), Lucien Gaillard (1861–1933), Henri (1854–1942) and Paul (1851–1915) Vever, Edward Colonna (1862–1948), Archibald Knox (1864–1933), Oliver Baker (1859–1938), Jessie King (1875–1949), John Paul Cooper (1869–1933),

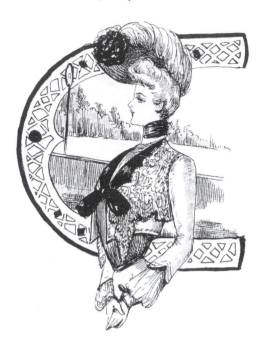

A young Victorian woman dressed for the day. Note the choker collar, a typical Art Nouveau look, popularized by Queen Victoria's daughter-in-law, Alexandra, who wore a choker to hide an ugly scar on her neck. Courtesy of Dover Publications, Inc., NY.

Arthur (1862–1928) and Georgina (1868–1934) Gaskin, Henry Wilson (1864–1934), and Omar Ramsden (1873–1939).[4] In the United States, the leaders in Art Nouveau jewelry production were Louis Comfort Tiffany (1848–1933), the Gorham Silver Co. of Rhode Island, and Krementz Jewelers of New Jersey.

Like the Edwardian period of jewelrymaking, the Art Nouveau movement suffered and nearly disappeared once the first shots of World War I were fired. It was already expensive to create during the latter part of the nineteenth century, and its extravagance was too much for the economy to bear during and in the aftermath of the war. The cheaper, streamlined modern jewelry that was new on the scene would eventually have its sway, and the mythic and fantastic elements of

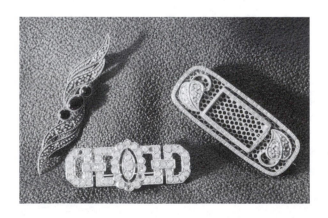

Victorian-era and modern marcasite pins. Copyright © 2007 by Anthony F. Chiffolo.

this fanciful era would disappear once again into books and favorite recollections, only to be "rediscovered" by eager collectors nearly a century later.

☞ DID YOU KNOW?

Though made popular in the Victorian era, marcasite became ubiquitous and was a favorite of Nouveau designers, who set it into sterling silver to accent its brilliance, thereby enhancing their creations. Marcasite, whose name is derived from the Arabic word for the mineral pyrite (to which it is similar), is found today in great quantities in Germany, the Czech Republic, Slovakia, Guanajuato (Mexico), Joplin (Missouri), and Tavistock (England). One of the greatest modern designers of marcasite jewelry is Judith Jack.

NOTES

1. This period overlaps with several other periods of jewelrycrafting, most notably the Victorian and Edwardian periods and the Art Deco movement. The high point of the Art Nouveau era was probably the years between 1892 and 1902.

2. Bing opened his shop in 1896. See the article on Art Nouveau at http://en.wikipedia.org/wiki/Art_Nouveau

3. Ibid.

4. To be sure, designers such as Georg Jensen, Theodore Fahrner, Sybil Dunlop, and Harold Stabler were important figures in the Art Nouveau jewelry world, as well. However, since their work overlaps the Art Deco era, they are discussed in more detail under that heading (see **Art Deco Jewelry**).

Arts and Crafts Jewelry

Period: 1870–1900

Birthplace: England

Origins: the work of British poet, artist, and architect William Morris (1834–1896)

Influences: critique of mass production and Victorian decorative design; medieval themes; A. W. Pugin's (1812–1852) Gothic revivalism;[1] the philosophy of John Ruskin (1819–1900); the search for a new English style; the work of the pre-Raphaelites, such as Dante Gabriel Rossetti (1828–1882)[2]

Much like Art Nouveau jewelry, the jewelry of the Arts and Crafts era was more of a reactive creation than a functional or adaptive enhancement of previous or current styles. William Morris, whom many perceive to be the founder of the Arts and Crafts movement, was angry and frustrated by Victorian designs of the day, which he considered busy, garish, overmechanized, and dulled by mass production. He longed for an end product that was handwrought, uniquely individualized and appreciative of the designs found in nature—work in which the imperfections of human error would come to be understood as part of the artistic process, items that were "of the people, for the people."

Morris found many allies among the craftspersons of the day, both in England and in the United States. Spurred on by the philosophy of the movement to attempt to create a new aesthetic sensibility, the artisans of this period experimented with new or heretofore unconsidered materials for their handicraft. Copper, brass, aluminum, silver, and wood were used in jewelrymaking that revealed the hammer marks of its creator. Atypical gemstones, such as translucent moonstones or opals, and turquoise were used and cut *en cabochon* (a rounded, polished surface with a flat back). The emphasis in Arts and Crafts jewelry when choosing gemstones was on color and style, not on monetary value; hence, diamonds and other very precious stones were rarely used in Arts and Crafts jewelry; neither were platinum nor gold fashioned for the base metals of pins and rings and bracelets: Arts and Crafts jewelry was all about innovation. In fact, one might say that it was a "think-tank" process, where the philosophies and energies of the artists and craftspersons acted synergistically to create a product that was meant to elicit a response of awe in the buyer, who, coveting such rarity of beauty and form, would be moved to own the work of art at any cost. Unfortunately, the end result was a product that paid so much attention to detail that the labor involved meant it was often unaffordable to the middle or poorer classes; so Arts and Crafts jewelry, in England at least, was primarily in demand by and purchased by the wealthy.[3]

It is difficult to point to any one style of jewelrycrafting that defines the Arts and Crafts movement, especially because the work was often the creation of several or many hands. But there were some common themes that were popular among artisans of this period. Influenced by the thinking of John Ruskin (1819–1900), probably the most influential social and artistic critic of the times, much of the jewelry of the Arts and Crafts epoch featured nature and organic forms, such as flowers, birds, leaves, and the like. Winged scarabs, thistles, peacocks, ivy, and Scandinavian designs were often themes of the artisans of the day.[4] Natural pearls were popular accents, and ivory, malachite, carnelian, lapis, green garnets, quartz crystal, and enamel were common elements of the creative process.

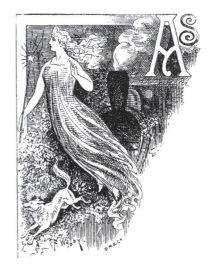

Arts and Crafts–era woman with her dog, a common jewelry design motif. Courtesy of Dover Publications, Inc., NY.

Because much of the handiwork in creating jewelry during the Arts and Crafts period was the work of guilds of artisans, each of whom played some part in the many processes that created the jewelry of this movement, it is not easy to speak about key artistic players of Arts and Crafts jewelrymaking. A major inhibitor to identifying significant contributors is that many of the pieces of this era went unsigned. Still, there are a few stars who merit special mention: Nelson (1859–1941) and Edith Dawson, Arthur (1862–1928) and Georgina (1868–1934) Gaskin, Alexander Fisher (1864–1936), Frederick J. Partridge (1877–1942), Bernard Cuzner (1877–1956), and C. R. Ashbee (1863–1942) undoubtedly helped to shape and perpetuate Arts and Crafts style and design. Ashbee, in particular, is a standout; he founded the Guild of Handicraft in 1888 and designed most of the work so that guild crafters could set about to create it.

Because of the fine quality of handiwork and its unique style, Arts and Crafts jewelry is highly sought after by collectors, and, not surprisingly, it is still expensive!

☞ DID YOU KNOW?

The Arts and Crafts movement, though British in origin, was popular and manifested itself in various ways in other European countries as well during the latter part of the nineteenth century and into the twentieth. The Amsterdam School (1900–1940) was very active; its influence was Indonesian and Moorish, with a decidedly Muslim slant. Jewelry was crafted in hammered copper or silver or set in enamel using cabachon cuts of stone, such as agate, carnelian, and other members of the chalcedony quartz family. There were also prominent Arts and Crafts movements (or schools) in Germany and Austria, which had a profound influence on jewelrymaking both in Europe and around the world.

NOTES

1. "Gothic revival in its Victorian form started with the publication of Augustus Pugin's book, *Contrasts: or, A parallel between the Noble Edifices of the 14th and 15th centuries and similar buildings of the Present Day; showing the Present decay of Taste* (1841). Before this, Gothic revivalism had been a consequence of the romantic and picturesque movements in art. Pugin's book lamented the decline of taste in architecture, resulting in bland classical buildings with no individuality. Pugin proposed the idea that English architecture had taken a wrong turn at the end of the 16th century, and suggested that architects go back to earlier forms, out of which a more correct style, or one appropriate to the nineteenth century, might evolve" (G. Bulmer, "The Battle on the Styles of Victorian Architecture" at http://everything2.com/index.pl?node_id=1511999).

2. The Pre-Raphaelites were a group of nineteenth-century artists who sought to "rediscover" the painting styles of their brethren who lived earlier than the sixteenth-century Italian artist Raphael (1491–1528). Dante Gabriel Rossetti, though not a founding member of the movement, was a key player in perpetuating its philosophies.

3. This is indeed a "rich" irony (pardon the pun), as the entire movement was based on creating a grassroots product that would be affordable to everyday people.

4. Etruscan, Celtic, and Renaissance designs were also common.

Assyrian Revival Jewelry

Period: 1840–present

Birthplace: ancient Mesopotamia and the Near and Middle East, including
parts of Northern Africa

Origins: discovery of the ruins of Nineveh in 1840

Influences: the Great Exhibition of London (1851) showcasing new jewelry
incorporating Assyrian designs

Perhaps less well known than their neighbors in Egypt, Assyrian artisans created
fascinating and intricate body adornments that are among some of the earliest
examples of jewelry uncovered by modern archaeological digs. "Assyria" refers to
the area in the upper regions of the Tigris valley, stretching at times as far north
as Armenia and as far south as the ancient city of Thebes during the period between 1900 B.C.E. to roughly 627 B.C.E. Its history boasts capitals as diverse as
Babylonia and Sumer, a distinct Semitic language form and alphabet (Aramaic),
unequalled architectural form, and the use of document cylinder seals, an art
form in themselves. This expressive diversity of culture, language, and innovation
had a profound influence on local artisans who experimented with form, style,
movement, and graphics to create unique and greatly copied works of art, many
of which were replicated in the jewelry of the period.

Archaeologists investigating the ruins of the ancient city of Nineveh in the
1840s uncovered artifacts with Assyrian motifs: lions, winged bulls, decorated
horses, and turbaned men with curly beards. It is apparent that craftmaking was
an important job in Assyria, not only by the fine work that was unearthed, but in
the dedications uncovered to the many "craft" gods that were part of the Assyrian pantheon. There was Nin-ildu the carpenter, Gushkin-banda the goldsmith,
Mummu the craftsman, and Nin-agal—the patron of smiths. By the grace of
their gods, Assyrian craftsmen worked lead, tin, textiles, and gold into finery that
was coveted by citizens and foreign trading partners alike.

Among the treasures that have survived the ravages of time and are now located
in museums and private collections around the world are *ugal,* or headdresses,
worn by royal women; small, carved mountain crystal (a type of quartz) objects
inscribed with the owner's name; gold earrings in the shape of pine cones; beaded
collar and spider-web choker necklaces; anklets; decorative hairpins; beaded
bracelets and rings; many types of jewelry crafted in the shape of cylindrical seals;
and animal amulet figures of gold and silver, or decorated with gemstones.

The rediscovery of these jewelry forms as a result of the Middle Eastern
archaeological excavations of the nineteenth century gave rise to a new fashion
known as Assyrian Revival. Soon after the British archaeologist Austen Henry
Layard (1817–1894) returned from his excavation of Nineveh (modern-day Iraq)

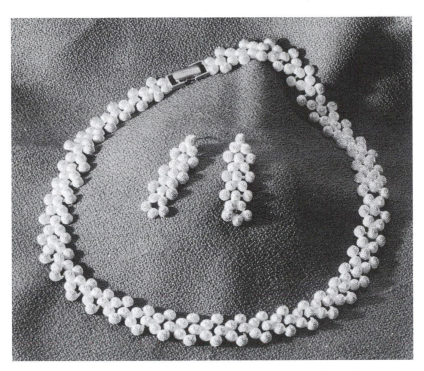

Twentieth-century Assyrian Revival gold-tone necklace and matching drop earrings.
Copyright © 2007 by Anthony F. Chiffolo.

in the mid 1850s, English and Continental jewelers began to copy the architecture
and other art forms that were part of the works that Layard had donated to the
British Museum. The interest in these ancient pieces created a major shift of
focus in the fashions of the day, a welcome reprieve from the rather dull and mor-
bid Victorian staid conservatism in comportment. Gold bracelets, awash with
the scenes of an Assyrian lion hunt, or exotic brass-feathered drop earrings now
appeared on the scene.

Coupled with the Egyptian Revival trend that at the same moment was dawn-
ing, the Assyrian Revival movement was one of the major forces that helped to
create and define the Art Nouveau period in jewelry design. In the 1980s, when
the Metropolitan Museum of Art in New York City was promoting its catalog
business, these Middle and Near Eastern jewelry pieces of long ago enjoyed yet
another renaissance.

☞ DID YOU KNOW?

Thanks to the movies and history books, we probably can conjure up in the mind's
eye some visuals of ancient Egyptian history and culture without too much trouble.
Doing the same with Assyrian history is a bit more challenging. But due in great
part to the archives and diligence of the museum community, who have preserved

large bites of ancient Assyria, we have come to understand the motifs of Assyrian sculpture, and it is these motifs that influenced nineteenth–twenty-first-century jewelers to create the Assyrian revival jewelry on hand today. Assyrian sculptors were detailed artisans who were able to painstakingly recreate every nuance of their subjects. From the wisps of a feather to the grains in wood, Assyrian reliefs invite one to touch them to make sure they are not "real," but rather a fine representation. Cypresses and date palms, lilies and grapes, animals of all shapes and sizes, and riders and their chariots pulled by plumed horses appear with amazing detail in these ancient Middle Eastern remnants. Victorian jewelers, undoubtedly appreciative of the fine handiwork of such talented crafters, copied all they saw, and with the same attention to detail. The resulting handiwork created a new niche in the jewelry market that still has strength today. Then, as now, Assyrian-style pins, necklaces, and bracelets are some of the most unusual and visually compelling jewelry pieces available for purchase.

Birthstones

A birthstone, when first you dropped by;
A grindstone, your nose to apply;
A gravestone, no doubt,
When you're spirited out;
And some brimstone, for after you die.
(Mephistopheles at *The Omnificent English Dictionary in Limerick Form*)

Craftspersons from all parts of the world make jewelry for special occasions, or upon the request of an individual benefactor or client. Perhaps the most requested "special orders" of jewelry are items that are made from the wearer's birthstone, a precious material that symbolizes the month or day of the week or sometimes the zodiac sign related to one's birthday. Of course, "birthstone" is somewhat of a misnomer, as all the materials used or associated with them are not "stones"; for example, pearl, the official birthstone for the month of June, is not a gem; amber, which is on some lists, is actually petrified tree resin. Yet whatever the material, these precious and semiprecious gifts from the land and sea have found a special place in the history of jewelry, especially for their talisman effects, which are said to both endow the wearer with magical gifts and protect from a wide variety of demons and ill happenings.

Nearly everyone knows what their birthstone is, or they have some idea. If not, one can consult the Jewelers of America's official list, adopted in 1912, which today is the most widely used list in the United States, Australia, and Thailand, as well as in many other countries. In this traditional list, birthstones are assigned as follows:

JANUARY: GARNET

Though commonly thought of as a red gem, garnets are actually available in every color except blue. They are most commonly found in Brazil, Madagascar, Sri Lanka, India, Siberia, Africa, and the United States. In the religious traditions of the Jewish people, garnets are said to have been one of the twelve gems of Aaron's breastplate. For Christians, the blood-red color is said to symbolize the passion and death of Christ on the cross. For Muslims, garnets illuminate the Fourth Heaven in the writings of the Koran. In Teutonic folklore, garnets are believed to endow the wearer with special night vision; it was said that Noah himself hung a large garnet in the ark so that he might see during the rainy 40 days and nights. The ancient Egyptians held the belief that garnets placed on the body were antidotes for snakebites and food poisoning.

FEBRUARY: AMETHYST

Amethyst is a transparent purple variety of quartz. It is most commonly found in Mexico, Brazil, Canada, Uruguay, Italy, Germany, Russia, Sri Lanka, Zambia, and the United States (notably in the Lake Superior area, Maine, Texas, Pennsylvania, North Carolina, and Yellowstone National Park). Its brilliant lavender color has been the favorite of royalty and can be found therefore in many state crowns and scepters. Fine amethysts are featured in the British Crown Jewels and are said to also have been a favorite of Russia's Catherine the Great (1729–1796) and the pharaohs of Egypt. For centuries, the Church embraced its mythic properties, and most bishop's rings today are made of amethyst (as are rosary beads), because it is believed to encourage both celibacy and piety. It appears as the birthstone for February probably due to its association with St. Valentine; therefore, amethyst has often been worn to attract love. In antiquity, amethysts were primarily used for intaglios. Ancient tradition maintained that those who wear amethyst will know peace and calmness of mind, so it was favored by soldiers who carried it on the shafts of their spears as they marched off to war. In the folklore of the peoples of Northern Europe it is thought of as a charm against witchcraft, poison, and evil thoughts. In Tibet, amethyst is considered to be sacred to Buddha.

MARCH: AQUAMARINE

Named after the clear blue "sea water" of some of the tropical locations where it is found, aquamarine is a beautiful beryl (like emerald) that is said to represent youth, fidelity, hope, and fine health. It is most commonly found in Brazil, Nigeria, and Zambia. Legend has it that those who wear an aquamarine will experience love and affection and be endowed with knowledge, foresight, and inspiration. Because of its link to the sea, it is greatly favored by sailors, who carry it to keep them on course and guide them to safe harbors. Bloodstone, which could not be more different from aquamarine in both texture and color, is an alternative birthstone gem for those born in March.

APRIL: DIAMOND

Whether or not they are "a girl's best friend," as the maxim goes, diamonds are the hardest of all known gemstones, which makes them both rare and desirable to own and just perfect for engagement rings, as they represent strength (in love) and endurance. They are found primarily in Australia, the Democratic Republic of Congo, Botswana, Russia, and South Africa. It is said the ancients believed that diamonds were splinters of stars fallen to earth, or tears of the gods, or crystallized lightning, or even hardened dewdrops. In Greek mythology, Cupid's arrows were rumored to be tipped with diamonds, which allowed him to pierce even the hardest of hearts. Rulers of ancient civilizations throughout Asia Minor and Africa wore diamonds as a symbol of courage and invincibility. Though we actually know very little about how diamonds are formed, they have a very simple composition: pure carbon.

White topaz is an alternate April birthstone.

MAY: EMERALD

Called by jewelers "the Queen of gems," emeralds, a type of beryl, have long been an important stone in jewelrymaking. They are found primarily in Colombia, Brazil, Zambia, and Zimbabwe. The most prized examples are pure green or bluish-green, which most often under magnification flaunt all types of inclusions—crystallized bits seemingly trapped within—making a truly clear emerald very rare. In ancient times, emeralds were held in great esteem. They were believed to sharpen the mind and the eye, to protect the wearer on long and dangerous journeys, and to allow discerning souls to predict the future.

JUNE: PEARL

The only "gem" in the list of birthstones that is not a stone, the pearl holds its own when it comes to natural beauty, desirability, and great worth. The rarity value of real pearls just a little over 100 years ago was such "that an American skyscraper exchanged hands for the price of a pearl necklace."[1] Pearls are found in many locations worldwide, but they are mainly the product of Japan and China, Indonesia, and Australia. Pearls are created when a grain of sand or some other foreign irritant makes its way inside the shell of an oyster, which then produces a covering, called nacre, that eventually develops into a small, roundish orb. The rounder and more lustrous the orb, the better the pearl. Pearls range in color from bright white to black and can be cultured or natural. Besides the popular round shape, pearls come in other shapes and sizes, too: fresh water (elongated shapes); mabe (large and hemispherical); South Sea (very large); and other varieties. The pearl has been called the "gem of the moon." Tradition has associated pearls with symbolism of modesty, chastity, and purity, which is why they are often worn by brides, as they are said to portend a happy marriage.

Both moonstone and alexandrite are alternative birthstones for June.

JULY: RUBY

In the *Wizard of Oz,* the main character, Dorothy, wears ruby slippers. It's no wonder she never wanted to take them off: Rubies, rich red members of the corundum family (which includes sapphires), can be worth two to three times the value of a large diamond of equal size and quality. Rubies are mined primarily in Myanmar, Thailand, Kenya, Tanzania, Cambodia, Sri Lanka, and India. They are extremely durable, with a hardness factor surpassed only by that of diamonds. The ancient Greeks and Romans believed that rubies contained a bright spark struck from the planet Mars. These same civilizations prized rubies for their reputed ability to cure illness and reconcile quarreling lovers. In the Hindu tradition, rubies were called "the Lord of the Gems" and were said to possess in them an inextinguishable fire so hot that it was capable of boiling water.

AUGUST: PERIDOT

Varying in color from yellow-green to brilliant light green, the peridot is sometimes called the "Evening Emerald" because under artificial light it is said to glow a bright green. Peridot is quite abundant and found in many places where volcanos have been active, such as in Hawaii, where crystals have been sifted from the black sands of Kauai and Maui. It is most often found in Myanmar and parts of the mainland United States. The peridot symbolizes eloquence and persuasiveness; it was worn to ward off terrors of the night and bad dreams and was considered a powerful talisman against all types of evil. It is said that it was especially favored by pirates. In the Christian tradition, peridot was dedicated to St. Bartholomew, whose feast day is August 24.

SEPTEMBER: SAPPHIRE

Though we think of them as primarily deep-blue in color, sapphires, members of the corundum family of minerals, are found in nature in every color. The one exception are red stones, which are classified as rubies (see above). Rare orange, pink, and lavender sapphires, along with those deep, deep blue varieties, are the most expensive. Sapphires are native to Sri Lanka, Australia, East Africa, and the countries of Southeast Asia. In ancient folklore, they were reported to have the power to stop bleeding and cure diseases of the eye and were noted for their importance as an all-around cure for many ailments, as well as a crucial antidote against poisons. Other folk legends claimed that they would not shine if worn by the wicked or unfaithful. In Judaism, it was said that God wrote the Ten Commandments on tablets of sapphire.

OCTOBER: OPAL

It is rumored to be bad luck to wear an opal if it is not your birthstone. Nevertheless, opals are purchased and worn by millions of persons born in all months who are attracted by the opal's tremendous color spectrum and its "fiery" self-presentation. Opals are found chiefly in Australia, Mexico, and the United States.

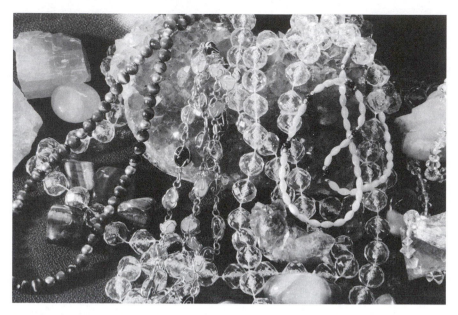

Strands of agate, pearl, amethyst, and quartz: Birthstones are a favorite jewelry choice. Copyright © 2007 by Anthony F. Chiffolo.

Their reputation as symbols of hope, innocence, and purity has made them a favorite with young brides. In the Middle Ages, opals were believed to render the wearer invisible, should the need arise. The ancient Romans prized the opal, calling it the "King of all Gems" due to the presence within the stone of all the colors of the rainbow.

The alternative birthstone choice for October is tourmaline.

NOVEMBER: CITRINE

Citrine, so named because of its lemony color, is a variety of quartz found mainly in Brazil. It is very durable, available in nearly all jewelry markets around the world, and can be found in large quantities for very little money. It comes in colors from pale yellows to brown to a kind of blood red and is often confused with topaz, which has many of the same color strains. People once carried citrine to ward off the plague, bad thoughts, and skin conditions like psoriasis, eczema, and leprosy. It was also used as a charm to protect against the bites of venomous reptiles.

DECEMBER: (BLUE) TOPAZ

The color for the month of December is blue, and so a variety of stones make the "official list," among them turquoise, lapis lazuli, blue zircon, and, most recently, tanzanite. However, the most popular of choices for December birthstones, due, one supposes, to availability, cost, and the brilliance of the stone itself, is topaz. Topaz is mined mainly in Brazil, Nigeria, and Sri Lanka. It comes in many colors, from clear to golden yellow to red to dark brown to light green to pink to December's blue. For thousands of years in many varied civilizations, topaz has been favored as a gemstone that holds vast curative powers. The ancient Greeks favored it with high esteem, as they believed it gave them strength; the ancient Egyptians praised its glow as the emanation of the power and presence of their sun God, Ra. It was believed to cool tempers, restore sanity, cure asthma, relieve insomnia, ward off sudden death, allow the wearer to become invisible in case of danger, and detect poisons. If you are looking to own a rare topaz, seek out a stone that is pink or orangish-red.

☞ DID YOU KNOW?

There is an astrological version of birthstones, using zodiac signs instead of calendar months.[2] There is also a list of birthstones assigned to each day of the week, as follows:

Monday: pearl
Tuesday: garnet
Wednesday: cat's eye (agate)
Thursday: emerald
Friday: topaz
Saturday: sapphire
Sunday: ruby

NOTES

1. Thomas, Pauline Weston, "Jewellery in Costume and Fashion History" at http://www.fashion-era.com/jewellery.htm

2. To see a copy of this list, go to http://www.bernardine.com/birthstone/zodiac-birthstones.htm

Body Piercing

> Tongue, ears, lips, nose, brow, nipple, navel, genitals, chin, neck, hands, stomach . . . nearly any part of the body can be pierced. (Memory Lane Antiques)

Human beings have been piercing parts of their bodies for religious or other cultural reasons for thousands of years. The mummified body of Ötzi the Iceman, for instance, found in an Austrian glacier and dating back more than 5,000 years, showed signs of ear plugs 7 to 11 millimeters in diameter. Both nose and ear piercing are mentioned in stories about the earliest peoples of the Bible. In

Genesis 24:22, Abraham's servant gives his daughter-in-law, Rebekah, a "golden earring," or *shanf* (in Hebrew, "nose-ring"). This practice is still followed among the Berber and Beja nomads of Northern Africa, where the size of the ring denotes the wealth of the family: The husband gifts the ring to his intended bride, and it is her security if the marriage is dissolved.

It is possible to pierce nearly every part of the body, and various cultures throughout hundreds of centuries have been known to promote piercings as body adornment, as a religious practice, as a means of spiritual enlightenment, to mark rites of passage (such as puberty or marriage), to honor the dead, for sexual pleasure, as anesthesia (or for other medical reasons), and for purely practical reasons. From the eyebrows to the genitals and at many body parts between, piercings throughout all of history have also been a major trend of fashion. The ancient Egyptians were fond of earrings, particularly of gold, often crafted in the shape of lotus blossoms. The Aztecs, Mayans, and other native Americans practiced tongue and nose piercing, both for religious reasons and to make them look more fierce to their enemies. The custom was also common among many of the tribes in New Guinea, who used bone and feathers as symbols of pride, wealth, and, among the men, virility. In Central and South America, lip labrets for women were meant to attract the opposite sex, and the bigger the labret, the greater the beauty (not unlike the use of collagen among some women today).

Legend has it that sailors believed that piercing one ear would improve their long-distance sight, so it soon became fashionable among sea explorers of the late Middle Ages and early Renaissance period in Europe to wear at least one earring, a practice that spread to the male nobility. Diamond studs or large drop earrings with a huge gemstone were an obvious way to advertise one's wealth and social standing, especially for a young man on the lookout for a wife. As fashions in Europe changed and necklines for women plunged, thanks in great part to the Queen of Bavaria (1376–1434), who was fond of wearing very little above the waist, nipple piercings became a more common way for women to show off their jewelry. It is said that by the 1890s, it was almost expected that women would have their nipples pierced, not only as a fashion statement and a sexual enhancement, but as a body modification recommended by doctors to improve breast-feeding conditions among childbearing women.[1]

Perhaps the most common and overall "acceptable" form of body piercing today is to have holes made in the ears in order to wear jewelry specifically designed for that purpose. Though ear piercing has been known since ancient times, it is only fairly recently that it has gained popular acceptance in the West, among women and men. As a result of both the cultural and sexual revolution of the 1960s in the United States, pierced ears—which used to be thought of as the fashion plate of only "hippies" or the LGBTQ community—are so common in most Western communities as to be considered mainstream—for both sexes. In recent years, nose, eyebrow, tongue, and navel piercings are seen more frequently and are promoted by fashion designers and trendsetters. But jewelers and craftspersons are today supplying the market with rings and studs for other parts of

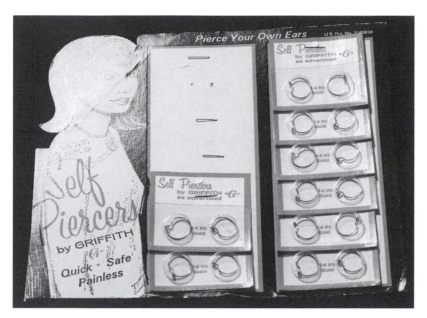

A 1960s advertisement for self-piercing earrings. Ouch! Copyright © 2007 by Anthony F. Chiffolo.

the body as well, parts that were traditionally and more frequently covered, such as the nipples and genitalia. On the whole, body piercing is a major presence within the modern jewelry market. Even Tiffany & Company, the jeweler to the jewelers, sells belly button rings for navel adornment (in titanium, no less).

Many jewelers who sell gold and sterling jewelry as part of their inventory are practiced in and equipped for ear piercing. This is usually accomplished by creating an opening in the earlobe using a piercing gun, a technique that has both pros and cons but is favored by retailers and consumers because it is a fast and fairly safe method of ear piercing. (Piercing guns should not be used on upper parts of the ear, where cartilage is involved, as they can cause excessive pain or discomfort.) Other piercing methods, especially for large-gauge jewelry, involve internally threaded jewelry, where the ball ends of the jewelry screw into the bar, rather than the bar screwing into the jewelry; dermal punching, whereby a circular area of tissue is removed in order to place the jewelry in the skin hole; scalpelling, which employs a medical scalpel to cut a slit in the skin; indwelling cannula method, which places a hollow plastic tube at the end of a needle, allowing both to be pulled through the opening to set the jewelry in place; tapering, a process that uses a steel bar to set the gauge of the opening; and the fairly stan-dard needle method, which makes an opening with a hollow medical needle. All these piercing methods are invasive procedures and carry some risk of infection and therefore should only be performed by professionals. Aftercare using a sea-salt or medical saline rinse are recommended; hydrogen peroxide and isopropyl alcohol are often effective but too strong for fresh piercings, so should be used sparingly, and results will vary.

☞   **DID YOU KNOW?**

There must be something in the water in California that provides entrepreneurs with insights regarding the latest trends. Leave it to two ingenious self-proclaimed rebels at Ledesma Enterprises to come up with the idea of body armor for your car. At www.pierceyourride.com, you can arrange to have your car personalized with rings or studs, or in the case of your bumper, car piercings. The piercings come in a range of different finishes and designs and in just about any metal that one could imagine. (They don't do tattoos—however those are available at some other California sites.) No word yet as to whether the car feels any pain or the rates of infection, but the recovery time is said to be minimal.[2]

NOTES

1. See Roberts, Lucy P., "The History of Body Piercings—Ancient and Fascinating around the World" at http://ezinearticles.com/?The-History-of-Body-Piercings—Ancient-and-Fascinating-Around-the-World&id=2948

2. Source: www.autoblog.com/2006/10/03/car-piercing-youve-got-to-be-kidding/

Bracelets

Kissing your hand may make you feel very, very good but a diamond and sapphire bracelet lasts forever. (Anita Loos [1888–1981], U.S. screenwriter and author of *Gentlemen Prefer Blondes*)

Bracelets (from the Latin *bracchiale*, "armlet") are arm ornaments that have been worn by both men and women since before recorded history. In ancient times, when worn by men they were often a sign of rank. Bracelets have been made of nearly every type of material, from metal to stone to gemstone and leather. In ancient China, bracelets made of jade were popular, as were those made of inlaid wood. The Mogul emperors of India wore bracelets as part of their royal costume. Shell bracelets were common in the Ban Koa culture (2000–500 B.C.E.) of what is now southern Thailand and Malaysia. In the Americas, Aztecs and Incas wore a variety of wrist cuff ornaments. In ancient Egypt, four bracelets were usually worn—two on each arm, with one above the elbow and the other at the wrist. They were sometimes plain gold bangles, or more often they were constructed of gold and glass beads with gold wire. In the later Ptolemaic and Roman periods of Egypt's history, bracelets were often fashioned in the shape of serpents. The bracelet was also an important feature of ancient Roman and Greek fashion: Bracelets of pure gold, some set with gemstones, as well as coin armbands and wrist

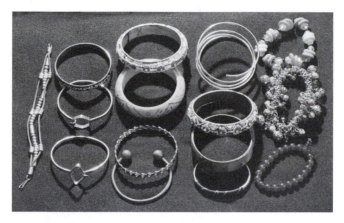

Bangles, cuffs, wristbands, and cling form—bracelets are made in many formats to appeal to nearly every taste in fashion. Copyright © 2007 by Anthony F. Chiffolo.

adornments made of glass, have been uncovered at many classical archaeological dig sites. Roman, Greek, and Egyptian pottery and other artwork depict men and women with bracelets decorating their arms. Some were obviously made to slip simply over the wrist; others were fashioned with a hook and eye or were cut to merely wrap or tie about the arm (known as cuffs).

Following the decline of the Roman Empire, bracelets among European peoples seem to have lost their appeal. This was due in part to changing fashions in the eras of long-sleeved daily costume, as well as differing sentiments regarding jewelry. The dawn of the Renaissance in Europe and the move to emulate classicism brought the wearing of bracelets full circle: Pomander bracelets with jewelry oils and scents, serpentine bracelets, bracelets with cameos of mythological figures, and bracelets studded with gemstones were all part of the resurgence of bracelet wearing in the post–Middle Ages. By the seventeenth century, bracelets were out of vogue again in Europe, but by the Victorian era, they were once again popular fashion accoutrements.[1] This was the defining moment for the plain gold bangle bracelet (ca. 1870), though pearl bands, elegant diamond wrist wear, gemstone cuffs, and strands of a loved one's hair, woven to be worn near the hand, were innovations of the era.

Today, all sorts of bracelets are made for men, women, and children. Some of the more interesting twentieth-century bracelet trends included:

CHARM BRACELETS

A charm bracelet is a band, bangle, or chain worn about the wrist from which hang decorative pendants or trinkets that often carry important significance to the wearer (for instance, names of children, tokens of places visited, school ring, and so forth). Its history goes back thousands of years to the ancient Egyptians, whose burial rites included necklaces or wrist bands with charms as keys to the next life: Each trinket would instruct the gods of the underworld as to the wearer's status, role, and position so that they would be recognized for who they were in the afterlife. But it was Queen Victoria of England (1819–1901) who made charm bracelets wildly popular late in the nineteenth century; she wore a charm bracelet of small gold lockets with photos of family members enclosed. Following World War II, returning soldiers would bring home remembrances of places stationed and visited; a popular souvenir was a foreign charm or coin, which U.S. jewelers attached to a sweetheart bracelet. Thus, by the 1950s, charm bracelets were all the rage. The craze died out in the late 1960s. Recently, Italian charm bracelets, featuring individual pieces that have been soldered flat onto the bracelet (versus dangling, as with traditional bracelets) have become a major fashion trend.

POW BRACELETS

In the early 1970s it was fashionable, both as a sign of protest against the Vietnam War and in solidarity with families whose loved ones were either prisoners of war or missing in action, to wear bracelets engraved with the name of a POW. This was done in a spirit of hope that they one day might return alive to be with their families. The bracelet concept originated with a California student-based organization called VIVA (Voices in Vital America) through their contact with the wives of missing U.S. pilots whose planes had been downed over some part of Southeast Asia. Organizers Kay Hunter, Carol Bates, Steve Frank, and Gloria Coppin first had ten sample bracelets made with the name, rank, and date of loss of local POW/MIAs, and from there sought funds to produce the bracelets on a larger scale. After being turned down by a number of big-time celebrities, including H. Ross Perot (1930–) and Howard Hughes (1905–1976), they took some of their own funds and had bracelets made by a local metalsmith of nickel and copper at a cost of about 75 cents each, selling them on average for $3.00 (the cost of a student movie ticket at the time). On Veterans Day, November 11, 1970, they officially kicked off their bracelet program at a news conference in the Universal Sheraton Hotel. The public response was overwhelming. At one time, more than 12,000 requests for bracelets came in per day. In all, nearly 5 million POW bracelets were distributed during a six-year period.

Since the terrorist attacks of 9/11/2000 in the United States, bracelets are once again being produced to keep the memory alive of those who have died at the hands of terrorists or who are fighting overseas in the Iraq war, as a way of offering moral and financial support to their families and loved ones.

COPPER HEALTH BRACELETS

Though copper bracelets have been used as currency for more than 400 years in places like the Philippines and Africa, since the 1940s they have been aggressively marketed as a popular natural remedy for arthritis. The origin of copper's healing properties probably dates back to the era of the Eber Papyrus (circa 1552 B.C.E.), an Egyptian document that entreats sufferers to combat inflammation of the joints with pulverized copper. The discovery in 1939 that miners in Finland were found to be unaffected by arthritis as long as they were working in the copper mines helped to fan the flames of copper's positive properties for the Modern Age. Dr. Helmar Dollwet's health book, *The Copper Bracelet and Arthritis* (Vantage Press, 1981), helped to popularize the healing effects of copper (though the American Arthritis Foundation calls copper bracelets an "unproven remedy"), to the point that millions of copper bracelets are sold around the world today (particularly in Europe) as a pain-relieving essential. Copper bracelets with magnets (a purported healing additive) are also popular, particularly in the New Age movement. Copper bracelets are also the stuff of comic book action heroes, who depend on them often as the source of their incredible strength and resilience.

LIVESTRONG BRACELETS

Livestrong bracelets are colored rubber wristbands made popular by seven-time Tour de France champion Lance Armstrong (1971–). In 1996, Armstrong was diagnosed with testicular cancer, which also spread to his lungs and brain. With only a 50 percent chance of recovery and following two surgeries and chemotherapy, he decided "to stand up and take stock of his life" and turn the cancer death knell into something positive. Armstrong went on to establish the Lance Armstrong Foundation to fund cancer research and provide support programs to other patients suffering as he was. As part of that program, Lance launched a project with the sports giant Nike to market yellow synthetic silicone rubber bracelets, printed with the word "LIVESTRONG," in the hope of raising awareness about cancer and to show solidarity with those who are its victims. The wristbands are considered "hip," especially in the athletic world, and are popular with men, women, and children. To date, the Lance Armstrong Foundation has sold more than fifty million bracelets, a modern phenomenon.

TENNIS BRACELETS

A tennis bracelet is a thin, in-line bracelet that features a symmetrical pattern of diamonds. It takes its name from an unusual moment in tennis history. It seems that tennis great Chris Evert (1954–) was playing an event in the 1987 U.S. Open when her Harry Winston (1896–1978) diamond bracelet (as described above) broke and the match was held up momentarily to allow for the diamonds to be collected.[2] This incident created a new name for that style of diamond bracelet; it also sparked a jewelry trend, making tennis bracelets one of the top selling jewelry items of the latter part of the twentieth century.

☞ DID YOU KNOW?

The Swiss jewelrymaker Chopard has recently come out with an incredible timepiece that is sure to catch the attention of those who must have the most expensive gift under the Christmas tree.[3] It is composed of three heart-shaped diamonds: The pink diamond is 15 carats, the blue diamond is 12 carats, and the white diamond a mere 11 carats. But the bracelet upon which the diamonds sit is what makes this piece of jewelry worth its weight in krugerrands! It is encrusted with white and yellow-fancy shaped diamonds clustered to create a bed of flowers, with a TCW (total carat weight) of 163 carats. So, how much for 201 carats of diamonds on one bracelet?

A cool $25 million.

And it tells time to boot!

NOTES

1. See Mason, Anita and Diane Packer, "Bracelets" in *An Illustrated Dictionary of Jewellery,* 41.

2. See the news article "Bling, Tennis and Wimbledon" on the Diamond Bug Web site at http://diamondbug.blogspot.com/2005/06/bling-tennis-and-wimbledon.html

3. Source: http://www.tyler-adam.com/97.html

Brass

Composition: alloys of zinc and copper with other metals; there are 16 major brass types, some of which are alloyed with tin, aluminum, lead, nickel, silver, gold, silicon, and arsenic to make varying strengths of brass metal

Origin of name: possibly from Old English *braes* or Middle English *bres* or *bras,* circa 1200 C.E.; perhaps akin to French *brasser* ("to brew") or *braser* ("to solder") since it is an alloy

Primary usages: musical instruments, primarily trumpet, tuba, trombone, saxophone, harmonica, euphonium, and organ pipes; springs, screws, rivets; gunmetal, metal hoses and bellows, cryogenic containers; jewelry, decorative adornments, sculpture; pre-1940: used in fan blades, fan cages, motor bearings

Brass, a metal alloy of zinc and copper (and often other metals), has been known and used for many millennia. Both the ancient Egyptians and Greeks appreciated its malleable properties, and the Romans were fond of it for coinage and for the durable gold-like color it lent to the helmets of their soldiers.[1] It was the Romans in particular who produced a grade of brass (from 11 percent to 28 percent zinc) that allowed for a variety of decorative colors for the production of all types of ornamental jewelry. However, the zinc in their jewelry and other items was a by-product and was probably not intentional. For more than a thousand years, through the medieval period, there was no source of pure zinc, meaning that the only way to intentionally produce brass or a brass color was to process calamine, which naturally contains both copper and zinc, in order to obtain the desired brass result. One of the top sources for calamine was found in the Mendip hills of Somerset in South Wales. It is from this source that many wonderful brass monuments and memorial plates set into the floors of British churches originate; they can be viewed yet today.

In pre-industrialized Europe, the principal users of brass were those in the woolen trade. Later the pin trade came to depend heavily on brass: Because brass was easily worked and could stand up well to corrosion (the more zinc or tin that was added), it was the ideal substance for all sorts of clothing and fashion accessories. Yet this was not the only commercial usage of brass during the period. From the late 1500s through the Renaissance era, brass was also a major component of clocks, chronometers, watches, and navigational aids. For any instrument that required precision, brass parts were in demand and stood the test of time: Many clocks made in the 1700s are still in good working order and show very little wear, despite three hundred years of use.

For the next several hundred years, the process of making brass was refined, primarily in an industrialized England, which had the industry, inventiveness, necessity, and mining know-how to make brass a key element of all kinds of metal production, both within its borders and beyond.

The history of brass jewelry is rather complex. Diverse civilizations have used brass (intentionally or not) for body adornments and for ritual purposes since ancient times; in the past 200–300 years, brass has come to be used more as a finish over other metals in European jewelry. In the Americas, though it was often used in Native American crafts, brass has not had a wide appeal. However, for at least five centuries, if not longer, brass has been the major metal in jewelrycasting throughout Africa and Asia. Much of what today is sold as "ethnic jewelry" has a brass underskin or is entirely made of brass.

Most African jewelry came to be made of brass due to climate and economics. A good portion of Africa is so dry that making any type of metal jewelry is nearly impossible. However, there has long been commerce in brass jewelry thanks to

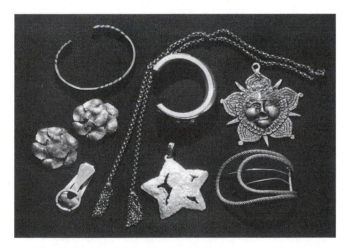

Brass is a popular metal alloy used to create many types of jewelry, from pendants to chains, rings to bracelets. Copyright © 2007 by Anthony F. Chiffolo.

trade routes between north and west Africa. These routes have allowed for animal skins and other desert products to be traded for brass and copper, affording one group the luxuries of another. Since the early fifteenth century C.E., along the edge of the equatorial rain forest and the savannahs, gold and ivory have been traded for glass beads, copper, coral, and brass. One of the peoples that have long taken advantage of these trades has been the inhabitants of Benin, a tiny kingdom located in the rain forests of Nigeria. The tribespeople, known as the Yoruba, have been making brass jewelry since the thirteenth century C.E. through a process known as the "lost wax method." By this method, a wax model of the jewelry piece is made first; then a mold is formed around the wax model; next it is cast with the metal; finally it is cooled and finished. Many thin-plaited brass bracelets are still made by the Yoruba using this process. The bracelets are wide and are worn by women all throughout Nigeria as both an expression of celebration and to attract the opposite sex.[2]

In addition to African jewelry, much of the brass-based or brass-made jewelry on the market today comes from Middle Eastern countries (sometimes referred to as West Asia), India, Nepal, Tibet, Thailand, the People's Republic of China, Sri Lanka, the Philippines, and Indonesia. The Internet features thousands of sites selling modern brass jewelry from these markets.

There are also many do-it-yourselfers when it comes to making brass jewelry, as it is not a difficult process, provided one has the correct materials. To make brass jewelry, crafters use a variety of tools, including soldering elements, copper tongs, sandpaper, hydrogen peroxide, rolling mills, jeweler's saw, ring clamps, jeweler's files, anvil, center punch, rawhide mallet, drill, pliers, buffing wheels, rouge polish, spray lacquer, flush cutters, Ball-peen hammer, crimpers, pickle pot with pickle solution, and other tools as well. Although brass for jewelrymaking can be purchased in rods, sheets, foil, and wire, much of today's brass on the market is recycled scrap, which can be purchased at reasonable prices in comparison to other jewelry metals, making brass an ideal material for crafters.

☞ DID YOU KNOW?

In 2007, many of the countries of the world have coins that are made of brass or some other copper alloy (such as cupro-nickel). Brass is a traditional coin metal, appearing as early as the eleventh century B.C.E. in China. Jewelry buyers have long been fascinated by brass coins, and many bracelets, belts, rings, earrings, and belly dancer costumes have featured brass coinage that really catches the eye.

Some of the most collected brass coins come from countries that had a short existence. One recent example is the country of Rwanda-Burundi, which received its independence from Belgium in June 1960. It issued just one coin, a brass franc that featured a walking lion, struck in Brussels. It hardly had the time to make the rounds of the country, as Rwanda and Burundi separated into two distinct nations on July 1, 1962.

Speaking of brass coins: The new U.S. Golden Dollar, though gold in color, is actually a manganese-brass alloy that is 12 percent zinc; but there's not an ounce of gold in it. Seems as though it's going to end up on a lot of bracelets in the near future!

NOTES

1. The Greeks called brass *oreichalcos;* the Romans *aurichalum.*
2. See Camera, Lucille, "The History and Aesthetics of African Jewelry" at http://www.yale.edu/ynhti/curriculum/units/1993/4/93.04.02.x.html

Buttons

The world is made up of two kinds of people: those who lose buttons, and those who collect them . . . (Memory Lane Antiques)

Though in the twenty-first century we have come to take them for granted, buttons were once prize pieces of jewelry and high on the fashion end of must-have accessories. The word *button* comes from the French *bouton,* a small piece of metal or some other material used to connect different parts of a garment. It is thought that buttons originated in southern Asia around the Indus Valley about 2000 B.C.E. and that they were used primarily as a decoration (pins and belts are what held clothes together). Archeological evidence has unearthed seashells from this period that were carved into geometric shapes and pierced with holes so that they could easily be attached with string or thread to clothing. The ancient Greeks and Romans were fond of shell and wood buttons, and other ancient cultures made buttons of ivory, bone, gemstones, gold, and silver. But it wasn't until the thirteenth century C.E. in Europe that the button and buttonhole made their fashion marriage debut, thanks to the availability and usage of more delicate fabrics. Pins left ugly holes in fine silks and velvets, and something more functional was needed. Thus the buttonhole was invented, and buttons became the epitome of style (for those who could afford them).

For the next three to four hundred years, between 1300 and 1700, buttons served fashion and style more than practicality. Diamond buttons, especially for men, were not an unusual sight in the royal courts of Europe. During the Elizabethan era, handmade covered buttons were popular, especially with the Queen herself. Gemstone buttons completed the perfect outfit. At the start of the eighteenth century, wooden buttons covered with embroidered patterns made their way onto men's coats and waistcoats. It wasn't until the late 1700s that we see a major shift in button trends, when the bigger, metallic steel varieties appear on men's clothing.

The year 1802 was perhaps the most important year in the development of buttons. Abel Porter and Company became the first button-making factory in the United States, established to provide a growing native garment industry with domestically made metal buttons, since imported buttons were hard to come by and very expensive. Porter was the first to make cast brass wire loops in buttons. Meanwhile, B. Sanders in Birmingham, England, made what is thought to be the earliest known machine-covered button, and with a metal shank to boot. It was in 1802 as well that the now ubiquitous flexible shank button was born.

Though the button industry struggled to keep up with the advances of the Industrial Revolution, it came into its own in the 1840s with the invention of the porcelain button (1840), threefold linen buttons (1841), and the first completely U.S. manufactured button (all parts by machine) in 1848, through the genius and engineering of Samuel Williston (1795–1874) in Easthampton, MA.[1] Williston factories soon opened in Waterbury, CT, Philadelphia, and New York City.

In 1860, Johann Hille set Vienna on fire with the introduction in Austria of hand-colored buttons made from discarded South American ivory nuts. Herman Donath of Schmolln, Germany, traded hand-carved ivory umbrella handles for manufacturing buttons made of ivory nuts, and Schmolln became the center of the ivory button industry. In the years that followed, vegetable ivory button factories were established in England, in Massachusetts, and in Ontario.

Queen Victoria's (1819–1901) years of mourning for her beloved Prince Albert (1819–1861) had a profound effect on the button industry. Victoria started a fashion revolution soon after Albert's death in 1861 by appearing in public with black jet (polished coal) buttons sewn on to her royal wear as a symbol of her grieving. An imitative but poor public (who could not afford the expensive mineral) found an acceptable substitute in what is sometimes called "French jet," and this onyx-colored glass, though fragile, was cheap and looked respectable. Today, black buttons of either kind from the Victorian period are greatly prized by collectors.

In 1869, the first celluloid buttons were introduced. During the Art Deco period, Bakelite buttons were the rage, and after World War II, buttons made of

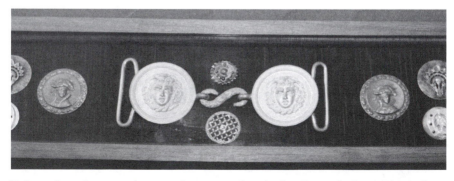

Eighteenth- and nineteenth-century buttons in a box display. Copyright © 2007 by Anthony F. Chiffolo.

every conceivable material became available, particularly in plastic (post–1953). Today, buttons are a big collectible item, with some buttons of age and rare material bringing thousands of dollars on the resale market. Of particular value are habitats, metal-backed, glass-domed buttons with dried plants or animals (whole insects, for instance) creating a kind of mise-en-scene effect. Uniform buttons, especially military samples, are prize finds. Another uncommon but much sought after type are livery buttons, worn by English house servants, usually with the crest or coat-of-arms of their employer emblazoned on the button surface. So check out grandma's sewing kit—there's probably a small fortune staring from within!

☞   DID YOU KNOW?

Who says buttons are not jewelry? King Francis I (1494–1547) of France ordered 13,400 gold buttons to fasten a black velvet outfit for a rendezvous with King Henry VII (1457–1509) of England to discuss an alliance. King Louis XIV (1638–1715) of France is rumored to have spent $600,000 in one year on his buttons and nearly $5 million on buttons during his lifetime.

And have you ever wondered why men's and women's clothing button on opposite sides? The practice supposedly originated in the fifteenth century. Men generally dressed themselves, and as most were right-handed, it was faster to button right to left. Women who were wealthy enough to afford buttons on their clothing had dressing maids, and as most were right-handed it was more expedient to have a mirror-image reversal. Tailors complied and the custom remains to this day.[2]

NOTES

1. Williston helped to invent the press, stamp, and engine for button molds; he used ground animal bones and hooves as filler. He was so successful that within in a few years of having opened his first factory, he was making buttons for half the world.

2. Source: Joan Kiplinger, "Vintage Fabrics—In Search of Warp Ends," at www. fabrics.net.com

Cameos

Cameos: Imperial messages in agate . . . (Dutch scholar A. N. Zadoks-Josephus Zitta)

A cameo is a portrait or scene carved in relief (bas-relief) with a contrasting colored background. It has a long history as an objet d'art of jewels: It is said that Queen Elizabeth I (1533–1603) had a large collection of cameos, and that Catherine the Great (1729–1796) did also. Greco-Roman cameos have been

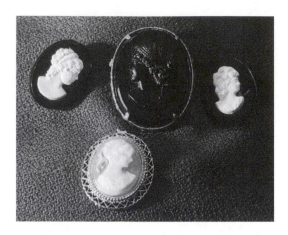

Twentieth-century cameos made from a variety of materials. Copyright © 2007 by Anthony F. Chiffolo.

found that date to as early as 200 B.C.E., when they were used on helmets and military accessories, such as breastplates and sword handles, or on vases, cups, and dishes.[1] Hellenistic young women were purported to have used cameos as charms to express desire. Yet their original purpose was most likely utilitarian (as seals on documents), though they were often used as decorations on the ceremonial robes of the Roman emperors.[2] However, cameos gained a greater popularity as adornment during the Renaissance in Europe, when they were worn only by royalty and clergy. The height of cameo fashion came during the reign (1837–1901) of Queen Victoria (1819–1901) of England. In fact, cameos are still popular today; many women have the pieces that were handed down in their families through the generations, and they prize these superb works of art for their beauty and delicate crafting.

Cameos can be made of a wide variety of materials: stone, ivory, French jet (glass), English jet (polished coal), lava, coral, wood, gemstones (agate, onyx, sardonyx, turquoise), and plastic or other synthetics. In eighteenth-century England, Wedgwood was producing molded stone cameos (much of their current Jasperware is produced in cameo style), and Bilston produced enameled versions. However, since about 1805, the large majority of cameos have been carved from shell, particularly conch, mollusks (mother-of-pearl), coral, or abalone. It was in that year that the French emperor Napoleon I (1769–1821) founded a school of stone carving to promote the production of cameos, and had his coronation crown decorated with them.[3] Today, the majority of the world's cameos are produced in Italy, particularly in Sicily, Pompeii, and the area around Naples, where one can visit cameo factories and hundreds of merchants plying the trade.

"The capital city of cameos" is called Torre del Greco, in southern Italy. Were one to visit the more than 5,000 cameo artisans that reside there today, an entire world of superb crafting on display, as it has been since the fifteenth century. For hundreds of years the occupants of this small town have been involved in coral and shell diving and have harvested lava (from Mt. Vesuvius nearby),

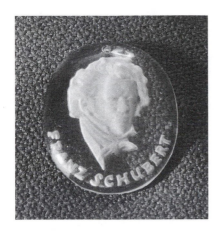

A glass intaglio of the musician Franz Schubert.
Copyright © 2007 by Anthony F. Chiffolo.

coral, and conch—three of the primary materials for making cameos. Select-ing only the best materials for a cameo background that is free of cracks and flaws, the cameo artisan takes the piece to be engraved and mounts it with wax on a wooden stick. Once a sketch is made of what needs to be carved, the engraving process begins using steel burins. As the engraving is finished, the cameo, usually no more than 2 millimeters in width, is wrapped by hand, usually with gold metal ribbon (known as bezel or gallery wire) around the perimeter that is then folded over the edges of each piece. Usually oval in form, the bezel is then hand-decorated with gold moldings, ribbons, braids, ropes, or pearls, then further embellished with filigree work or diamonds. It is an ardu-ous and painstaking process of exquisite detailing with results that are truly breathtaking.

Cameos often feature a portrait of the "ideal woman" of her époque, some-times decorated with small silver or gold chains, minute diamond pendants, earrings, or a tiara. These jeweled and decorated cameos are called *habilles* (French for "ornamented" clothing). In Victorian times, the perfect gift for a woman was to receive a cameo after her likeness; yet thousands upon thou-sands of cameos have been produced of an anonymous female with upswept hair, high lace collar, upturned nose, and ivory-colored skin. Some cameos portrayed important historical figures of the day, such as George Washington (1732–1799) or Louis XV (1710–1774) of France, or leading ladies, such as the popular nineteenth-century actress, Sarah Bernhardt (1844–1923). When cameos did not feature an individual portrait, they often depicted pastoral or mythological scenes—perhaps the Three Graces of Greek mythology—or a biblical heroine, such as Rebecca or Ruth. Victorian cameos also included flowers, trees, and bridges—all that was idealistically sylvan, natural, and clas-sic. They were most often worn as pins or as pendants on a black velvet ribbon and were set in bezels of gold, silver, pinchbeck, and/or brass. Some bezels were further decorated with filigree, tiny gems, seed pearls, or marcasite. Most cam-eos of this era were also fixed with a back mounting so that they could double as either a pin or pendant. Victorian-era cameos also appear in rings, earrings, bracelets, and stickpins.

Cameos are yet today one of the most purchased and collected jewelry items of modern fashion.

For those who enjoy the art of jewelry, the Walters Art Museum in Baltimore, Maryland, has a wonderful collection of stone cameos.

☞   **DID YOU KNOW?**

An intaglio is a portrait or scene carved below the surface of shell or gemstone or other product. It is the opposite of a cameo. In ancient times the intaglio was used as an official seal on papers or as a way to mark property.

NOTES

1. See "Collecting Cameos: Ancient Beauties," from *Antiques Roadshow Tips of the Trade* at http://www.pbs.org/wgbh/pages/roadshow/tips/cameo.html Wikipedia claims that "cameos of great artistry were made in Greece dating back as far as the sixth century B.C.E." (See "Cameo" at http://en.wikipedia.org/wiki/Cameo)

2. These "cameos" were actually what is known as intaglios.

3. See the "Evolution of Jewellery" at http://www.jewellerycatalogue.co.uk/antq/evolution-of-jewellery.php Monica Beth Fowler in her article "In Praise of Cameos" (*Antiques and Art around Florida*, Winter/Spring, 1998 at http://aarf.com/ferame98.htm) writes that about this same time (1805), "the first public school for the study of cameo engraving was opened in Rome. The school was funded by the Vatican through Pope Leo XII (1760–1829) and met with much success."

Carats

1 carat = 100 points = $\frac{1}{142}$ ounce = $\frac{1}{5}$ gram = 200 milligrams
1 pound = 454 grams = 2270 carats

In biblical times, precious commodities were sold and measured according to their equivalent weight in carob seeds extracted from the pods of Middle Eastern locust trees.[1] Carob seeds were used because of their reputation for having a uniform weight. In classical times they were known as siliqua, and one siliqua was equal to three barley corns or four wheat grains. Johnson's *Dictionary* of 1755 defines a carat as four grains.

Yet not all carob seeds weigh the same, and there was a lot of variation in countries using the metric system as to just how many milligrams equaled one carat. By the mid-nineteenth century, a carat was 199.1 milligrams in Lisbon, 205.1 milligrams in Amsterdam, yet 207 milligrams in Venice. As measurements became more precise, a universal standard was needed. In 1877, the principal

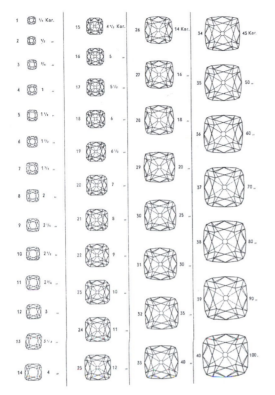

A chart showing approximate gemstone sizes, from ¼ carat to 100 carats. Antique Jewelry by E. Steingraber, copyright © 1957. Reproduced with permission of Greenwood Publishing Group, Inc., Westport, CT.

merchants of the gem trade in Europe met and agreed that one carat should equal 205 milligrams. Yet this standard did not prevail. It was finally decided in 1914 by the International Committee on Weights and Measures that traders, buyers, and sellers would accept the metric standard of one-fifth of a gram (200 milligrams = 1 carat) for diamonds and other precious gemstones.[2]

Gemstones are measured to the nearest hundredth of a carat, called points.[3] So as to distinguish a carat (with a "c") from a karat (with a "k," that is to say the amount of gold mixed with alloys in fine jewelry), a carat is now frequently referred to as a metric carat and is abbreviated as "ct." The weight of multiple small stones in one jewelry item is expressed as a whole amount and is written as "total carat weight" (or TCW).

In the case of diamonds, stones that are less than 20 points are called melee, grain, or, sometimes, grainer. A grain is equal to one-quarter of a carat: therefore a three-quarter carat (or 75 point) diamond may be referred to as a "three grainer," and a one-carat stone may be listed as a "four grainer." Loose stones are easily weighed on a scale, but for stones that have been mounted into a setting, an estimated weight is often given using a jewelry-standard mathematical equation. Jewelers also use a chart that estimates carat size by measuring the diameter of the diamond and comparing it to a size chart such as the one on the next page.

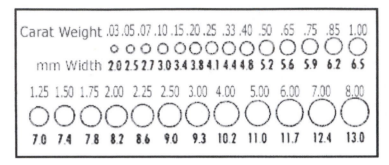

Another quick way of estimating mounted round diamonds is by measuring the diameter of the diamond and comparing it to a size chart. Carat weight measuring chart courtesy of A. Fishman & Son, 580 Fifth Avenue, Suite 419, NY, NY 10036. Used by permission of Josh Fishman.

Carat weight is only one characteristic that should be considered when buying a high-end precious stone. Rubies, emeralds, diamonds, and other gemstones are graded according to the 4 Cs: carat size, color, clarity, and cut. All are important in assessing the worth of a particular stone. It is also important to remember when assessing the value of precious stones that weight and size are not the same thing. Because precious stones are rarer as they increase in weight, the larger the stone, the more valuable and costly it is. Therefore, all things being equal (keeping in mind the 4 Cs), a three-carat diamond will always be more expensive than three one-carat diamonds.

☞   DID YOU KNOW?

The largest fine-quality, colorless diamond ever found was called the Cullinan. It was mined in South Africa and weighed 3,106 carats. This rare find was then cut into 106 jewels and produced the finest, largest gemstone ever, known as the Star of Africa, which weighed 530.2 carats.[4]

NOTES

1. Karat (or carat) is a Middle English word, from the Old French, from the Medieval Latin *quarâtus* (carob bean); from the Arabic *qirât,* a bean pod or a weight of four grains; from the Greek *keration,* a weight, which is also the diminutive form of *keras,* a horn.

2. The relationship between weight and size varies with each family of gemstones. For example, rubies and sapphires are both heavier than diamonds and have a higher specific gravity; therefore, a one-carat ruby or sapphire is smaller than a one-carat diamond. Pearls, once measured by carats also, are more regularly sold according to size in millimeters.

3. It is not totally accurate to say that a carat is always equivalent to 100 points. Because not every stone can be cut to the same exact measurements and weight, a point should always be understood as the best approximate value.

4. Source: http://en.wikipedia.org/wiki/Diamond

Celtic Jewelry

Period: Stone Age to present

Birthplace: Ireland, Scottish Highlands, Wales

Origins: Coptic manuscripts (partly)

Influences: Saxon and Pictish traditions of abstract beast forms; nature and zoomorphs; designs found at Skara Brae in the Orkney Islands; Druid religious practices

The Celtic people (or Gauls, as the Romans called them) have their roots in Eastern Europe. Following the rivers that led north and west, they eventually settled in what is today Ireland and Scotland, though at times their numerous tribes were the chief inhabitants of Germany, Austria, Switzerland, parts of France, and Russia as well. They were well known as fierce warriors, often engaging in battle in the nude, their bodies painted with interlocking designs and animal motifs using woad, a type of blue, wood dye that they believed made them appear a more formidable foe.

The jewelry of the Celtic peoples, some of which has been discovered in sites believed to be more than 5,000 years old, is fashioned after the ancient symbols that were used to decorate their burial sites, pottery, and other artifacts. Ancient Celtic jewelry was made of stone; at Iona, where the rock is so old that there are no fossils, green serpentine marble known as St. Columba's tears (or Iona greenstone), and bloodstone were hewn to make adornments for the body. Later, bronze, pewter, silver, and gold, sometimes decorated with enamel or gemstones, were used. The most common motif in the jewelry from this period was a single spiral, which may have represented prosperity. In various forms it carried the meanings of night and day, winter and summer; when Christianity came to the Celts, a triple spiral came to symbolize all things good, all things of God (based on belief in the Trinity). Other common symbols were wild animals that looked like wolves with pointed muzzles and long tails. Interlacing knotwork, a symbol of eternity, was also a popular theme.

Because the ancient Celts did not have a written culture, they expressed themselves primarily through their symbols. Celtic jewelry is long on symbolism, especially forms that emanate from the animal kingdom and nature. One of the oldest representations found on Celtic jewelry is the snake, signifying rebirth, healing, the connection between heaven and earth, and fertility. Horses (elegance, strength), dogs (loyalty, protection from danger), roosters (courage, a new day), rabbits, geese, and cranes were also common. Trees (long life and good health) and their branches, especially the oak (a Celtic priest, called a "Druid," means "oak-knower"), were frequently depicted, as were horns (renewal, nourishment, welcome), swords (strength, triumph, skill), and *triskells* (triadic forms that represent life, birth, and death).

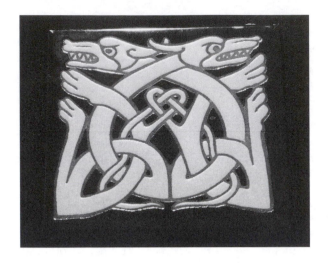

Celtic jewelry features all kinds of ancient symbols taken from the animal kingdom and nature, such as the one found on this tile. Copyright © 2007 by Anthony F. Chiffolo.

In modern parlance, "Celtic jewelry" includes pieces that are mainly Scottish, Welsh, and Irish, and as one might expect, there is a lot of overlap. Jewelry from all three geographical locations and cultural traditions is now sold as "authentically Celtic." It would not be unusual, therefore, to find Celtic jewelry with a uniquely Scottish influence, such as torques (neck rings), penannular brooches (kilt pins), fibulas (cloak pins), bracelets, and pendants—many with traditional Scottish heather, leeks, thistles, or Queen Mary's crown;[1] or Celtic jewelry with a Welsh influence, featuring daffodils, dragons, lovespoons, or the harp; or Celtic jewelry of a particularly Irish influence, with a shamrock, cross, or claddagh (crowned intertwined hands as a symbol of love, friendship, and integrity).

In the twenty-first century, Celtic jewelry is one of the most popular styles worn by both men and women.

☞ DID YOU KNOW?

In the Wales of centuries past, a young man would carve a spoon to symbolize his intentions towards a woman he wished to court. It was important to show his intended (and her family) that he was a good craftsman and that he could (and would) provide all that she might need in their new life, from furniture to kitchen utensils. A fancy spoon carved with horseshoes (good luck), bells (a wedding), a wheel (a pledge of hard work), balls in a cage (children, or a long marriage), or hearts (true love) said all that needed to be said. It is from this tradition that the expression "to spoon" is taken (to hold hands or embrace as lovers).

NOTE

1. Marie Stuart (1542–1587), Queen of Scotland, executed in England during the reign of her cousin, Elizabeth I (1533–1603).

Chains

Round her neck she wore three chains, which reached to her knees. (As quoted in
Dining with the Sultana by Lady Mary Wortley Montagu [1689–1762], 1718)

A chain is a series of rings, links, beads, or discs, usually of gold, silver, or some
other metal, that have been link-crafted to one another. They have been used
since the earliest of times and were very common among ancient populations,
particularly the Egyptian and Greco-Roman civilizations. Heavy gold chains were
also very popular during the Renaissance and Victorian eras in Europe and during the Victorian era in the United States. It was the luxury goods firm of Bulgari
who introduced the use of handmade gold chains in the twentieth century as a
staple of modern jewelry. Chains of all types found a new buyer's market in the
late 1960s and 1970s and were an important fashion style of the disco dance era.
Today, chains are also a vital symbol of all that is cool among hip-hop aficiona-
dos. In early times, chains were handmade; since the Middle Ages, they have
been both machine-made and handcrafted, usually by bending a piece of wire
and soldering the ends together to create links that are themselves connected to
construct a chain.

As neckwear jewelry goes, chains are in a class by themselves. In the twenty-first
century, they are constructed of nearly every available precious metal, as well as metal
alloys like brass, steel, and pewter. Worn by men, women, and children, there are
almost as many types of chains as there is jewelry to wear on them. Of course, many
chains are so lovely that they are worn as a solo piece to show off the craft of the designer. Some of the top chain types made by jewelry craftspersons today include:

Book chain: A book chain is a heavy, link chain, usually made of gold, gold-
fill, or silver, with each link crafted into a rectangular shape by folding
the metal in a way that resembles a book. The book chain was very
popular in the Victorian era.

Box (Venetian): A box chain is made up of wide and square links resembling
a box. The links are closely connected to give the appearance of an
uninterrupted and smooth surface.

Byzantine: The Byzantine link features two pairs of oval-shaped pieces that
are connected yet divided by a third, larger and thicker link attached to
each pair.

Cable chain: The cable is perhaps one of the most common chain designs
in which uniform round rings are linked, one to another. Because the
links are connected in opposite directions, this type of chain will not
lie flat.

Curb chain: The curb chain shows intricate work of oval-shaped twisted links
that are often diamond cut so that they lie flat.

Figaro (3-in-1) chain: A very popular style, Figaro chains alternate curb rectangular and circular links, usually set as one long rectangular to every three smaller, short, circular links.

Figure-8 chain: A small oval link is twisted into a figure-8 shape and serves as a connector between curb links to form this attractive chain.

Foxtail chain: One of the most recent innovations of jewelrycrafters, the foxtail chain is woven with two rows of oval links facing each other at a 45-degree angle connected by a center row of flat rings that have been set flush.

Herringbone chain: Very popular look, herringbone is made with a series of short, flat, and slanted parallel links set in two or more rows, with the slant of the links alternating from row to row.

Marina chain: The marina chain (not to be confused with the mariner chain [see below]) is made up of a series of small, round, diamond-cut links set very close together.

Mariner chain: For sea lovers, the mariner chain picks up a kind of nautical theme, sporting oval links with a bar set in the middle, dividing the link from top to bottom. The *figogucci* chain is a variant of this style.

Omega chain: A difficult chain to make and wear, the omega is constituted of rectangular, smooth metal plates placed side by side and crimped along the end onto a strip of metal mesh.

Rolo chain: A rolo chain is very similar to the cable chain except that its links are formed from half-round wire—versus whole-round wire—of different gauges. This gives the chain a heavier look using less metal content.

Rope chain: For a rich, textured look, the rope chain weaves together two thick chains, giving the appearance of a spiral.

Serpentine chain: Named for its "s" shaped links, the serpentine chain is crafted with small, flat S-shaped links that are placed close together; to hold their form, a twin set of links is set below them.

Snake chain: Not to be confused with the serpentine chain, from which it varies greatly, the snake chain shows a series of round, wavy metal rings joined side by side to form a smooth, flexible kind of tubing. The snake chain gets its name, some say, from the way the pattern of the waves resembles snake skin.

Wheat chain: A wheat chain is composed of oval and twisted oval links that are connected and intertwined, resulting in a strong chain with visual texture.

Other popular chains found on today's market include the Ball, Barleycorn, Barrel, Belcher, Benoiton, Brazilian, Butterfly, Cord, Cuban, Diamond Trace, Fetter, Jaseron, Loop-in-loop, Mesh, Strap, and Trace chains. Chains can also be linked to make clothing; known as chain-mail, its strength has made it a natural armor for warriors and soldiers from the Middle Ages to modern times.

☞ **DID YOU KNOW?**

In the spring of 1999, visitors to Dubai in the United Arab Emirates could gaze upon the longest gold chain in the world. The piece, created by the jewelers

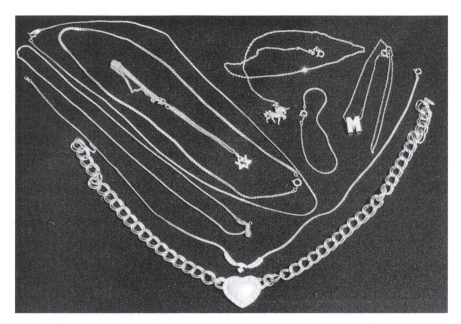

Chains of varied widths and sizes, for both men and women. Copyright © 2007 by Anthony F. Chiffolo.

at AngloGold in 22k yellow gold, measured 4.1 km (2.5 mi.) and weighed 200 kilograms. At the time, the chain was said to be valued at US$2 million. As part of a worldwide gold promotion, the Dubai Shopping Festival sold 3.12 km of the chain, which had been divided into more than 9,000 pieces for customers who had pre-booked their portions and had them fashioned into bracelets, necklaces, and the like. But those who didn't make reservations ahead of time were not left out of the incredible deal: The final kilometer of the chain was sold the same day to visiting tourists eager to participate in a moment of jewelry market history.[1]

NOTE

1. Source: "The World's Longest Gold Chain" at http://thelongestlistofthelongest stuffatthelongestdomainnameatlonglast.com/long283.html

Coin Jewelry

It could be a medal (no value listed on its face), or a token (a value is given), but if it were issued by the government for use in commerce, it's a coin. . . . (Memory Lane Antiques)

The use of coinage in jewelry goes back about as far as the minting of coins themselves. Some of the oldest known coins are from the kingdom of Lydia (see **Gold**), in what is modern-day Turkey, dating to circa 650 B.C.E. These first coins were made of gold and silver. Following in the footsteps of their Lydian neighbors, the Greeks and Romans minted coinage, and as the centuries progressed and competition between city-states increased, coins became more elaborate and took on a new role; not only were they the stuff of barter, but they quickly became a propaganda tool to promote the politics of the era. Eventually the owl-adorned coins of the Greeks and the mythological motifs of the Romans gave way to portraits of the ruling political figures of the time; as a testament to their self-ego and their place in history, the rulers began to add dates to the coins to better record their accomplishments. From the time of Alexander the Great (356–323 B.C.E.) to the era of the Caesars (first century B.C.E.–third century C.E.), coinage was the most powerful propaganda tool of kings, queens, emperors, and empresses. The quality of Roman Empire die work and the architecture of their coins, both in aesthetic style (overall appearance) and durability (many of them still exist today) as well as their ubiquity are unrivaled.

In Asia, the Chinese were minting coins as early as the Zhou (1122–255 B.C.E.) and Ch'in (255–206 B.C.E.) dynasties. This coinage seems to have consisted primarily of round copper pieces with square holes; also what is known as "spade" and "knife" coins were common in this period. The round coins, sometimes called "cash coins," were prominent in all the countries of Asia. The hole in the middle of the coin had a very practical usage, as money was often transported on strings rather than in a purse or pocket. The strings were usually tied in units of 100, 300, or 1000, which made counting and trading easy. Interestingly enough, there did not appear to be any problem with exchange rates—even the name of the coin was nearly identical in all the countries and provinces where it was used.

About the same time as the Lydians and Chinese were minting their coins, the first coins were being made in India. Referred to in modern parlance as punch-mark coins, they seem to have developed independent of outside influences and, as such, are quite different from their Lydian and Chinese counterparts. The first Indian coins were nearly all uniface and without any defined shapes; yet they all bore symbols of various types, hand-punched onto silver pieces of a specified weight.

When one studies old coinage, it is easy to see the important role coins played in the history of ancient civilizations. Coins also teach us a lot about how civilizations operated and what was important to them. It is interesting to observe the move from coin usage as a trade commodity to its first use as jewelry. Obviously, coinage has to be a long-established community fixture before its primary function is abandoned, if only in part, for another use. It is said that the peoples of ancient Rome were responsible for the popular usage of coins in jewelry. In the Roman Empire, the first coins used in jewelry appear to be first- to third-century C.E. gold coins (*aurei*) in pendants or amulets, often set in a gold frame of open filigree work, worn about the neck by both men and women, usually with a gemstone (the favorites of the time were emeralds, opals, and beryls) in

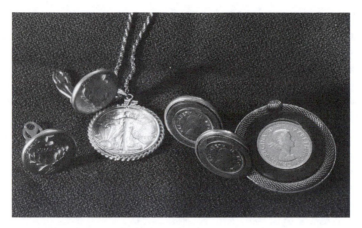

Jewelry items made from twentieth-century U.S. and foreign coins.
Copyright © 2007 by Anthony F. Chiffolo.

the setting.[1] Gold coin rings with the image of Marcus Aurelius (121–180 c.e.),
armbands with coins of Caracalla (188–217) and his wife Plautilla (d. 212), and
a belt made with coins bearing the images of Roman emperors also appear in museum and private collections as among the first examples of Roman coin jewelry.

It's a big jump, but suffice it to say that throughout the next 1,600 years or
so, coins were used as a jewelry art form in nearly every country where they were
minted; also, as folks traveled and traded, and coins were picked up or used in
commerce, they made their way to neighboring territories. The Danes, for example, were famous for taking coins of foreign places they visited as a payoff against
invasion. Most of the coins ended up in buried hoards back home. But not all
of them. Some were made into beautiful pendants for loved ones or were melted
or crimped and taken home as booty or tribute. This was especially true of silver,
which the Vikings prized above gold. The pieces of silver were melded with other
finery and made into jewelry.

Many of us have images in our minds of tribal and ethnic jewelry worn by
Middle Eastern women or by gypsies going back hundreds of years. While coins
in jewelry became more common in the late Middle Ages, the belly dancer image
of lots of jangling and dangling coins is a recent reconstruction or, at best, an
amalgamation of many styles over several centuries.[2] While it is true that many
ethnic groups in Africa, the Middle East, and Asia are associated with coin necklaces as part of daily wear, most of these groups have come by the fashion only in
recent years.[3] A majority of coin jewelry on the market today, even that which is
called "ancient" or "antique," contain coins that have age but have been incorporated into modern settings. Whatever was holding any coin pendants or earrings
of yore has, in most cases, long since disintegrated.

Somewhere about 1880 in the United States, coin jewelry took on a whole
new chapter. It became the fashion at the time for male soldiers and travelers
abroad to etch and decorate foreign coins to bring back to their girlfriends (or

mothers), in what came to be known as "sweetheart jewelry."[4] The coins were worked by hand to create floral motifs or to emblazon initials or meaningful names, dates, or designs. Often the coins were soldered into a bracelet or made into a love token in a metalsmithing art form called "piercing." It was not unusual in the late nineteenth century to encounter small gold pieces that had been pierced with holes to wear as charms. Sometimes the coins would be set using a technique called pyramiding, whereby the lettering and the design seemed to float inside the rim of the coin. Most times the coins were set inside a bezel or wire-wrapped so that they could hang from a necklace, earrings, or a bracelet. For more than 100 years, much Native American jewelry of the Southwest was made with melted-down silver coins (called "coin silver") or, at times, coin cut-outs. Today, many Native American artisans use coins in their jewelry, usually wrapped in a bezel so as not to deface them.

It has also become popular of late to purchase foreign gold coins and wear them as jewelry in rings, belts, necklaces, earrings, bracelets, and body jewelry (in piercings). Rare gold pieces, such as those recovered from shipwrecks, have also been offered and sold with great frequency; usually they are wrapped, although sometimes they are pierced for wear.

☞   DID YOU KNOW?

Never an industry to shy from competition, and usually cutting-edge, the watch industry has found a way to employ coinage to its greatest advantage, using gold and silver coins for watch faces. One of the most popular watches in recent years has been the Corum US$20 Liberty Eagle (gold coin) man's wristwatch. Using mint coins, Corum carefully cuts them in half, and in between the obverse and reverse of the coin, a high-quality movement is installed. Yet, the Corum Coin Watch, first introduced in Basel in 1965, almost did not make it past the drawing board. The U.S. law prohibiting the "mutilation" of government-minted coins, even those long out of circulation, required an exemption on behalf of the Swiss watchmaker. The solution: The cutting work of the coins was to be carried out in Switzerland and not in the United States.

Corum's persistence with the U.S. government has not gone unnoticed. U.S. Presidents Ronald Reagan (1911–2004), Harry Truman (1884–1972), and Lyndon Johnson (1908–1973) actively wore Corum $20 Liberty Eagle watches while in office. The price tag: on the average, in 2006, $12,500. They're selling well. And why not: Corum has a very clever advertising slogan: "Time Is Money."

NOTES

1. Levine, David, "Ancient Coin Jewelry" at http://www.shopnbc.com/product/?familyid=C19516&storeid=1&track=1&taxid=1&propid=974

2. See "Mistress Safia's Middle Eastern Garb Do's and Don'ts," at http://www.willofyre.com/OriginalSite/Clothing/periodmideastgarb.html She writes, "There is one very early Persian tile that looks as though two dancing girls, pouring wine while performing, are

wearing coin belts. ('Wall Painting,' Jausay al-Kahaqani Palace, Samarra, 836 c.e., from *Islamic Art and Architecture,* Robert Hillenbrand, Thames and Hudson, 1999, p 47.) This is the main reference used in the coin argument. The problem is, the only parts of the tile that are actual surviving period pieces are tiny shards. The rest of the tile was reconstructed in the 1920s. So, this can obviously not be used for garb documentation."

3. Though it is recorded that the Rai women of Nepal have long used silver and gold coin jewelry as part of their adornment.

4. Foreign coins were used, as it is illegal in the United States to deface any government currency (although it is frequently done, and the Secret Service does not actively pursue violators).

Conceits

Objets de Luxe: The House of Fabergé produced hundreds of . . . utilitarian things like the frames for lorgnettes, spectacles . . . fan handles, cane heads, cigar and cigarette cases, match holders, opera glasses . . . and dozens of other relatively insignificant things that became important when the House of Fabergé gave them the benefit of its genius.[1]

A conceit is a jewelry term used to describe any unusual or strangely contrived accessory that was conceived as a way to flatter or complement one's vanity. Conceits differed from **necessaries** (items deemed to be necessary to carry on one's person, such as a comb, brush, or mirror), although the terms were often interchangeable, depending on just who was doing the observing. Often, conceits were merely a high collar or a flower on a hat, or a brooch on a ribbon round the neck (now called a choker). Engraved children's bib pins, sterling-encased mustache combs, key rings, umbrella straps, lingerie pins, trunk or baggage identification tags, armlets and garters, parasols, and shoe and dress clips were all considered conceits. The scatter pins of the 1950s and 1960s, worn all over the body on various parts of one's wardrobe, as well as sweater clips, were often described in fashion commentaries as conceits. Just about anything can be a conceit, from buttons to buckles, cloche pins to ankle bracelets; but some of the more unusual items meant to bolster one's vanity include(d) the following.

BELT BUCKLES

Why does a firefighter wear red suspenders? Every child knows the answer to the riddle: to keep his pants up. But when it comes to belts, and particularly belt buckles, more is at stake than just the ability to support one's britches. Belt buckles are big fashion and have become one of the major jewelry conceits of the twenty-first century. Their origin begins in the Bronze Age: The Metropolitan Museum of History has samples of buckles dating to the third and second century B.C.E.; also in their collection is a Visigothic belt buckle (ca. 500–600 C.E.) that is made of a copper alloy, cells with garnets, glass, lapis lazuli, and cuttlefish bone. Both appear to have been worn by men. In fact, throughout history, it is rare that women's fashion styles included belt buckles, the exceptions being during some parts of the Middle Ages, Mantuan dress of the seventeenth century, and skirt/blouse combinations in the United States circa 1910. The use of belt buckles as a dress staple by men appears to have begun with British sailors, who were looking for something that could outlast string and fasteners on clothing that was being eroded by salt and weather. It is said that modern buckles were the sailors' invention, and that Puritan countrymen copied their dress, wearing large buckles to highlight their personal disdain for buttons, which they considered to be "vainglorious."

Currently, belt buckles are experiencing a kind of fashion revival. The Western films of the 1920s put cowboy buckles on the radar of every well-dressed Western gentleman. Designers such as Don Ellis, Michael Srour, Al Pecetti, William Nelson, John McCabe, Les Garcia, Edward H. Bohlin, and Robert Schaezlein made quite a name for themselves designing belt buckles to outfit all aspiring cowboys. Many of their creations cost upwards of a thousand dollars. Native American buckles made of turquoise, coral, silver, and other materials can sell for even greater sums. Whatever the material—plastic, silver, wood, diamonds, rhinestones, gold—buckles are made to be seen. Often they denote profession and status: Military and police/firefighter buckles are a proud part of the uniform. Not to be left out, the designers of women's fashions have been producing great-looking belt buckles for nearly 100 years. Every major designer, from Dior to Cartier, makes buckles for women, many of which are designed to match other jewelry accessories. The Internet at present boasts over three million importers/exporters of women's belt buckles!

All of which goes to prove that though the firefighter once needed a belt to hold up his britches, these days it's the buckle that ultimately matters, no matter who's wearing the pants!

CIGARETTE HOLDERS

Perhaps one of the most recognizable of conceits is the cigarette holder. Who can forget Audrey Hepburn's (1929–1993) character in *Breakfast at Tiffany's,*

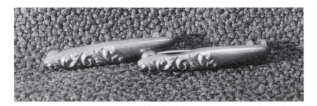

Lingerie pins: A typical late nineteenth-century conceit. Copyright © 2007 by Anthony F. Chiffolo.

Holly Golightly, and her elegant telescopic holder, poised with dramatic flair in her white-gloved hands? It is said that the cigarette holder completed the Hollywood diva look. As much of a fashion statement as they might be, cigarette holders, constructed of every conceivable element, but most usually plastic, wood, ivory, ebony, teak, gold, silver, platinum, amber, tortoiseshell, Bakelite, or horn, are functional and somewhat practical tobacco filters. These tubular creations are used by smokers to prevent their lips from touching the cigarette and to keep their hands clean of tobacco stains (they unfortunately did very little to protect the teeth). Cigarette holders were considered an essential part of women's fashion from the early to the mid-twentieth century and are sometimes of quite simple design; or they may be incredibly ornate, with gemstone or mother-of-pearl inlays. Today cigarette holders are still widely popular on the Japanese fashion scene.

DOG TAGS

Dog tags (not the canine variety) are identification markers worn around the neck by U.S. military personnel so that they might be recognized and named in order to inform loved ones upon their demise. The practice of making an effort to ensure one's identity while on the battlefield goes back at least as far as the Civil War, when General George Meade's (1815–1872) troops pinned paper tags to their clothing prior to battle.[2] By 1913, U.S. Army regulations made ID tags mandatory, and by 1917, all combat soldiers were wearing aluminum versions on chains around their necks. Many ex-soldiers wear their ID tags today as a symbol of pride and as a badge of having survived the ravages of war. In modern times, as iconoclastic (or some might say "insensitive") as it may seem, dog tags have found their way into the youth jewelry market as a kind of military chic. One can purchase ID tags with the same look and feel as the military versions and have them inscribed with personal details in classic aluminum or copper, brass, stainless steel, silver, or gold.

FANS

Ever since the days when a large banana leaf was waved over a panting member of some royal court to bring cool relief, fans have been both a status symbol and a useful ornament, and a ceremonial adornment that became a customary fashion conceit as well. One of the earliest recorded uses of fans hails from the era of the ancient pharaohs: Tutankhamen's (reigned 1333–1323 B.C.E.) tomb contained gold fans decorated with ostrich feathers. In the Americas, ancient Mayan, Aztec, and Incan civilizations left drawings of plumed fans made of eagle feathers and those of other birds. The ancient Greeks, Romans, and Etruscans used hand fans as cooling devices and in religious ceremonies. Roman ladies are often depicted holding gilded and painted circular wooden fans.

Fans were present in Chinese culture for at least two centuries before the start of the Common Era and usually denoted social status.

The folding fan with which we are most familiar today was invented by the Japanese sometime between the sixth and eighth centuries C.E. It was made by tying together thin strips of cypress wood with thread; the number of strips of wood indicated social rank. In the modern era, Shinto priests still use fans as part of formal costume attire, as does the royal family of Japan.

The height of fan fashion in Asia was during the Ming dynasty (1368–1644), and the city of Hangzhou was the center of the folding fan industry. The fan slats, made of ivory, bone, mica, mother-of-pearl, sandalwood, or tortoiseshell, were carved, covered with paper or fabric, and then hand-painted. The stylized usage of fans during this period was a highly regarded feminine art.

The folding fan made its way to Europe in the late sixteenth century and became hugely popular, especially among the aristocracy. Rigid fans from an earlier period of fashion were worn, hung as conceits on the skirts of ladies, and were often decorated with feathers and jewels. A contemporary portrait of Queen Elizabeth I (1533–1603), a major fashion scion, shows her carrying both a rigid and a folding fan, no doubt a gift from one of her suitors, probably accompanied by a pair of jeweled gloves.

From this time forward in Europe, fans were a major part of fashion and industry, usually made by artisans who were specialists in the trade. Folded fans began to appear in lace (especially in Spain and Belgium), silk (France), and parchment, taking their place alongside earlier models made from other materials of elegance. The courts of Europe were replete with fan-holding gentlewomen, and an entire fan language was created to convey favors and connote attachments and invitations to those gentlemen whose attentions were required.

LINGERIE PINS

As women's fashions changed in the nineteenth century, and a woman showed more and more of her shoulders to an adoring public, the need arose for a way to hide all the thin straps of lingerie and other underclothing. A quite inventive conceit of this period were lingerie pins, narrow, small bars, usually of 14k gold, often with an imbedded pearl or small gemstone, that were designed to align the strap of the dress with the strap of the slip and the strap of the brassiere. They were sometimes worn on top of the outer garment, or underneath the dress to keep the lingerie from "peeking out." With the invention of the halter top and other new dress styles in the 1920s, lingerie pins went out of fashion.

LORGNETTES

A lorgnette is a pair of eyeglasses or opera glasses with a lateral handle, invented in the eighteenth century by George Adams (1750–1795), an Englishman, probably as an adaptation of the scissors-glass, which was a double-eyeglass on a handle. Many lorgnettes were elegantly decorated with mother-of-pearl or rhinestones, as were their cases, especially those that folded in half into their handles. Lorgnettes were a typical conceit of the Art Nouveau and Art Deco periods, since most owners did not need glasses to actually see better; it was merely better to be seen holding a pair as an expression of "the ultimate" in fashion. Most women's fashionable eyewear of the 1950s and 1960s, as well as sunglasses from the 1970s to the present, continued the deception.

For men, the conceit of similar usage was the lorgnon, also known as the eye ring or monocle. Developed in the eighteenth century in Germany, it was introduced in England around 1800 by a young Austrian optician, J. F. Voigtlander (1759–1839), of the same family as the camera manufacturers). He took the monocles he was making in England to his homeland in 1814, and soon they were the rage in Germany and Russia among aristocratic men. Perhaps two of the most well-known monocle wearers were President Teddy Roosevelt (1858–1919) and his cousin, Franklin (1882–1945); however, following World War II, the monocle fell into disrepute, no doubt due to its use by many members of the Nazi party in Germany.

VINAIGRETTES

A vinaigrette was a small accessory usually carried by expectant mothers. It was often made of silver or gold, with small perforations on top. Vinaigrettes were so named because they housed a liquid solution, usually aromatic smelling salts, spirits of ammonia, or fragrant vinegar, as an aid in case of feeling faint. They were popular from the Victorian era through the 1940s.

☞   DID YOU KNOW?

Undoubtedly one of the top conceits of the past two hundred years made its appearance when modern-day celebrities began to carry their pets as an accessory (the Gabor sisters and Paris Hilton [1981–] with their miniature dogs come to mind). As a further conceit, these animals, some of whom have become celebrities themselves, are constantly photographed as divas of pet fashion sporting very expensive dog collars, not a few of which match the jewelry of their owners.

Recently the Hollywood film studio Warner Brothers launched a luxury range of dog collars for pampered pooches. The collection, inspired by the success of the cartoon character Scooby-Doo, includes a $1,700 satin dog coat studded with Swarovski crystals and lined in pink silk, and a diamond-encrusted platinum dog-collar pendant embossed with the initials S D costing $22,300. The collection also features crystal-studded collars and leads ($1,168 a set), travel cases with brushes, nail clippers and flea powder ($1,100), and "unisex" pillows and beds—blue on one side, pink on the other ($280).[3]

NOTES

1. Troute, Elaine, "Fabergé: The Perfect Gift," at http://www.fabergetheperfectgift.com/objetsdeluxe.html

2. However, some claim that the practice of wearing some sort of identification around the neck was common among soldiers in ancient Sparta.

3. Milner, Catherine, and Victoria Gurvich, "Bling-bling for dogs," *The Age*, December 9, 2003, at http://www.theage.com.au/articles/2003/12/08/1070732142445.html

Copper

Periodic table symbol: Cu

Atomic Number: 29

Origin of name: from the Greek *cupros* (the island of Cyprus), called "Cyprian brass," known to the Romans as *cuprum*

Important historical background information: known and used by various civilizations dating back more than 10,000 years

Geographical location of element: found worldwide; the major copper-producing countries are Chile, the United States, Indonesia, Australia, Peru, Germany, Russia, Canada, China, Poland, Kazakhstan, Mexico, Zaire, and Zambia; also found in various ores such as chalcopyrite, chalcocite, cuprite, and malachite

Copper is a reddish-colored metal with a bright metallic luster. It occurs naturally throughout the environment and is found in rocks, soil, water, and air. Copper is an essential element in plants and all animals, including human beings, making its consumption through eating, breathing, and drinking necessary for healthy living. In addition, because of its high electrical and thermal conductivity, and the fact that it is malleable, sectile, and ductile, it has become one of the most important metals known to humankind. Copper is used extensively in electronics, in structural engineering, in the production of coinage, in household products (pots and pans, doorknobs, gutters, flatware), in the making of musical instruments, and in surface coatings in hospitals to help protect against the spread of disease (copper is biostatic). Copper is considered by some to be very helpful in pain relief due to arthritis. It also has a reputation as a good "conductor" of energies from otherworldly sources—hence its purpoted healing qualities.

Copper is most often found near bright-blue/green stains in the earth, called "copper blooms." The copper extracted from these stains is usually a brightly colored blue or green. In this natural state, copper is one of the few metals that appears as an uncompounded mineral; therefore, it can be mined and processed without having to spend a lot of time and trouble extracting it from other ores, as with many precious metals. Copper was used by some of the oldest civilizations in the Middle East, Anatolia, and China. The Ancient Greeks and Romans associated copper with the gods Hermes (the blacksmith) and Aphrodite (love), so copper often took on the properties associated with these deities: quick wit, high intelligence, and the ability to balance and stabilize difficult situations. Wearing copper as jewelry or adornment was thought to enhance one's metaphysical abilities and to imbue the wearer with god-like sensibilities.

Therefore, in jewelrycrafting, copper has long been popular. A copper pendant was found in what is now northern Iraq that dates to 8700 B.C.E. In the Americas, copper was being mined as early as 600 c.e.; Native Americans of Michigan's Keweenaw Peninsula were among the first to discover some of the richest copper mines in the world at this location and have for centuries made jewelry and tools from copper. They discovered, as have many other crafters, that copper wire is ideal for stringing beads, since it is easily worked and can be pounded thin. Copper beads have a ubiquitous presence in both native and homespun crafts, particularly in bracelets, earrings, and necklaces. A high polish helps to bring about a burnished gold hue in the beads.

Modern copper jewelrycrafters can buy copper in many formats, including bars, foil, granules, insulated wire, mesh, plates, powder, rods, sheets, shot, turnings, wire, and, "evaporation slugs," a liquid copper state that when exposed to a high heat or light source leaves behind a deposit of the metal. To execute their jewelry designs, copper jewelrymakers use both high-tech power tools and standard hand tools, including (but not limited to) propane torches, pliers, copper rods, wooden sticks, pipe cutters, drill/driver and spade drill bits, wooden hammers, steel shots, bench shears, anvils, grinders, sandpaper, and heat-sustainable gloves.

Perhaps two of the most famous and innovative copper craftsmen of recent times were Frank Rebajes (1906–1990) of New York and Jerry Fells of California. Fells was known for two lines of copper jewelry, one marked Renoir (founded in 1946, it produced plain copper pieces), and the other called Matisse (established in 1952, it made enameled jewelry). Both lines imitated the look of the earlier Arts and Crafts era, using contemporary abstract designs that had a hand-hammered, hand-finished look. Fells' companies closed their doors in 1964. Rebajes worked in New York City from the 1930s until his death in 1990. He began his career selling small sculpted pieces made from tin cans. His early fame led to an exhibition of his works at the 1939 World's Fair, and many years later he opened a spectacular Fifth Avenue store. At one time, he claimed to have more

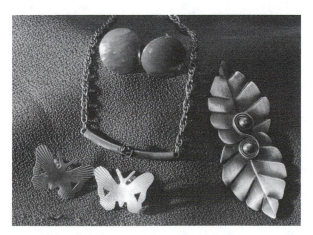

Wearing copper jewelry is said to have beneficial health effects. Copyright © 2007 by Anthony F. Chiffolo.

than 100 crafters working for him and carrying out his designs. Rebajes' most popular medium was undoubtedly his copper works, though in later years he was crafting jewelry out of every kind of material, from natural pyrite and uncut emeralds to wood and river rocks. Though other companies of the mid-twentieth century produced copper costume and better jewelry on a limited scale, Renoir/Matisse and Rebajes pieces are the most sought after by collectors today.

☞   DID YOU KNOW?

Without a doubt, the finest copper crafters of the twentieth century could be found at the Roycroft Studios in East Aurora, New York. Though not particularly known for creating copper jewelry (although their copper jewelry boxes sell in the thousands of dollars today), some of the pins created by original Roycrofters have surfaced on the contemporary resale market. A rare Walter Jennings pin was sold in auction recently, and jewelry by Dard Hunter (1883–1966) and Alburn Sleeper is mentioned in many publications about these wonderful Arts and Crafts artisans. If you're a copper jewelry collector, look for these Roycroft names; their jewelry is worth hundreds even for small pieces, despite the fact that they are rarely recognized as important by anyone other than the most astute collectors.

Costume Jewelry

The difference between false memories and true ones is the same as for jewels: it is always the false ones that look the most real, the most brilliant. (Artist and designer Salvador Dalí [1904–1989])

Though imitation jewelry has been around ever since the Egyptians first discovered that coated glass beads could be passed off as precious stones more than 3,500 years ago, the commercialization of fake jewelry as an acceptable alternative to the real thing is a fairly modern advancement in jewelrycrafting. Perhaps the most famous jewelry "forger" or deceptor of all time was the Frenchman Georges-Frederic Strass (1701–1773), who understood better than anyone at the time the potential of English hand-blown leaded glass to stand in for expensive diamonds. Known as paste, it could be hand cut to look just like a diamond; the "stones" were then foiled with a type of aluminum, set in silver, and backed in gold, in the same way as their more expensive counterparts. During the late eighteenth century, Strass was single-handedly responsible for establishing paste jewels as creations in their own right by crafting them to be spectacular imitations of highly valued pieces.[1] He knew his market well. The upsurge in highway robberies and the faux pas of wearing high-end jewels after the French revolution meant that anything paste was greatly desired by the wealthy, most especially European royalty!

While paste was still wowing them in France, in Bohemia some hundred years later, Daniel Swarovski (1862–1956) was perfecting the polishing and cutting of beautifully colored stones, especially crystals, as a kind of "replacement" jewelry. A native of the area near the river Rhine, his elegant handmade "brilliant-cut" creations came to be known as rhinestones. Swarovski was one of the first to mass-produce rhinestones and was a leading force of the imitation jewelry market of the nineteenth and twentieth centuries.

The term *bijouterie* ("costume jewelry," sometimes called "fashion jewelry") comes from the French *bijou fantasie* and the designs of René Lalique (1860–1945) at the end of the nineteenth century. It is said that Lalique was the inventor of costume jewelry.[2] Lalique and his contemporaries, among them Louis Comfort Tiffany (1848–1933), were innovators of design and substance, employing a wide variety of imaginative ornaments, precious metals, and unrelated natural and handcrafted materials (including some pre-plastics) in the making of jewelry. Their knowledge of glass and its properties and their eye for color made their creations highly desirable (and often unaffordable to any but the rich, even today). La-lique and Tiffany were fine artisans, but they were not designing for the mass market.

The golden era of costume jewelry design and production was from 1930 through the end of the 1970s. Prior to World War I, couturiers Paul Poiret (1879–1944) and Madeleine Vionnet (1876–1975) were the first European designers to showcase costume jewelry along with their fashion designs: Poiret at his lavish parties; Vionnet with her private clientele and eventually at her own fashion house on the Avenue Montaigne in Paris. But it was the likes of Coco Chanel (1883–1971) and Elsa Schiaparelli (1890–1973) who made costume jewelry all the rage in the 1920s and 1930s, as they began to promote it in very small quantities for their customers, often combining costume pieces with authentic jewels for a new look. For inspiration they did not have far to look: Most of their jewelry was an amalgam of ornamentation and materials they were already using in their haute couture designs. Once again, form and substance followed design. It seemed as though their approach to crafting jewelry took little effort; yet if the truth be known, they were hard-working women with a lot of vision.

Vision and an eye for talent: Schiaparelli hired artists such as the surrealists Salvador Dalí (1889–1963), Jean Cocteau (1889–1963), and Alberto Giacometti (1901–1966) to design jewelry for her collections. During her reign as one of the

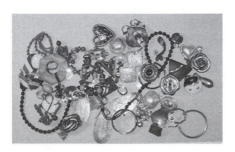

Costume jewelry is attractive, affordable, and fashionable. Copyright © 2007 by Anthony F. Chiffolo.

queens of jewelry design, she made a name for herself with outrageous and witty creations: earrings shaped like telephones, bracelets of porcelain vegetables, huge necklaces of fantasy paste stones. Chanel, for her part, had an entire retinue of designers working for her, known as La Maison Gripoix, the most famous of whom is probably Karl Lagerfeld (1938–), the man responsible for the revival of Chanel's costume jewelry line in the 1980s. Chanel made her name using the opposite tack of Schiaparelli: Her costume jewelry was luxurious in its simplicity, famous for its blacks and whites, gold and bead chains, charm bracelets, and understated jeweled belts. She hated "big" and promoted elegance. Today, the work of both these European designers commands sums of money beyond those of semiprecious and precious "fine" jewelry. ("Fine" is obviously in the eye of the beholder!)

Perhaps no one had a greater effect on the early costume jewelry period in the United States than designer Miriam Haskell (1899–1981). A friend of Chanel, Haskell made her mark beginning in the 1920s creating irregularly shaped, high-quality fake pearls, often in colors other than white and off-white. She backed her creations with an interwoven and overlapping fusion of metalwork, mixing gold and silver tones on a copper base. One might say her work was "riveting," as the piece work of every pin, necklace, and pair of earrings holds together like the inner workings of an unmoving machine. The backings of her jewelry are often as interesting to marvel at as are her frontispiece hallmark pearl mountings. Haskell's company was sold after her retirement in 1950, but one can still purchase designs only months old that have re-created her style and commitment to quality and endurance. At present, vintage Haskell pieces sell in the hundreds—sometimes thousands—of dollars.

Haskell was not the only designer making a name for herself in U.S. venues. Following the crash of the stock market in 1929 and the ensuing Depression era, coupled with the austerity of the war effort, jewelry designers took their cue from the happenings of the day and sought to create fun and affordable and fantasy pieces that would capture the eye and the aspirations of the buying public. In this landscape some of the most important names and figures of jewelry design opened their doors: Corocraft, Eisenberg, Carnegie, Weiss, Regency, Hobé, Boucher, and Joseff are just a few who became household jewelry names during this period.

Today there are literally thousands of jewelry designers and production houses making billions of jewelry items per annum. Years ago, few pieces were ever "signed"; if they were, they were expensive and of high quality. Nowadays, just about everything has a label, and the age of design *dis*tinction appears to be fast approaching *ex*tinction. Where are Elsa and Coco and Miriam when we need them?

☞ DID YOU KNOW?

Though the most expensive piece of "fine" jewelry ever sold at auction remains a white diamond that went for US$16.5 million at Sotheby's auction house in 1995, what is the record for costume jewelry?[3] It might just be a three-strand fake pearl necklace that originally belonged to Jackie Kennedy Onassis. At the auction of her personal items in 1996, a giant copy of a photograph of John-John Kennedy pulling on his mother's necklace helped the sale tremendously. Originally valued at $200–$300, it sold for $211,500.

NOTES

1. Grant, Lucille, "Fabulous Fakes," *Antiques & Collecting Magazine,* February 1999, 88ff.

2. Ibid.

3. Source: Solis-Cohen, Lita, "The Jackie O. Sale: A Marketing Triumph," *Maine Antique Digest,* June 1996, at http://www.maineantiquedigest.com/articles/jack0696.htm

Crosses

> In the 15th Century, Emperor Zara Ya'Eqob of Ethiopia decreed that every Christian should wear a neck cross so that they could be recognized among the . . . masses.[1]

As ubiquitous as crosses are in fashion today, their appearance as a piece of jewelry is a relatively new phenomenon. This may be due to the admonition in the book of Exodus that warns against the making of graven images, undoubtedly a deterrent to enterprising jewelers and other craftspersons. Concomitantly, neither the cross itself nor the crucifix were symbols employed by the Church to represent Christianity until sometime in the fourth century C.E., when tradition has it that the Emperor Constantine had a vision of a large cross in the sky along with the written instructions "In this sign conquer."[2] (Up until that time, the symbol for Christians and the Christian church had been a fish and, later, a lamb or the Greek letters *Chi* superimposed on *Rho*.) In the fourth century, pieces of what was called "the True Cross" (supposed relics of the cross upon which Jesus was said to have been crucified) were embedded in gold or sometimes inserted into a smaller cross: These were known as an *enkolpion,* from the Greek word for an item worn on the breast (later called "pectorals"). The eulogy for the sister of Gregory of Nyssa (circa 335–after 394), who died in 379, speaks of her "iron cross and an iron ring, which . . . were worn on a chain close to her heart."[3] John Chrysostom (347–407), bishop of Constantinople, wrote that "both men and women had relics of the cross enclosed in gold and wore them around the neck."[4] It was reported that crucifixes (a cross with the body of Christ on it) were in use in some Christian circles in Egypt by the fourth century.

The orders of the Sixth Ecumenical Council (680 C.E.), which required that all representations of Christ must include the entire corpus, meant that crucifixes, large and small, institutional and personal, could soon be found throughout

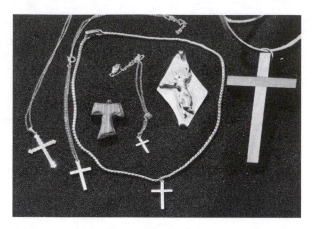

Once merely a religious symbol, in the twentieth century, crosses became fashion jewelry as well. Copyright © 2007 by Anthony F. Chiffolo.

much of Christendom. During the rule of the emperor Justinian II (669–711; ruled 685–695), the first coins were minted that featured a portrait of Christ.[5] Some Byzantine reliquary crosses (hinged boxes with what was thought to be a relic [piece of bone, hair, clothing] of one of the saints inside) from the second half of the first millennium have been uncovered, yet these probably belonged to clergy or members of religious orders. Celtic pendant crosses dating from as early as 500 C.E. have been discovered in ancient English burial grounds.[6] It is also said that Byzantine soldiers wore crosses as part of their armor to ward off death and evil as early as the eighth century, a practice that continued in Europe with soldiers of all countries up through the end of the Middle Ages.

Generally speaking, from the twelfth to the fifteenth centuries, the styles and morals in Europe discouraged the wearing of jewelry, except for nobility. There can be little doubt, however, that the Crusades had a strong influence on the wearing of religious jewelry. Coupled with the rise of infectious and life-taking disease during the Middle Ages, the making and selling of religious amulets, particularly religious cross pendants, was big business. Crosses appear for the first time at the end of rosary knots or beads as early as 1160: The remains of St. Rosalia (1132–1166), discovered by a hunter in a cave at Mt. Palermo in 1625, included a little string of little beads that ended in a cross.[7] The royal inventory (1380) of King Charles V (1500–1558) included "'nineteen Rosaries made of rose tinted amber and coral with pearls for markers' . . . gold beads, and jet beads with eleven gold crosses."[8] And by 1550, there is record of a rosary called the Three Fifties with "a pendant . . . that ends in a cross."[9]

During the European colonization of the Americas, beginning in the sixteenth century, silver crosses were among the gifts given to Native Americans who converted to Christianity. They soon became popular among the tribespeople as a nonreligious form of adornment: Small silver crosses were fashioned into earrings;

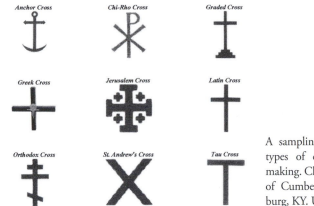

A sampling of the many different types of crosses used in jewelry-making. Chart of cross types courtesy of Cumberland College, Williamsburg, KY. Used by permission.

larger ones were worn on the chest. Cross jewelry soon became a very popular trade item with the fur companies in and around the Canadian border.[10]

So, exactly who is responsible for the "cross-over" from religious devotion to fashion accessory when it comes to crosses? Was it the sudden fascination with Egyptian jewelry (thanks to archaeological digs in the 1840s)? Was it commerce with Native American people who were trading silver wares by the late 1870s?

Probably two factors contributed greatly to the popularity of wearing a cross as a kind of jewelry. The first was due to King Frederick VII of Denmark (1808–1863), who presented a copy of an ancient cross (known as the Dagmar) to his daughter Alexandra (1844–1925) upon her marriage to the Prince of Wales (later Edward VII [1841–1910] of England). There was such a demand for a copy of the cross soon after that jewelers could barely accommodate the requests for a replica. The second factor was undoubtedly the invention of the camera and the ability to reproduce photos on a widespread scale by the 1880s. Since many of the photos were merely headshots, women were often pictured with their best but most modest jewelry; many Victorian photographs exist of properly dressed women, hair severely pulled back, with a lace blouse proudly supporting a cross pendant, demonstrating both virtue and a fine upbringing.

In modern times, crosses have become commonplace as jewelry for both men and women. The pop singer Madonna (1958–) is particularly well known for using cross jewelry as a fashion statement, a move quick to be imitated by other singers and video stars. There are many types of crosses available on the market, such as the primary examples depicted above.

☞   DID YOU KNOW?

Long before it was associated with the Nazi regime in twentieth-century Germany, the swastika was a common Christian symbol with origins that go back more than 3,000 years. It was used by nearly every culture and religious group through the ages as a symbol of life, sun, power, health, and good luck. It is frequently found on Native American jewelry of the early twentieth century, as well as Masonic pins and emblems. The swastika is based on the Greek Cross (*crux quadrata*) or Gamma cross (for the third letter of the Greek alphabet), as it is composed of four intersecting gammas.

NOTES

1. PalaceGallery.net, "Coptic Crosses" at http://home.sprynet.com/~gipsyped/brooches.htm

2. Some scholars claim that the situation was different in Egypt, which had another type of cross, the ankh, a symbol in use there for nearly 2,500 years before the birth of Jesus.

3. Stiver, Stanley L., and David J. Stiver, "Enkolpion" at http://www.crosscrucifix.com/glossaryhome.htm

4. Ibid.

5. Excavations in recent years have uncovered coins with piercings or small holes, which is thought to indicate that religious pilgrims wore the coins around their neck, either as a talisman or a symbol of devotion.

6. See for example "Medieval Jewelry" at http://www.swordsofhonor.com/celcrospenwn.html

7. See the article on "The History of the Rosary" at http://www.rosaryworkshop.com/HISTORYjournalingBead.htm

8. Ibid.

9. Ibid.

10. See "Trade Crosses" at http://www.overstockjeweler.com/history.html

Cut Steel Jewelry

> *For sale*: Cut Steel Salamander Antique Brooch: What wonderful whimsy! For centuries animal motif jewelry has long been held in favor. Whether in the form of a talisman or in a naturalistic theme so loved by the Victorians, this charming piece may be one of the last traces of that long tradition of cut steel jewelry created to imitate the sparkle of diamonds. (Amazon.com jewelry ad)

Cut steel jewelry is composed of and fashioned just as one might suspect, given its name, which is to say that jewelry of this type is made up of pieces of steel that have been cut to produce a specific design, often with small facets in a structure that is reminiscent of the way in which rose cut diamonds are produced. In actuality, each cut is a series of polished steel studs that are riveted with a post at its back and inserted very close together into a brass or metal frame. The result is a work of art in miniature that resembles fine bead work. The intent in creating cut steel jewelry was to imitate the brilliance of diamonds, and the craftspeople that excelled at the skill were highly sought after. During the height of

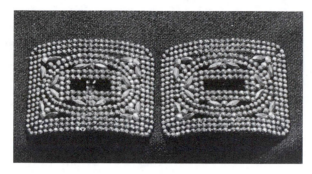

A pair of late nineteenth-century cut steel shoe buckles. Copyright © 2007 by Anthony F. Chiffolo.

its popularity, shoe buckles, knee buckles, buttons, bracelets, earrings, necklaces, hair ornaments, chatelaines, and other jewelry were fashioned in cut steel.

Making its debut as early as the sixteenth century in Europe, cut steel was immediately *en vogue* due to its practical versatility to accessorize and add a bit of glamour to everyday clothing. Besides, it was not some poor substitute for an expensive alternative (like zircons or paste are for diamonds). Its remarkable blue-gray coloration made it the prize possession of the lucky owner, satisfying tastes as varied as the upper-crust English wife and the queen consorts of France and England, who were said to have extensive collections. Cut steel found its greatest market in the eighteenth and nineteenth centuries, though early in the nineteenth century the quality of cut steel work was diminished and was stamped out in strips instead of being individually cut and riveted. Its popularity waned in the period just prior to World War II.

The zenith of cut steel production can best be seen in the work of Matthew Boulton (1728–1809), an eighteenth-century factory owner in Birmingham, England, who became the major purveyor of cut steel in his time.[1] He and other English jewelers exported this sparkling commodity, and soon France, Italy, Prussia, Spain, and Russia were also producing it.

Today, cut steel pieces are somewhat hard to come by. Though composed of a hard metal, the cut work made it vulnerable over time, and consequently quite brittle. Most examples from early periods have not survived the ravages of time. If one is fortunate enough to own a cut steel piece, it should be stored between pieces of cloth and kept clear of moisture (it rusts). Facets can be cleaned with a child's paintbrush (never use a toothbrush), but one should avoid excessive handling.

☞ DID YOU KNOW?

Sometimes confused with cut steel work is Berlin Iron Work jewelry. Manufactured for just a short time between 1796 and 1850, it was a very fine, lace-like product made primarily by Prussian foundries from molten iron. Iron work jewelry had auspicious beginnings. In the early part of the nineteenth century, Prussia found itself at war with France. To support the war effort, requests were made by the Prussian royal family for donations of gold jewelry. Those who contributed were given iron jewelry as a replacement. (Hence the common expression of the era, *Gold gab ich fuer Eisen,* or "I gave gold for iron.") When Napoleon (1769–1821) defeated Prussia in 1806, the patterns were sent to Paris, and iron work jewelry soon made its way across Europe.

Berlin Iron Work jewelry can be differentiated from cut steel jewelry easily: Whereas cut steel work sparkles like diamonds and has a blue-gray color, iron work pieces have a heavy black appearance caused by a linseed oil coating that was used to preserve castings during the manufacturing process.

NOTE

1. Interestingly enough, Boulton later formed a partnership with James Watt (1736–1819), who was responsible for the commercial success of the steam engine. Boulton was not an inventor, per se, but he was an astute thinker, and his ingenuity and creativity enabled, among other creations, the reproduction of oil paintings through a mechanical process; the patent for raising water on the principle of the hydraulic ram; copper coinage for the Sierra Leone and East India Companies, as well as for Russia; and other innovations.

Cuts (Diamonds)

The jungle is dark but full of diamonds. A diamond is rough and hard to the touch. (U.S. playwright Arthur Miller [1915–2005])

Diamond cuts[1] and diamond shapes—contrary to popular parlance, they are not the same thing. While it may be true that it is necessary to cut a diamond in order to give it shape, when diamond experts talk about cut, they are referring to the depth, width, and uniformity of its facets. All these features have an effect on its brilliance, its strength, and its overall character. In fact, when it comes to precious gems, diamonds are a "cut above the rest."

In order to fully understand diamond cuts, especially those of antiquity, it's important to learn a bit of the diamond-cutting vocabulary. Modern diamonds are described by gemologists as having three main parts: the top of the diamond, called the crown; the middle of the diamond, known as the girdle; and the bottom half of the diamond, referred to as the pavilion. Diamonds are further divided into facets, or polished surfaces: The flat part across the top is known as the table. Modern brilliant cut diamonds have about 57 additional facets. The facet at the very bottom of the diamond is called the cutlet (if a diamond comes to a point, there is no cutlet). So now add to depth, width, and facet uniformity the characteristics of table size, crown angle, pavilion depth, girdle thickness, polish, and symmetry, and one begins to understand why diamond grading is done by experts![2]

Interestingly enough, one cannot speak of antique diamond cuts in the same way as modern cuts. That's because throughout history, diamonds have been cut in a variety of ways, both according to what was available to cut them and the fashions of the times. One of the earliest known diamond cuts was the point cut, managed in such a way that the rough diamond became, in effect, nothing more than a polished octahedron. About 1538 C.E., the table cut was introduced into Europe; it remained popular till about 1650.

The rose cut was introduced at nearly the same time and found its greatest popularity in the late 1700s and early 1800s at the diamond centers of Antwerp and Amsterdam in the Netherlands. It is still one of the most popular cuts on today's jewelry market. It resembles the petals of a rose bud; its crown is dome-shaped; its facets meet at a point in the center of the diamond. A rose cut can have anywhere from 3–24 facets.

About 1640, the old single cut was introduced; when a few more facets were added, it was called a double cut.

Of course, once you've seen the single and double cuts, what improvements or innovations could be made? In Italy, a new cut, called the Peruzzi, came to

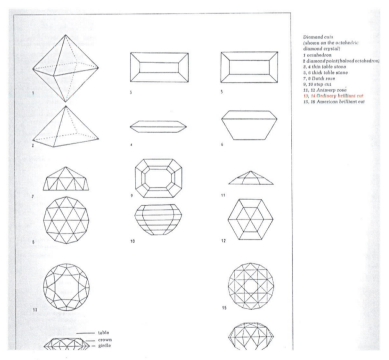

A sampling of sixteen diamond cuts; the last two are American brilliants, one of the most popular cuts among future brides in the twenty-first century. *Antique Jewelry* by E. Steingraber, copyright © 1957. Reproduced with permission of Greenwood Publishing Group, Inc., Westport, CT.

market. It was highly worked and became the forerunner of today's brilliant cut diamonds. Also known as a triple cut, Old Mine cut, Miners cut, or cushion cut, it was the earliest form of the brilliant cut. The Old Mine cut had a high crown, small table, a deep pavilion, and a large cutlet. It was the perfect look for a whole generation of new diamonds discovered in Brazil in the late 1700s. It is said that in a room full of diamonds, one can always pick out the Mine cut for the way it picks up the light. For that reason, it has been rediscovered in modern times by an ever-discerning buying public and is once again an extremely popular choice for newly engaged couples.

Equally well known, but perhaps not as popular, was the Old European (or Victorian) cut, with a small table, but a heavy crown, a circular girdle, and great overall depth. It never had a lot of play on the jewelry market, as the cutting process was being further refined, and at a quick pace. Soon after, the modern brilliant cut made its appearance in the early part of the twentieth century.

Diamond cuts went through a myriad of changes in the twentieth century. Single cut, rose cut, step cut, trap cut, baguette, king cut, baton, emerald cut, briolette (drop cut), scissor cut, cross cut, mixed cut, lentil cut, keystone cut, marquise cut, navette, lozenge, radiant cut, trillion cut, pear cut—the choices in buying diamonds are great. Today there are over 255 registered diamond cuts![3] To help buyers understand what is available, the Gemological Institute of America (GIA) now sorts diamond cuts into three basic categories, based on the style of diamond and the arrangement of its facets.

The first are brilliant cuts, which they describe as diamonds "with numerous facets shaped like triangles and kites."[4] The round brilliant cut is the most popular diamond, although a princess cut diamond (also known as a quadrillion or squarillion cut), which is square, is the second choice among buyers.

The second are step (or trap) cuts, which are used on transparent stones and are particularly appropriate with stones of great color.

The third are mixed cuts, a combination of any of the cuts mentioned above, often used on stones from Sri Lanka.

Diamond cutters use a variety of tools to accomplish their work, from diamond saws to lathes to burnishers and polishers. Today, the diamond industry is very high tech and one might say, somewhat insular. Why? What's one of the best things to use to cut a diamond? The answer: another diamond!

☞   **DID YOU KNOW?**

The largest faceted diamond in the world is the Golden Jubilee, weighing 545.67 carats. It is a fancy brownish-yellow color and "fire rose cushion cut." It is unusual also because it has a certain type of rare color banding. The second largest faceted diamond in the world is the Star of Africa, also known as the Cullinan I. It weighs 530.20 carats and is a pear shape with 74 facets. The third largest diamond in the world is the Incomparable. It is a golden yellow-orange color, pear-shaped, and weighs 407 carats. The fourth largest faceted diamond in the

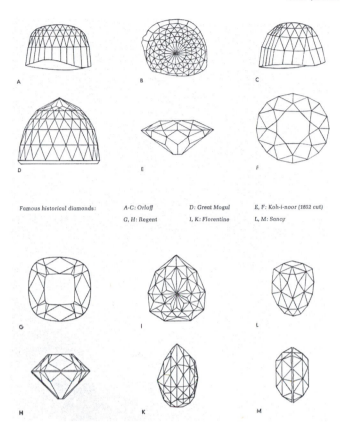

Famous historical diamonds: A-C: Orloff   D: Great Mogul   E, F: Koh-i-noor (1852 cut)

                              G, H: Regent   I, K: Florentine   L, M: Sancy

Famous diamonds of the past five hundred years. Note that each cut is different, tailor-crafted to enhance the overall beauty of the stone. *Antique Jewelry* by E. Steingraber, copyright © 1957. Reproduced with permission of Greenwood Publishing Group, Inc., Westport, CT.

world is the Cullinan II. It was cut from the same stone as the Star of Africa—aka Cullinan I. It weighs 317.40 carats and is a cushion cut.[5]

NOTES

1. For this entry, only diamonds will be examined, as they are the standard by which all other gems are measured.

2. See "Antique Diamond Cuts" at http://www.topazery.com/antique-diamonds.htm

3. "The World's Most Famous Diamonds," at http://famousdiamonds.tripod.com/famousdiamonds.html

4. See "About Jewelry/Accessories: Diamond Cut—Pictures and Facts about Diamond Cuts" at http://jewelry.about.com/od/diamondshapes/ss/cutting_styles.htm

5. Source: "The World's Most Famous Diamonds" at http://famousdiamonds.tripod.com/famousdiamonds.html

Diamond Look-alikes

There are many sham diamonds in this life which pass for real, and vice
versa. (English novelist William Makepeace Thackeray [1811–1863])

"Diamonds are a girl's best friend," croons Marilyn Monroe (1926–1962) in
the movie musical *Gentlemen Prefer Blondes*. But not every girl nor their best
friend can afford the precious gems, so diamond alternatives have always been in
demand. At first, crystals were cut to simulate diamonds, and good paste could
always do the trick (see **Costume Jewelry**). But as technology improved, so did
the ability to imitate nearly anything, and diamonds were at the top of many
"to-do" lists!

When speaking about diamond imitations, it's important to understand the
difference between synthetic ("put together") and simulant. A synthetic is a gem
made from the same raw materials as its natural counterpart, only it is grown in a
laboratory. Both optically and in its chemistry, it is identical to the natural gem.
Simulants are imitation gemstones that have been made from glass, ceramic, or
plastic. Though they may resemble the gems they are mimicking, simulants cannot duplicate a gemstone's inherent properties.

Thus one can purchase a lab-created or lab-grown diamond (that is to say, a
synthetic diamond), but it is very expensive. That's why so many other alternatives exist, as found below.[1]

NATURAL IMITATIONS[2]

Zircon (ZrSiO)

Zircon (from the Arabic, *zarqun* ["vermilion"], or Persian, *zargun* ["yellow-
colored"]) is a nearly ubiquitous crystal-like mineral found in igneous,
metamorphic, and sedimentary rocks within the earth's crust. Its natural colors
include yellow-golden, green, brown, red, and clear (or colorless); colorless
samples are sometimes referred to as Matara diamond, after the name of the
area where many have been found. Their brilliance and dispersion make them
a great diamond look-and-act-alike. Zircons are found in large quantities in
Canada, Madagascar, Italy, Norway, Sri Lanka, India, Myanmar, Thailand,
Australia, Cambodia, South Africa, the Ural Mountains, and the United
States.

Zircons are often heated to improve their color. Despite being one of the
heaviest of gemstones, they are very fragile and often are individually wrapped
when stored to prevent chipping. Hence it is easy to distinguish zircons from
diamonds, not to mention that zircons are double refracting as compared to diamonds, which are not.

Blue zircon is one of the birthstones chosen for December, and because it is relatively inexpensive, despite rarity, it is often the choice of jewelers over blue topaz, the official December birthstone.

Spinel (MgOAl$_2$O$_3$)

Spinel, from the Greek word for "spark," is a natural stone that comes in a wide variety of colors, including clear (or colorless). It so exhibits the qualities of other gemstones (such as rubies and diamonds) that it has often been called "the great impostor." It is found primarily in Sri Lanka, Tanzania, Tajikistan, and Myanmar, with some smaller versions emanating from India. Spinel has a hardness factor of "8" on the Mohs scale and therefore is frequently used in jewelry settings, as it is quite durable. However, spinels are relatively rare in nature. Therefore, since the early part of the twentieth century, spinels have been synthesized for use in jewelry and as a diamond imitation. Common commercial names include Corundolite, Lustergem, Magalux, and Radient.

White Sapphire (Al$_2$O$_3$)

Sometimes called colorless sapphires, these gemstones were an early diamond substitute; they are brilliant and second only to diamonds on the Mohs hardness scale (with a rating of "9"). White sapphires are found in Afghanistan, Australia, Brazil, Cambodia, India, Malagasy Republic, Malawi, Myanmar, Pakistan, Sri Lanka, Tanzania, Thailand, the United States, and Zimbabwe. They lack the "fire" of real diamonds, but are often used in a mixture or combination, where sheer volume and flashiness is the intended impression. Synthetic versions have been produced since the early twentieth century and were popular through the 1940s. Commercial names once used for these sapphires include Diamondette, Diamondite, Jourado Diamond, and Thrilliant.

White Topaz (Al$_2$[f,OH]$_2$[SiO$_4$])

White Topaz is a colorless topaz sometimes found in jewelry that has been crafted in Asia. Visually, it is less brilliant and has little "fire" as compared to the gemstone it is imitating. White Topaz has gradually built a name for itself in the jewelry market, claiming a place as an April birthstone alternative.

Herkimer Diamonds

Sometimes quartzes, when finely cut, can resemble good gemstones. Such is the case with Herkimer diamonds, which are not really diamonds at all, but wonderfully clear, doubly terminated quartz crystals with a fine luster. Also known as Middleville Diamonds or Little Falls Diamonds, they are found in Herkimer County in New York State. Herkimers are softer than diamonds, with a hardness factor of "7" on the Mohs scale.

Colorless Quartz, Topaz, and Beryl (Goshenite)

These natural gemstones have also been used as diamond imitations.

SIMULANTS

Cubic Zirconum (ZrO$_2$)

Cubic zirconum is an extremely rare mineral that in a synthesized format (known as cz) is widely used to simulate diamonds. Cz's are hard and optically flawless; though they come in a variety of colors, clear cz's (also called colorless) are particularly popular due to their diamond-imitative qualities. The discovery of cubic zirconia is linked to two German mineralogists, M. V. Stackelberg and K. Chudoba, who in 1937 first encountered zirconium oxide in zircons. This discovery, though noted by them, seemed unimportant at the time, and the material was not even given a name. Many years later, Soviet scientists were able to build upon the earlier German research and were able to demonstrate the value of cz's as a synthetic diamond. Their breakthrough work was published in 1973, and three years later, commercial production was underway.

Cz's have so many good diamond characteristics that it is nearly impossible for the untrained eye to distinguish them from diamonds, hence making them perfect for the jewelrycrafter who is looking for a much cheaper alternative to costly precious gems. Under 10x magnification, the truth becomes more evident. Because clear cz's are nearly flawless (and diamonds nearly always have some flaw), their perfection is a dead giveaway, as too their weight. Cz's on the whole weigh 1.7 times more than diamonds of equivalent size. And one should not be fooled by setting. Cz's are set into the finest gold, silver, and platinum with equally elaborate handiwork in comparison to much diamond jewelry on the market.

The key to figuring out what is real and what is not is usually price. As they say in the trade, there are no good deals in the diamond market. If it is a real diamond, it is always precious, and one will pay accordingly. Or perhaps another way of looking at it is to quote the old maxim, "You get what you pay for."

Moissanite (SiC)

Moissanite, named in honor of Nobel Prize winner (1905) Ferdinand-Frédérik Henri Moissan (1852–1907), is a mineral that was first discovered in a meteorite located at Diablo Canyon in Arizona. In natural form, it is extremely rare and primarily indigenous to the Arizona site alone. However, a synthetic version of moissanite, known as carborundum, is grown in laboratories and is used today as a diamond simulant. Its refractive properties and fire under a light source make it extremely hard to distinguish from real diamonds, even to the trained eye. Like a diamond, moissanite is also a superb heat conductor (unlike zircons or cubic zirconia), and because heat radiation has been the primary test for diamonds for so long, many an error has been made distinguishing between the two. There are other distinctions as well (color, shape, flaw structure), but average testing rarely takes into account so many steps and procedures.

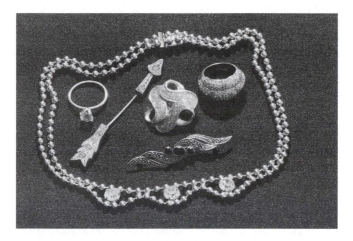

Diamond imitators: Everything from crystal to marcasite, cubic zirconia to just plain old glass. Copyright © 2007 by Anthony F. Chiffolo.

Though an "imitation" diamond, moissanite is not a cheap alternative, due to the high cost of manufacturing it and cutting it for gemstone use.[3] Plus, there is only one company making moissanite (North Carolina–based Charles and Colvard),[4] and lack of competition in the market always allows for higher pricing. Still, jewelers who are looking for less expensive materials for their buyers' market are finding moissanite has caught the imagination and pleased the pocketbook of many of their customers.

Strontium Titanite (SrTiO$_3$)

Strontium titanate is a rare mineral whose natural counterpart, Tausonite, in synthesized form, is sometimes used as a diamond simulant.[5] In years past it has appeared on the jewelry market as strontium mesotitanate, Brillante, Diagem, Diaomintina, Fabulite, and Marvelite. Tausonite was named for the Russian geochemist Lev Vladimirovich Tauson (1917–1989). It is found in small quantities in Siberia, Paraguay, and Japan.

Strontium titanite is both denser and softer than natural diamonds; yet its refractive index is nearly the same. However, its dispersion of light, which gives it its "fire," is nearly four times that of a diamond—a factor attractive to some, but which most jewelers consider overkill, making it appear cheap as compared to what diamonds offer. Nevertheless, large quantities of synthetic strontium titanite were manufactured beginning in 1955 for the sole purpose of providing a diamond alternative. The appearance of the cubic zirconia on the scene basically put an end to the marketability of strontium titanite, though it can still be found in some older pieces and through discerning jewelers who offer it to collectors, for the most part.

Synthetic Rutile (TiO$_2$)

Synthetic rutile was first produced in 1948. It has a high refractive index and in colorless form is an attractive diamond imitation. It is rarely used today in jewelry due to its slightly yellow luster that tends to show through under certain lighting. It was often marketed under the name Titania, as evidenced by many jewelry articles and ads of the 1950s. Other commercial names included Astryl, Diamothyst, Gava or Java Gem, Meredith, Miridis, Rainbow Diamond, Rainbow Magic Diamond, Rutania, Titangem, and Ultamite.

Yttrium Aluminum Garnet (YAG) [Y$_3$ Al$_5$ O$_{12}$]

Yttrium aluminum garnet is used as a diamond simulant in jewelrycrafting. YAGs are desirable due to their clarity (which makes them look like diamonds), durability and high refractive index (which makes them act like diamonds), and dispersion (which makes them shine like diamonds). According to some experts, the QVC diamond simulant Diamonique, in its earliest format, was most likely made from YAG.[6] Other commercial names used for YAG were Diamonair, Gemonair, Replique, and Triamond.

Gadolinium Gallium Garnet (GGG) [Gd$_3$Ga$_5$O$_{12}$]

Gadolinium gallium garnet is a diamond simulant used much in the same manner as YAG (see above). It is usually colorless. Commercial names for GGG have included Diamonique II and Galliant.

☞   DID YOU KNOW?

So why the need for counterfeit diamonds? Are diamonds really so rare? Aren't there enough *real* ones to go around? The truth is that the amount of diamonds on the market today is highly regulated by De Beers, the largest diamond mining company in the world. However, it is said that there are enough natural diamonds cut and ready for distribution to give every man, woman, and child in the world an entire cupful.[7]

NOTES

1. Throughout centuries past, there have also been a number of diamond simulants that have been used in small quantities and with varied success; many imitate colored varieties of diamonds. Some of these include colorless scheelite, carbonate cerussite, sphalerite, andradite (particularly the variety known as demantoid), and tsavorite, to name a few.

2. Other types of natural stones sometimes referred to as diamonds are the Irish diamond, Mexican diamond, Bohemian diamond, and Baffa diamond, all of which, though lovely, are merely rock crystal.

3. However, carat for carat, a moissanite gem is about one-seventh the cost of a diamond of the same size.

4. Charles and Colvard partnered with Cree Laboratories of North Carolina in 1995 to begin large-scale moissanite production.

5. Some titanites are referred to as sphene in jewelry parlance, though the nomenclature has been discredited by the International Mineralogical Commission on New Minerals and Mineral Names, which prefers titanite. However, sphene is still commonly used, especially when referring to older pieces.

6. See the article on "Diamonique" at http://www.24carat.co.uk/diamoniqueframe.html

7. Source: Thompson, Ryan, "FAQ's, Myths and Rumors" at http://famousdiamonds.tripod.com/faq.html

Diamonds

Chemical composition: Carbon (C_n)

Origin of name: from the Greek *adamas* ("invincible"); sometimes referred to as adamant

Important historical background information: known and used for more than 6,000 years; mentioned in the Bible (Exodus 28) and in third-century B.C.E. Buddhist texts

Geographical location: mined in South Africa, Namibia, Botswana, Angola, Tanzania, Sierra Leone, Russia (Siberia), Democratic Republic of Congo, Australia, Brazil, Canada, and India

Primary usages: abrasives, jewelry, electricity, cutting and grinding tools, semiconductors

The official birthstone for April, the gemstone diamond is the hardest known natural material. Diamonds are transparent crystals of pure carbon, and though not rare, are highly valued, not only for their excellent thermal conductivity, but especially for their use in industrial applications and jewelry. They are formed in the earth's crust by prolonged exposure of carbon-bearing materials to both extremely high pressure and temperatures. Diamonds that have made their way to the earth's surface from deep within are generally between 1 billion and 3.3 billion years old.[1]

Diamonds come in all shapes, sizes, weights, and colors, and are found on the market in natural, synthesized, and simulant formats (see **Diamond Look-alikes**). They were probably first mined in India as early as the third century B.C.E., though they were certainly known and used for several millennia prior (particularly in China). Due to the gems' fineness and beauty, many ancient civilizations believed that diamonds were the tears of the gods or fallen stars, and they used the stones to decorate their important religious icons and statues. Diamonds were symbols of heroism and strength and were thought to endow the owner with special protection. Perhaps for this reason alone, royalty were often gifted diamonds (particularly rarer colored stones), and for many centuries among some ancient peoples, only kings and queens were allowed by law to own them. There is credible evidence to support that diamonds were well known and used by the Greeks and Romans, the Chinese, and the people of Yemen early on as engraving tips for their tools and as drill bits to make holes through stone for jewelry purposes. In Europe, the use of diamonds disappeared for nearly 1,000 years until the late Middle Ages, first because the Church condemned the usage of cut gems as superstitious (they were used in amulets), and second due to Arabic trade restrictions between the eastern and western borders of their empire.

Beginning about 1300 C.E., the diamond trade reestablished itself in Vienna, and from there made its way to the Benelux countries. About the same time, the prohibition against cut stones died out, and soon there was a guild of diamond polishers established in Nuremberg (circa 1375). The first diamond wedding rings appear on the scene in 1477 (or thereabouts). For the next several hundred years, the history of diamonds concerns itself primarily with the introduction of new cuts (see **Cuts [Diamonds]**) every now and then, as fashion, politics, economics, and gem discoveries either allowed or dictated. To this day, the interest in diamonds by all sorts and conditions of women and men has remained unabated, and the diamond industry produces more than 30 million carats of cut and polished stones for the jewelry market annually, and an additional 100 million carats of both natural and synthesized stones for industrial use.[2] That translates to a buying market of more than US$9 billion per year.

One of the earliest examples of diamond jewelry is a Hungarian queen's crown, which was set with uncut diamonds circa 1074 C.E. By the 1300s French and English royalty were wearing diamonds also. By the mid-fifteenth century it was the fashion for women of means to wear diamonds as jewelry. The trend was undoubtedly started by Agnès Sorel (1421–1450) at the court of Charles VII (1403–1461) of France circa 1450; from there it spread to all the courts of Europe.[3] The tradition of diamond engagement rings came about via Archduke Maximilian of Austria (1459–1519), who gave a diamond ring to Mary of Burgundy (1457–1482) in 1477. Not surprisingly, the demand for diamond jewelry greatly increased. Soon after, cut diamonds used in or as jewelry first appear on record at Antwerp (the Netherlands, circa 1550). Just who exactly made the first cut is a matter of conflicting tales. Some say it was Lodewyk van Berquem, a Flemish lapidary;[4] others claim it was Jules Cardinal Mazarin (1602–1661), an Italian/French politician and known jewel collector, who caused it to happen.[5] In the total schema of diamond history, it probably matters little. Stones still had to be set once cut, and a greater demand meant that reliable sources had to be found. Until the eighteenth century, the only known source of stones for cutting and setting was in India. Yet later discoveries of diamonds in Brazil (1726) and South Africa (1867) meant that diamond jewelry was now available through a wider variety of markets. As jewelry gradually made its way into even some of the most modest of homes, the diamond variety was still a big investment.

All of that pretty much changed when a physicist named Marcel Tolkowsky (1899–1991) figured out the best way to cut a diamond in 1919. The Tolkowsky Cut, as it came to be known, was a mathematical schema that showed diamond cutters the way to achieve the perfect cut for any type of design they had in mind. To be sure, this revolutionized the diamond industry, and for many years to follow in the twentieth century, diamond prices, though on the rise, kept pace with the demand. This was due almost entirely to De Beers—the market authority, they established and introduced the criteria for evaluating diamonds by looking at four distinct factors. Known as the 4Cs (see **Carats**) for Carat, Clarity, Cut, and Color, each diamond used in jewelrymaking is evaluated according to these De Beers standards, which have now been accepted by the entire industry.

Today, 90 percent of the diamonds used in jewelrycrafting are mined in African countries, and between 65 percent and 85 percent of those diamonds are handled through De Beers. So though the diamond may come with a Tiffany or Van Cleef and Arpels box, it most likely originated in a De Beers operated mine, or it most certainly was fashioned at a De Beers cutting site.

All of which is to say that diamonds are a complicated business except for one factor. The price we pay is not a matter of speculation. All diamond buyers are getting the same deal across the board, more or less. And forget the paperwork. The industry has suffered greatly in recent years from a multiplicity of fake or false GIA (Gemological Institute of America) certificates, so it's important that the buyer be as educated as possible and not rely on guarantees or letters of provenance. That means that with many sellers, it's the "hype" that varies greatly. The best advice when diamond shopping is to buy from a reputable dealer who would not risk their standing among peers for a few hundred dollars of discount. In other words, whether the diamond is purchased at a New York Fifth Avenue department store or at a hometown jeweler, all things being equal, the price should be the same.

☞ DID YOU KNOW?

When it comes to hardness, diamonds are the measure by which all other natural substances are judged. On the ten-point scale of mineral hardness, diamonds are "10." To understand how other minerals rate, the Mohs scale was established in 1812 by German mineralogist Frederich Mohs (1773–1839) using key known minerals for comparison, as follows:

10. Diamond
 9. Corundum[6]
 8. Topaz
 7. Quartz
 6. Orthoclase[7]
 5. Apatite[8]
 4. Flourite
 3. Calcite
 2. Gypsum
 1. Talc

To understand how other modern-day items measure on the same scale, consider:

Fingernail	2.5
Gold and silver	2.5–3
Copper penny	3
Platinum	4–4.5
Iron	4–5
Knife blade	5.5
Glass	6–7
Steel file	7.5[9]

NOTES

1. See "Diamond" at http://en.wikipedia.org/wiki/Diamond
2. About 80 percent of mined diamonds are not suitable to be used in jewelrymaking; these diamonds, known as bort, find their way to the industrial market and are used in cutting, drilling, grinding, and polishing applications.
3. See Tolkowsky, Marcel, "Diamond Design" at http://folds.net/diamond_design/
4. Ibid.
5. See "Diamond History" at http://www.danforthdiamond.com/education/diamonds/4cs/diamond_history.htm
6. Corundum includes rubies and emeralds.
7. Orthoclase is a feldspar; chemically speaking, it is potassium aluminum silicate and is used primarily in the porcelain industry.
8. Apatite is calcium phosphate, used in fertilizer, composed of (among other things) ground-up bones.
9. Source: "Mohs Scale of Mineral Hardness," at http://www.amfed.org/t_mohs.htm

Earrings

And they gave unto Jacob all the strange gods which were in their hand, and all their earrings which were in their ears; and Jacob hid them under the oak which was by Shechem. (Genesis 35:4, KJV)

Earrings are ornaments that are worn on the ear, either from the lobe or attached to some other portion of the ear. They are believed to have originated in Western Asia some 5,000 years ago. Though evidence of their existence is longstanding, the oldest earrings recovered from antiquity date from circa 2500 B.C.E. and were discovered in graves at archaeological digs in the biblical city of Ur, the patriarch Abraham's home in the biblical accounts of the book of Genesis. Earrings of gold, silver, and bronze have also been unearthed at grave sites on the

Greek island of Crete, dating back to 2000 B.C.E., the height of the Minoan civilization.

Earrings were a popular adornment among the ancient Egyptians, who were known to wear earplugs, a type of earring that has a groove cut into it so that it fits snugly. These are featured prominently in the funerary mask of King Tut, who ruled during the fourteenth century B.C.E. The ancient Greeks were also fond of earrings, favoring particularly the pendant style, which swung from the ear. These earrings were usually made of paste, often with a depiction of the sacred birds of the gods: swans, peacocks, doves, and the like. Earrings that featured an image of popular demi-gods, such as Eros and Nike, were also common. During the Roman empire, earrings were worn by wealthy women as a way of displaying their riches: Hence, precious gemstones were placed into earrings more frequently by Roman jewelrycrafters in order to please their high-end clients.

In Europe from about the fourth century to the sixteenth century C.E., headdress and hair fashions among women often made the wearing of earrings impractical, if not unnecessary, as the ears were usually covered over by a hat, wig, scarf, or ornamental headpiece, as a sign of respect and proper morals. In the sixteenth century, Italian women began once again to wear earrings when backswept hairstyles came into fashion. It took nearly another 100 years for the fashions to change in Spain, England, and France, as high-collared vestments were still in vogue. By the mid-seventeenth century, most well-dressed European women were wearing some sort of ear adornment.

The seventeenth century in Europe heralded a new earring fashion. The small wire hoops and earplugs that had been so long a part of daily wear were replaced by a much grander design known as the girandole, a French word (from the Greek, *gyrus,* or "circle") for a kind of chandelier-style hanging earring with a surmount that fixed to the ear, suspended from which were three drops, usually with the largest at the center. These earrings, often made of gold or silver with rich paste or gemstone appointments, were exceedingly heavy; yet, they remained

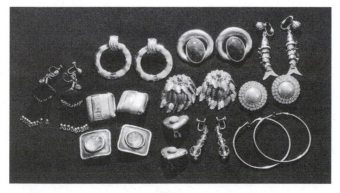

Clip-on, screwback, and pierced earrings: All popular styles of the twentieth century. Copyright © 2007 by Anthony F. Chiffolo.

a staple of fashion for several centuries. Another kind of earring popular at this time was the *pendeloque*,[1] lighter and longer earrings that acted as a kind of counterbalance to the higher and thinner hairdos worn by many women of wealth and high society.

By the nineteenth century, jewelrycrafters began to use more and more gemstones in the earrings they created. But because gold and other fine metals were scarce and not available to the general public, most European women of the pre-Victorian period wore simple gold wires that were fashioned into lacework patterns. By the 1840s, earrings with repoussé work in silver, gold, and other materials made their way onto the scene. Soon after, as hairstyles once again changed with the times both in Europe and in the Americas, earring-wear took a back seat and nearly disappeared.

As if on a 20-year cycle, hairstyles changed again and earrings came back into fashion with the upswept look of the 1860s. In one of the most inventive periods of jewelrycrafting, silversmiths, lapidaries, and manufacturers produced some of the wildest of creations, from light-hearted novelty earrings to intricate bead-work girandoles. The Art Nouveau movement and the Arts and Crafts experiment allowed jewelry designers the freest of reign, and many wonderful samples of exquisite ear decorations were fashioned for women of the day.

The twentieth century saw the advent of the screw-back earring. Most collectors today own earrings with a screw backing that belonged to some grandparent or distant relative; not to mention that the tag sales of many religious institutions are replete with earrings of this era, the alternative to piercing, which even in the time of suffragettes and the women's right to vote in 1919 was considered barbaric. But enter the 1920s flapper dresses and hairdos, and everything jewelry changes once again. (By this time, we can begin to trace the effect of hairstyles on the wearing of earrings in a measured way.) The Art Deco movement had a great influence on earring styles: Gone were curvaceous, glittery pendeloques; in style were straight, angular, long chandelier ear garb. And if it moved and matched one's dress, even better!

Earrings of the 1930s were a new creation: The clip-fitting earring (called "clip-ons" [vs. the screw-backs of earlier decades]) challenged every woman to wear ear decorations—no excuses! The clip-back earring was the queen-bee of fashion for more than 30 years. Yet no one, not even the most astute of designers, could have anticipated the fashion changes that came about in the 1960s, not only in the United States but worldwide. In the 1960s, earrings became not only daily wear, but with more and more women (and men!) piercing their earlobes, earrings became day and night wear, or better said— all-the-time wear.

Not much has changed since the 1960s, except that earrings are a fashion standard for both men and women, gay, straight, or what have you—it's just the materials that get more outlandish, and other parts of the body now sport what was once reserved solely for the earlobe.

DID YOU KNOW?

For all the trivia fans out there, here's a jewelry question of extraordinary esoterica. Which of Wonder Woman's accessories allows her to breathe in outer space? Is it (a) her tiara; (b) her bracelets; (c) her magic lasso; (d) her earrings? If you're at the end of this entry, you know the answer! That's right! Wonder Woman's earrings produce oxygen, allowing her to breathe in outer space.

NOTE

1. A pendeloque is also the name of part of a glass-shaped ornament on a lamp or chandelier. These earrings had a kind of length and movement that might remind one of a pendulum.

Edwardian Jewelry

Period: 1901–1910 (period sometimes referred to as "the Belle Époque")

Birthplace: England

Origins: Victorian England

Influences: Art Nouveau movement; late eighteenth-century; French designs of the court of Louis XVI (1754–1793)

When Edward VII (1841–1910) came to the English throne upon the death of his mother, Queen Victoria (1819–1901), he was already 60 years old. Once out of his mother's long overpowering shadow, he and his queen, Alexandra (1844–1925), instituted a respectful but elegant change in all things British, and these changes had a profound effect on the world around them. Some of the finest jewelry ever made was created during the Edwardian era.

Though Art Nouveau motifs were still strong throughout Europe, fashions were changing. Alexandra, born in Denmark, had her own sense of style, and as consort to the new king, she became the focus of all things fashionable. Alexandra popularized the "dog collar" necklace, or choker, which she used, interestingly enough, to hide a scar on her neck. But never mind; soon chokers were the stuff of haute couture, and every proper woman of fine society was seen wearing one. Edward likewise had his own influence on what folks were wearing in the early part of the twentieth century, particularly men. An avid sportsman all his life, he encouraged the use of sporting motifs in jewelry design. Lapel stick pins and watch backs, cufflinks and collar buttons, rings and men's fine accessories decorated with/or in the shape of horseshoes, wishbones, doves, laurel wreaths, fish, jumping horses, foxes, ducks, and hunting themes became the sign of a well-dressed and well-heeled gentleman. Edward also helped to make the peridot (his good luck charm) very popular.

Other characteristics of Edwardian jewelry, perhaps mimicking the late eighteenth-century French court of Louis XVI (1754–1793) and Marie Antoinette (1755–1793), included the popularity of drop earrings and pendant necklaces, often in pear shapes. Elegance was defined by all that was delicate and airy, such as handcrafted lace, yet with movement, so that the light would catch the whiteness of the platinum, diamonds, and pearls that were set into many Edwardian pieces. Open-work and scalloped-patterned edges were the hallmarks of good jewelry of this era, as were knife-edge wires, thin blades of metal with a sharp edge facing upwards, so that only a fine "knife-edge" of metal was visible.[1] Black French jet (onyx glass) combined with clear crystal created a "black and white" look that was also de rigueur.

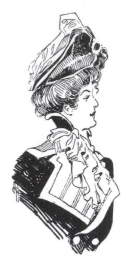

The Edwardian look: A bit simpler than Victorian fashion, but still quite elegant. Courtesy of Dover Publications, Inc., NY.

A few of the fancies of the Victorian era represented themselves during Edward's reign, but in a different package, so to speak. The bow, long a Victorian standard, was reproduced in platinum in a honeycomb of tight mesh as a complement to the lacy fabrics and embroidered silks of women's daily wear. For those who could not afford diamonds or the best of gems, rhinestones of glass and "good paste" made jewelry accessible to the masses. To simulate richness in form and style, shoe adornments were made of cut steel in ways that made them appear to be of greater value than their cost. Unique to the Edwardian period are items of tricolor gold, white gold, camphor glass, silver filigree, and bohemian glass, all of which make their first appearance as jewelry must-haves for the rich and poorer classes alike.

A few Edwardian design innovations that were rather short-lived included the "negligee" pendant, a necklace with two drops of unequal length, usually on a thin chain. The *sautoir*, a long necklace of pearls ending in a tassel, was also briefly popular. Handkerchief-style pendants, stomachers,[2] and *resille*[3] necklaces made shortstanding appearances.

Still, during the few years of Edward's time on the throne (and for several years that followed, up through the end of World War I), jewelry styles and fashions went through enormous changes. The Edwardian period heralded the advent of multistrand necklaces; bar pins and brooches; bangle bracelets; photo fobs; watch fobs; sash pins; cross-over, half-hoop, snake-ringed, and gold-chain bracelets; and tiaras for women who were nonroyalty. It was the age of elegance and of the Houses of Cartier and Fabergé; it was the era of Charles Dana Gibson (1867–1944) and "Gibson Girl" upswept hair, plunging necklines, and tiny waistlines; it was the prime of couturiers Jean Philippe (1856–1926) and Gaston-Lucien (1853–1924) Worth; it was the premiere of department and catalog stores like Sears and Roebuck, Montgomery Ward, and Wanamaker's.

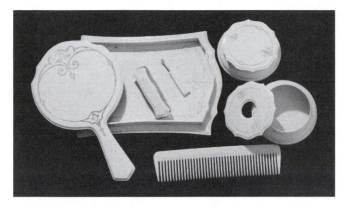

A late nineteenth-century celluloid dresser set. Celluloid was very popular but highly flammable, and was too delicate for long-lasting durability; it was soon edged out of the market by a tougher resin called Bakelite. Copyright © 2007 by Anthony F. Chiffolo.

The death of Edward in 1910, the onset of World War I, and the demands of a strained economy were responsible for the end of an elegance in jewelry that has yet to repeat itself in modern times.

DID YOU KNOW?

One of the most important yet highly unlikely products used in the jewelrymaking of the Edwardian period was celluloid. Although it had been invented many years earlier, perhaps as an ivory replacement, it came to be widely used for pins, hair ornaments, and women's accessories during the first part of the twentieth century. In general, pieces made from celluloid tend to be very brittle and are highly flammable; they are also subject to spontaneous decomposition. Celluloid jewelry should always be carefully stored to ensure its preservation.

NOTES

1. See the article on "Edwardian Jewelry" by R. F. Moeller Jewelers at http://www.rfmoeller.com/estate/edwardia.htm

2. Stomachers were heavily embroidered or jeweled garments that were worn over the chest and stomach.

3. A *resille* was a net-like necklace popular during the Edwardian period.

Egyptian Revival Jewelry

Period: late eighteenth century C.E.–present
Birthplace: Ancient Egypt

Origins: Napoleon's foray into Egypt in the late eighteenth century;
subsequent archaeological discoveries of the nineteenth century

Influences: Culture, art, and architecture of the Pharaonic period (B.C.E.)

Long before the first Egyptian dynasty came to power (circa 3100 B.C.E.), the
Egyptian people had been using precious metals acquired by trade and spoils of
war from the Eastern desert area and from neighboring Nubia in their daily living. Among the finer things that made their way to Cairo, Alexandria, and some
of the other large cities along the Nile delta, enormous amounts of gold were
quickly put to use by Egyptian artisans in a variety of ways. The visitor to this
North African land might have encountered gilded wood and stone, small gold
statues of the gods, or plated and decorated ceremonial furniture and funerary
items, richly wrought and crafted in excellence to please the eye of the beholder.
Indeed, this is what the explorer and archaeologist Howard Carter (1874–1939)
discovered in 1922 when he unearthed the tomb of the great Egyptian pharaoh,
Tutankhamen (reigned 1333–1324 B.C.E.): gold in abundance as part and parcel
of nearly every portion of the tomb, its furniture, its funerary artifacts, and the
walls of this great boy king.

However, what Carter's discovery made more than adequately apparent was
that the greatest use for all the gold (as well as other precious items) that made its
way to Tutankhamen's kingdom was in the production of jewelry, both for living
subjects and, most importantly, for those who had died, like King Tut himself.
Egyptian burial customs demanded that the mummified corpse be well adorned
with the finest handiwork of native craftspersons, whether around the neck or
as headwear, decorating the chest or lining the waist—truly all that glittered at
graveside was gold!

Such was the importance of their skill and trade that the great workshops of
Egyptian craftspersons were attached to the temples and palaces, where their
work was under the control of high officials. It is interesting to note, therefore,
that though they had the power and wherewithal to requisition the finest of all
that Egypt and its trading partners had to offer, these craftspersons did not use
what we would consider precious stones in their creations; in point of fact, some
of their finest work was in glass and other handmade materials that imitated
authentic rubies and sapphires and emeralds. The colors chosen for their finery,
though at first glance understood as aesthetically pleasing, held a deeper secret:
Each color contained an underlying symbolism or the properties of a particular
magic. Red jasper (the color of blood) enhanced the words of the spell "you have
your blood, Isis; you have your power"; green was the color of new life, and
hence, resurrection; dark blue, the color of the all-protective night sky.

Egyptian stonesetters, known in the jewelry trade as lapidaries, were particularly fond of a small variety of semiprecious materials to complete their creations.
Of the green hue, they favored *wadj* (malachite), used mostly for painting and
as the main ingredient in eye-shadow make-up; *mefkat* (turquoise), which symbolized joy and delight; green jasper, green feldspar (sometimes called Amazon

stone), prase, chrysoprase, olivine, serpentine, beryl, and peridot. Of the blue hue, lapidaries employed *khesbed* (lapis-lazuli). For red hues, red jasper, carnelian (symbolizing sadness), and sardonyx filled their orders. Thus a piece of jewelry or a combination of jewels carefully arranged on the sarcophagi of the deceased told their entire story: the life once seen in their eyes; their powerful rule, like the night sky; their sad heart at the loss of a consort . . . .

Egyptian jewelrymakers were also among the first to use *nub hedj* (literally, "white gold"—what we know today as silver) and copper. They were also very fond of quartzes, such as amethyst, and silicates, like beryls and garnets. Employing all materials at hand, whether local (such as animal horn, feathers, or breccia, a red/white rock) or imported (silver and lapis), these talented craftspersons created a large array of fine and beautiful items, setting the stage for most of what we are still wearing today to decorate our bodies, demonstrate our fashion sense, ward off evils, express our love, and bury the dead: amulets, anklets, bangle bracelets, belts, collars, diadems, earrings, finger rings, pectorals, pendants, and torques.

However, years prior to Carter's discovery of King Tut's tomb, the archaeological finds of the latter part of the Victorian period had already introduced the world to Egyptian styles, symbols, and motifs through newspaper headlines and subsequent museum acquisitions. Victorian jewelers were quick to pick up on

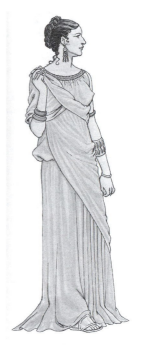

Egyptian queen Cleopatra (69–30 B.C.E.) in a Greco-Roman outfit. Note the armlets, earrings, and bracelet of the period. Used by permission of Tom Tierney from his book *Great Empresses and Queens Paper Dolls,* published by Dover Publications, 1982.

the fascination of the public with antiquities and, using their craft to study, copy, and interpret the handiwork of Egyptian artisans, launched an entirely unique jewelry trend known today as Egyptian Revival (also sometimes called Neo-Egyptian).[1] Soon, the public was presented with scarabs, asps, ankhs, sphinxes, languid Cleopatras, hieroglyphs, obelisks, and heads of the pharaohs embodied beautifully in all kinds of jewelry designs. The fascination has continued to the present day: One can find hundreds of sites on the Internet advertising and selling "Egyptian Revival jewelry," and many of the top designers of the last 50 years have made entire collections of jewelry with Egyptian motifs, most notably Kenneth J. Lane (1930–), MOMA, Cadoro, and Miriam Haskell (1899–1981).

☞ DID YOU KNOW?

One of the truly unique contributions to the history of jewelry from ancient Egyptian artisans was the introduction of the scarab, depicting the Egyptian

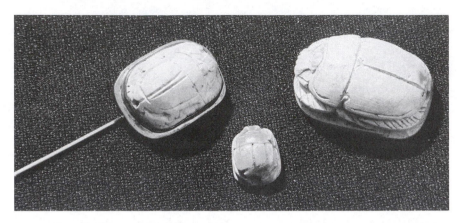

These are no ordinary beetle sculptures: Scarabs are believed to have a talisman effect and imbue magical qualities to those who possess them. Copyright © 2007 by Anthony F. Chiffolo.

beetle, carved in precious and semiprecious stones and the centerpiece of some of the oldest rings and pendants discovered at ancient archaeological dig sites dating back more than 5,000 years. The scarab symbolized self-creation and was often used as a protective amulet. Today scarab jewelry is extremely popular and can be found not only in rings but in bracelets, necklaces, and earrings, as well as other jewelry, both for women and for men.

NOTE

1. Some scholars subscribe to three distinct periods of the Neo-Egyptian trend: the first, a result of Napoleon's Egyptian campaign of the late eighteenth century c.e.; the second, the opening of the Suez Canal and the subsequent worldwide focus on Egypt; the third, Carter's discovery in 1922 of King Tut's tomb. In addition, Egyptian-style pieces are very popular in today's market. However, the interest of most modern collectors has focused on the work of the Victorian period.

Enameling (and Other Decorating Processes)

As we entered, I could not help being impressed by the wealth of articles in beautiful cloisonné enamel, in mother-of-pearl, lacquer, and champlevé. (*The War Terror,* Chapter XI, by Arthur B. Reeve [1886–1936])

Enamel is a nearly clear glass or a combination of various glasses (called flux) that has been melted together with flint or sand, red lead, and soda or potash, then mixed with metallic oxides to obtain a variety of colors. Originating in Byzantium, enameling jewelry is considered to be one of the finest and often most expensive methods of jewelrycrafting. Art Nouveau jewelers were particularly fond of enamel, with Carl Fabergé (1846–1920) undoubtedly the master enamel craftsman of his time (or any era, for that matter). "Enamel" is sometimes used to describe decorating techniques that use enamel or similar substances. There are various forms of enameling used in jewelrymaking, as follows:

CHAMPLEVÉ

Champlevé ("raised plane") is a French technique of enameling that is similar to cloisonné (see entry below). However, in contrast to the cloisonné method of soldering wire walls to a surface, champlevé items have troughs or cells that have been carved, etched, or gouged into an object, creating low areas that are subsequently filled with vitreous enamels or fine metals. Etching can be done with a hand tool, or by using ferric acid or some other type of acid to create a design.

Champlevé was a well-known process in Europe as early as the third century B.C.E., especially among the Celts and Romans. It was an extremely popular craft form in the Rhine Valley near Cologne and in Belgium in the eleventh and twelfth centuries C.E., especially among medieval metalworkers for use in jewelry and reliquaries. It was also used at times for bookbinding, though more for decorative effect than for strength. The enamelers Nicholas of Verdun (circa 1150–1210) and Godefroid de Claire (born circa 1130) were among notable practitioners of the era. As it is labor-intensive work, champlevé died out as a favored art technique sometime around the fourteenth century, though many buttons of later centuries sport champlevé work. Champlevé experienced a revival in the twentieth century thanks to Art Deco artisans (such as those at the Roycroft Studios [see **Copper**]) interested in its unique properties and format for decorating handcrafted items.

One highly developed form of champlevé is known as *basse-taille* (French for "low-relief"), a hand- or machine-chasing process whereby a figural scene is incised into the surface material, then "loaded" with translucent enamels in varying thicknesses in such a way that the highest point is lower than the surrounding metal. These differing levels produce tonal effects that give the impression of three dimensions to beads, jewelry, or other items.

Another technique, known as *émail en ronde bosse* (French for "encrusted enameling"), is a process by which small round objects or pieces made in high relief are covered with translucent or opaque enamels. This is delicate work, as the applied enamels are fragile and can detach easily if not carefully handled.

CLOISONNÉ

Cloisonné is a very popular but difficult form of enameling, using a technique in which very thin wires are solder-fitted as small walls (known as *cloisons,* or "cells") to form the outlines of a decorative pattern that has been traced onto a metal, glass, or ceramic surface. Colored enamels made of glass (known as frits) are then laid into the cloisons and baked in a kiln until they melt, filling the cells. Depending on the desired effect, this process may be repeated three to four times. After cooling, the enamel is polished to create a smooth surface that is level with the cloisons and is often electroplated with a thin film of gold to help prevent corrosion.

Cloisonné enamel, though often associated with Asia, was actually introduced to China during the Yuan dynasties of the thirteenth–fourteenth centuries C.E. by Egyptian traders and artisans. In the era of the Ching dynasty (1644–1911), cloisonné enameling had become an export ware for trade in Europe. Today, Beijing is the cradle of the cloisonné industry. Many jewelry pieces are made of cloisonné; of particular popularity are brightly colored beads for necklaces, bracelets, and earrings.

DAMASCENE

Damascene is the name given to the interlacing of gold and silver on the surface of objects. Though not an enameling process per se, damascening uses many of the same inlay decorating techniques to obtain a multilayered rich look on delicate metalwork, such as jewelry, desk items, and swords. The capital of damascene work is Toledo, Spain, though damascening was practiced by the Greeks, Romans, and Egyptians for centuries, usually as a forging method to temper *wootz* steel. It may have emanated at some point from Damascus (Syria, hence the moniker[1]), but its origins were most likely in India.

The damascene process begins by scoring the surface of an object with a series of slashes or nicks using a high-tempered steel awl in preparation for the introduction of gold and silver into the resultant small valleys. Next, designs (geometric patterns or flowers) are drawn on top of the indentations, and the precious metals are hand-hammered (using a *maceta*) into the defaced surface, resulting in a kind of "sunken" bas-relief. To further highlight the handiwork, a blackened background is created by oxidizing the nondamasked sections in a hot bluing solution. A final pass-over (*repasado*) of the object with a hammer, making light and delicate "chips" in the metal, gives the object a glistening quality. As a finishing touch, the product is hand-chased to bring out its beauty.[2]

Damascening has a long history in Japan, where it is known as *zogan,* or *shippou-zogan* (a kind of champlevé). Japanese jewelry produced by this method is called *shakudo,* from the use of a low-content gold alloy by that name used to create the dark background associated with damascene.

GRISAILLE

Grisaille (literally, "grey-ness") is an underpainting technique of enameling that uses a buildup of white overlays against a black background to create a monochrome appearance. The surface is dry-heated after each application, which helps to give it a three-dimensional look. Grisaille was a very popular jewelry design during the Victorian era in Europe and the United States.

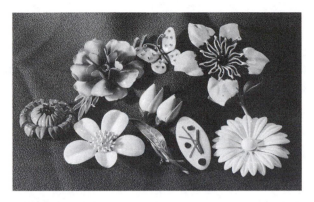

Enamel pins of the 1950s and 1960s are tops among today's collectors. Copyright © 2007 by Anthony F. Chiffolo.

GUILLOCHE

Guilloche (from the French word for "engine turning") is a kind of enameling in which fused, translucent glass is applied to a base metal that has been design-carved by a lathe or some other instrument. Guilloche was once a very popular method of decorating jewelry and watchcases.

JAIPUR

Carl Fabergé (1846–1920) may have been the master of enameling artistry during the latter half of the nineteenth century, but the artisans of Jaipur in India knew how to make some of the most beautiful and decorative works of enameled jewelry hundreds of years before Fabergé was born. In Jaipur to this day, a fabulous method of enameling is practiced to make *minakari* jewelry, in which ground-up precious gemstones are used to create a miniature "portrait" of brightly colored enamels that can be seen from the front and the back. These are set into an 18k–22k gold bezel or background. In the city of Nathdwara, a similar process is employed, using stamping and chasing, to make silver minakari jewelry. The city of Kundan also makes unique enameled jewelry.

JAPANNING

"Japanning" is a decoration style and preservative varnishing process that originated in Asia, probably in China. Once known as "Indiaware," the wood-finishing technique came to be associated with Japan (hence the name), from which some of the finest work of this type emanated. Prior to the seventeenth century C.E., japanning was accomplished by using natural lacquers to cover wood or another surface metal (tin, papier-mâché, glass) with a dark (usually black) color, then polishing it to a high finish after the item had been decorated with gold, silver, or some other glistening precious metal. The end product was not only visually stunning, but the base item, whatever it might have been, was now wonderfully preserved under layers of protective lacquer.

In the late 1600s, Europeans created their own japanning technique using *asphaltum*, a mineral pitch made of bitumen, which was prevalent throughout Europe, especially France, the Netherlands, Spain, and most particularly England. Once the pitch was applied, mineral pigments of reds, greens, and blues were superimposed, along with thin slivers of pearl, then heat-dried to create a rich design. The luster and hardness of the japanning technique are the result of polishing each coat of varnish or resin that has been applied. Japanning lost its popularity as an art form about the middle of the nineteenth century, due partly to the introduction of new materials to the handcrafts market and changes in taste and fashion; however, the discovery of electroplating as a preservative measure made lacquering seem old-fashioned and ineffectual.

In jewelrycrafting, japanning was frequently used to decorate ladies' conceits (see **Conceits**), such as snuff boxes and fan handles; however, japanning can also be found on brooches, necklaces, collars, and earrings from the eighteenth century in England, and right up to and throughout the modern costume era in the United States.

NIELLO

Niello is a deep-black, metallic mixture that is fused as an inlay onto metal for a decorative effect, creating a superb contrast between its darkness and matte or polished surfaces. Basically, niello work is a two-step process: The first involves making the mixture; the second is a matter of filling depressions or incisions that have been engraved, etched, stamped, rolled, or layered onto a metal surface. The recipe for niello is usually two parts silver, one part copper, one part lead, and a bit of borax. These are smelted in a crucible and then mixed with ammonium chloride to create a thin paste (called flux), which is then spread over the defaced surface, filling the cracks and crevices. The excess niello is then removed with a scraper or coarse file and burnished or polished, preferably with a leather stick or a felt wheel.

Niello is a technique that has been known since ancient times, originating most likely with the Egyptians. It was a common decorating technique in Europe until the sixteenth century, but its popularity waned soon thereafter, except in imperial Russia, where it had a popular following. In the twentieth century, niello jewelry from Siam (now Thailand) was frequently gifted by American soldiers stationed in Asia to their sweethearts back home. Many of the designs found on these jewelry objects were characters from the Hindu legend of Ramayama and/or typical cultural symbols from Siam's history. The most common niello jewelry items were necklaces, bracelets, rings, earrings, pendants, buttons, and tie bars.

PLIQUE-Á-JOUR

Plique-á-jour (from the French, "light of day") is a type of enamel process using ribbons of precious metal filigree or mesh wire to create a kind of stained-glass effect for jewelry and other fine pieces. With plique-à-jour, there is no backing for the vitreous enamel; instead, open spaces (called cells) are created using solder and a jeweler's torch. This is an especially vibrant technique for jewelry items that have a back-lit lighting source, such as dangling earrings. Plique-à-jour jewelry was very popular during the Art Nouveau period both in Europe and the United States.

TAILLE D'EPARGNE

Taille d'epargne is a type of enameling that uses black enamel to fill incised patterns on a gold background onto which a repeated pattern has been engraved. It was a very popular design method used by jewelrycrafters during the Victorian era in England and the United States.

☞ DID YOU KNOW?

And now for someone who has everything: Outrage! Deluxe, acknowledged by the *Guinness Book of World Records* to be the most expensive board game ever created. The laminated game board has a detailed map of the Tower of London; the playing cards are edged with gold leaf; the game pieces and coins are hall-marked British sterling silver, and the replicas of the Crown Jewels are 18k solid gold studded with real rubies, sapphires, diamonds, and emeralds. To add some color and panache to the set, each piece and flag has been individually colored in bright enamels to rival nearly any piece on the jewelry market today. The cost for the set: US$15,000, unless one wants it personalized: Then there is an extra cost for engraving. And for those who may doubt the veracity of any claims made about the game, each set comes with its own copy of the *Guinness Book of World Records* to silence the naysayers.

NOTES

1. Some sources say that the term comes from its perceived resemblance to the many varieties of rich silk damask patterns.

2. Hand-chasing is a technique by which an artisan details the front or top surface of a metal article with hammer-struck punches to assure that the pattern is firmly indented into the metal.

Findings

Not on one strand are all life's jewels strung. (English writer and designer William Morris [1834–1896])

Findings,[1] simply stated, are the component parts or materials that crafters use to make jewelry. The term itself probably refers to a time when jewelers had to "find" scrap pieces they needed in order to fashion a piece of jewelry; or if none were to be found, basics were created from what was at hand or what was left over from previous projects. Findings, therefore, are probably as old as the origins

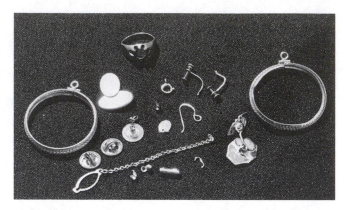

Findings are found on every jeweler's bench, as they are the stuff of jewelrycrafting. Copyright © 2007 by Anthony F. Chiffolo.

of jewelry itself: Without a way to attach beads, gemstones, and other items so that they could be worn, jewelrymaking would likely have remained rather one dimensional.[2]

There are three basic kinds of findings: functional, decorative, and hybrid.[3] Functional findings are those that have a mechanical purpose: to attach, join, or link, such as pinbacks, catches, posts, or screwbacks. Decorative findings are pieces that add beauty to a piece of jewelry; in handmade jewelry, these are often the parts that are created by the artisan, such as charms, filigrees, and festoons. Hybrid findings are pieces that serve both a functional and a decorative purpose, such as bead caps, bracelet links, and locket balls.

There are scores of findings used by jewelry artisans to make their wares. Some of the most important and notable types are:

Bail: A bail is a metal attachment that has been soldered or connected to a pendant so that it can slide easily on a chain, giving it some movement when worn. Bails are usually oval, tear-drop, or D-shaped and come in many varieties, depending on their intended function.

Barrel nut: A V-shaped or barrel-shaped clutch with a rubber insert that grips a stickpin or earrings to keep them from slipping out of place. When referring to earrings, the grip is sometimes also called a bullet clutch.

Bead caps: Bead caps are a kind of metal or plastic ornamentation that is glued or otherwise attached around the hole of a bead to hide inconsistencies or damage. Bead caps are a kind of hybrid finding, as they are both functional and decorative, and are often created in such a way that they accentuate the beads to which they are attached. With multiple strands of beads, a large cap called a bead cone is often used.

Bolo slide: The bolo slide is a component that has a flat surface with ends rolled into small tubes on its reverse side. The composition of the slide allows for space to which a bolo ornamentation can be attached, and the side-to-back tubes permit it to move easily up and down its affixed leather cords, making it a lightweight and attractive neckpiece. A hybrid finding used for this Western-style neckwear is the bolo tip (or ferrule), shaped as conical tubes, often of silver or plastic, that are glued to the end of the bolo to keep the leather from fraying.

Catch: For pins, a catch is the metal component that is fashioned to hook and lock in a pin-stem to keep the pin secure; for necklaces and bracelets, a catch is the lock or closing portion that fastens one end to the other.

Chain tag: A small, flat metal piece with a hole in each end that serves as the quality stamp or trademark of the manufacturer. In recent years, chain tags have taken on more of the personality of a conceit, an item designed to enhance one's status or fashion stature by its display.

Clip: On an earring, a two-part piece that is attached to the earring back so that it can be worn clipped to the front and obverse sides of the earlobe. The finding is spring-hinged and uses mechanical pressure for opening and closing. The clip was a variation of the screwback; today, many persons who cannot wear pierced earrings choose clips as an option.

Ear nut: The ear nut, or earring back, is a kind of holed clutch into which an earring post is inserted so that the earring can be secured to the earlobe.

Ear screw: Used most often for vintage earrings, an ear screw, sometimes called a screwback, is a U-shaped wire that tightens on a thread to secure earrings to the lobe.

Ear wire: An ear wire is a bowed loop with a bent catch that goes through the hole in the ear. It may be used plain or with beads or other ornamentation on the loop. Most ear wires today are made with hypoallergenic metals.

Enhancer: Enhancers are decorative crimped or molded findings that have been fitted over a strand of pearls or beads; molded findings contain a locking mechanism that can be opened and closed easily for added effect. Its opposite is the hybrid finding known as a shortener, most often a hinged ring that can fit across a doubled length of necklace or chain and hooked into place.

Extender: An extender does just what its name implies: It extends the length of a necklace or chain, which is helpful should it be too short for comfort or fashion style. Usually a short length of chain, the extender has a connector on one end and a small loop at the other for easy attachment.

Festoon: A pendant that has rings on both sides, a festoon becomes the centerpiece of a necklace when chain or cord is threaded through its rings. An old and decorative finding, the term has also become a jewelry verb: Items that are greatly and imaginatively decorated are said to be "festooned."

Filigree: Though rarely thought of as such, the ornamental nature of filigree work, with its intricate lace-like patterns formed of bent wire, is a very common finding, especially in jewelry from Asia. Filigree may be soldered, stamped, or cast and is often made of silver, copper, or gold.

French wire: Also known as a fishhook, this simple finding used to make earrings has a hooked end that is able to pass through the pierced ear, usually with an ornament or bead added for decoration at its opposite end.

Gallery: A gallery in jewelrycrafting functions much the same as it does in furniture making—as a decorative element that has a useful purpose. Galleries are continuous metal strips into which stones are set in a repeated design. They often line the entire rim of a jewelry item.

Joint, catch, and pin-stem: Not as complicated as it sounds, this three-part mechanism is used to affix jewelry, such as pins, to clothing. The joint is the fulcrum on which the pin-stem (a long pointed finding, often with a T-shape base) pivots, the catch a hook into which the pin-stem fits for a proper and tight closure.

Jump ring: The jump ring is a plain wire ring, usually round or oval, that is used to attach jewelry parts. The ends of the wire on jump rings are usually merely bent together, as opposed to similar findings that are soldered.

Kidney wire: One of the most popular findings used in making earrings, these wires have a kind of kidney shape to them and are often used to dangle beads or charms for pierced earrings. Kidney wires, with their closed endings, are different from fishhooks, which are generally open-ended.

Lanyard hook: This common finding, used as a pinback, is made wide at one end and thin at the opposite end; it opens and closes by thumb pressure to fit into or release from its hook.

Lever back: Sometimes called a Eurowire or German ear wire, a lever back is a hook-shaped ear wire hinged to a spring-loaded closing at the hook's base. While in an open position, the ear wire can pass through the earlobe hole. Once through, the closure mechanism can be snapped shut against the wire to keep the earring in place.

Link connector: Used primarily for cufflinks, this decorative finding is what locks cuff ends together. Most link connectors are bars that can be pushed horizontally through the button hole, then swiveled to a horizontal position and locked in. Other connectors, especially on vintage cufflinks, are simply chains.

Lobster claw clasp: The lobster claw clasp is a finding used to connect opposite ends of a necklace or bracelet. One of the ends has a wide, flat hook that resembles a lobster claw (hence the name), fitted with a kind of hinged "thumb" that is its spring. The opposite end has an open ring that the claw hooks to and is then made secure by closing the thumb of the claw. Lobster claw clasps are perfect for heavy chains or jewelry with lots of soldered appointments.

Pad insert: Pad inserts have been a welcome new addition to the findings category of jewelrycrafting, especially for those who wear clip earrings. Made of molded rubber or cloth, a pad fits over an earring back and provides the wearer with a cushion for greater comfort, especially with earrings that have new or tight hinges.

Pearl cup: A functional finding, pearl cups are designed to hold the pearl in place, either with glue or with a small peg (called a peg setting) that has been drilled into the bead for greater security.

Post: A post is one of the most common earring findings in jewelrycrafting. A pin-like element attached to an earring, it is designed to pass through a pierced earlobe, nostril, tongue, or lip and is usually made secure with a clutch to hold the earring next to the skin.

Ring guard: Anyone who has ever lost weight or decided to wear a family heirloom too big for their fingers is thankful for the invention of the ring guard, a finding that stretches across the inside of the band to temporarily reduce the diameter of the ring for a more secure fit. Ring guards are often made of the same material as the ring itself.

Safety catch, chain, clasp: Safety catches, chains, and clips, though distinct findings, serve a similar purpose: to safeguard a bracelet or necklace, often as a secondary backup, to ensure that valuable jewelry is not lost when it comes unclipped or accidentally disconnected. Safety "measures" of these types are especially important for heavier pieces, which tend to slip or slide more easily than lighter jewelry.

Scarf clip: Sometimes called a scarf ring, scarf clips are used as a decorative device to shape the material into folds or to create a fashion moment by their placement. Scarf clips operate much on the same principle as a bolo slide, though many scarf clips are tightly hinged in order to limit the movement of the scarf within the ring.

Shank: The shank is a finding on an item of jewelry, such as a ring, by which it is attached to another jewelry piece. Shanks are often found on cufflinks, button links, and at the end of chains. In jewelrymaking, a shank is also the part of the ring into which a gemstone can be set.

Spring ring: The spring ring is a nearly circular tube with a coiled spring inside pressing on the inner end of a curved wire. This wire, projecting from the tube, is what completes the circle. The wearer presses on a small lip, which allows the wire to be pushed back into the tube so that the ends of bracelets, necklaces, and links of chain can be attached.

Tallis clip: Sometimes called an alligator or sweater clip, a tallis clip is a hinged finding, often with "teeth," that secures one piece of clothing to another, such as button to buttonhole sides of a sweater, or a tie to a shirt seam.

Tassel: A tassel is a gathering of threads, cord, or chains of equal lengths into an ornamental tuft that hangs loosely from the knot that ties them together. Tassels were a very popular finding in the medieval and Renaissance periods, as well as in the 1920s flapper era.

Toggle clasp: A toggle clasp is a rigid metal bar inserted through a ring that is used to attach necklaces or bracelets. As the bar is turned sideways, it is not able to slip back through the ring, thereby securing the two attached pieces.

☞ DID YOU KNOW?

Beads, whether a finding or a primary jewelry element, are without a doubt one of the oldest jewelry elements known to humankind. Some scholarly sources claim that beadmaking as a craft dates back anywhere from 20,000 to 100,000 years. The first beads were probably made by perforating shells, carved pieces of animal bone, minute stones, and seeds. Beadmaking and stringing was not only

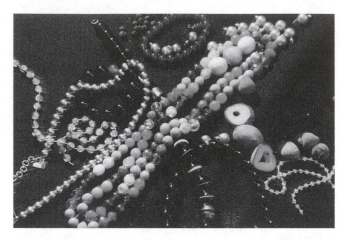

Beads, without a doubt, are the oldest known jewelry findings. Bead-stringing is a handicraft dating back nearly 100,000 years. Copyright © 2007 by Anthony F. Chiffolo.

a matter of adornment: Beads became an important trade item, a keen way to communicate themes and spiritual insights, and, through carving, a talisman against the perceived evils of the ancient world. Today beads are made from all types of materials, and they are collected by jewelrycrafters and hobbyists alike. For those interested in the history of beading, there are entire museums dedicated to beads and bead crafts in Glendale, AZ, Washington, DC, Carmel, CA, and Detroit, MI. Plans for a bead museum in Thailand are currently under way.

NOTES

1. Some other types of jewelry findings include bolt rings, chandelier findings, comfort discs, cufflink actions, ear cuffs, ear threads, eye pins, French hooks, fusion posts, jackets, omega clips, pelican clasps, screw eyes, split rings, and swivels.

2. Beads themselves are sometimes considered findings, as are the strings or chains on which they are strung.

3. For an excellent explanation of these three types and important glossary of findings terms, see "Jewelry Findings Glossary" at http://www.guyotbrothers.com/jewelry-findings-glossary.htm

Georgian Jewelry

Period: 1714–1830 (1837)[1]
Birthplace: England

Origins: French rococo/Italian Gothic

Influences: Ancient Greek motifs; rococo, Gothic, and Neoclassical designs;
   trends toward opulence and self-indulgence

The Georgian era[2] of jewelrymaking covers a wide expanse of years and styles during the eighteenth and nineteenth centuries. Like the Victorian period that follows it, it is perhaps best understood by dividing the time into thirds: early Georgian, mid-Georgian, and late Georgian. Each third represents a distinct approach to fashion and style, with jewelry fabricated to complement the times.

The style during the reign of the English kings George I (1714–1727) and George II (1727–1760) was decidedly rococo, in imitation of the finery of the French court. The emphasis seems to have been one of largesse: earrings, crosses, hair combs, buckles, aigrettes, and tiaras with grand stones were de rigueur. Shell, floral, and foliate motifs were common, with real shells often used as decoration. Opulence and luxury were the intended effect. In the early part of the rococo era, the hair was worn in curls; the colors were pastels and, later, rich blue and red tones; white cotton caps of varying shapes adorned the head; sleeves had large cuffs. Women who could afford such finery chose necklaces, earrings, and bracelets that matched their outfits in color and shape.

About 1740, during the reign of George II, fashions changed, and the *Robe à la Française* replaced the earlier style of dress known as the *Contouche* (a loose front-closing robe with large back pleats and a matching skirt, called a *jupe*). The bodice of this gown showed a close-fitting front with a waist seam. Filling out the midsection was a steel-boned stomacher, a large "brooch" that covered the gown from the low-cut neckline down to the waist. The skirts that completed the outfit were trimmed with ribbons, flowers, embroidery, and pearls. Hence, the jewelry chosen as good measure included chatelaines—long chains worn at the waist with dangling work implements (such as scissors, knives, decorative fobs, keys, and small purses [see **Necessaries**]); silk ribbon necklaces with drop pendants made of pearls or shimmery stones (such as diamonds and agates); bow brooches and girandole (chandelier-style) earrings (see **Earrings**). By 1750, new stones and materials like ivory, garnet, and topaz were worn along with emeralds, rubies, and sapphires. Lava, onyx, and carnelian were popular as well. Jewelry of the early and mid-Georgian period always followed the fashion in clothing; hence Georgian jewelers were often "second-tier" consultants in the employ of garmentmakers and tailors, their pieces crafted to order (especially if they were made of paste) to match the apparel of the customer.

Soon after George III (1738–1820) came to the throne in 1760, another fashion shift took place. The 1770s saw the introduction of the *Robe à la Polonnaise,* a looped-up overskirt with small side hoops (and later with hip pads). By 1780 skirts were smaller and hairstyles grander. Enter the *Robe à l'Anglaise,* with its tight bodice and stripes of all widths and colors. In this latter part of the century, hair fashion reached a zenith with wigs and mounted extensions

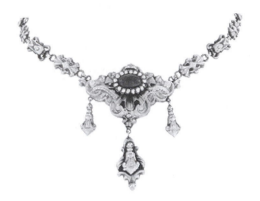

A Georgian 9k yellow gold link necklace, featuring a central scrolling foliate motif with an oval cabochon garnet surrounded by seed pearls with three gold scrolling drops. Courtesy of Lang Antiques and Estate Jewelers, San Francisco, www.langantiques.com

(some even with built-in bird cages or sailing vessels) fashioned to excess. Silk stockings (white or colored), fans, flowers, hoods, and tall walking canes made luxurious jewelry a necessity for the sake of continuity and balance. A few of the innovations of the late Georgian era include the *ferronire,* a head ornament with a jewel that sat on the forehead; and following the years of the French revolution, the wearing of a thin, red ribbon around the throat to simulate the cut of the guillotine.

Throughout all three portions of the Georgian era, some common element designs can be noted. All Georgian jewelry was handmade; ring settings often featured crowns and hearts as tokens of enduring love; high-karat gold was the precious metal of choice; stones set in jewelry pieces had a closed back lined with foil to reflect the light or enhance the color; mine cut and rose cut diamonds were the norm (a carryover from the Gothic period); marcasite and cut steel were common materials in nearly all jewelry; cameos became a craze (a revival from the late-Gothic period); and designs based on archaeological discoveries of the day (a Neoclassical contribution) were the rage. Many pins, earrings, and bracelets featured acorns; mosaics, such as "pietra dura," were introduced; miniature, heart-shaped lockets were *the* gift between lovers; and men were often as bedecked by jewels as were their female companions.

☞ DID YOU KNOW?

The French Revolution of 1789, which ended the reign of Louis XVI (1754–1793) and his wife, Marie Antoinette (1755–1793), took place during the latter part of the Georgian era. As both a fashion statement and as an act of remembrance, pieces of the wall of the famous Bastille prison were made into jewelry and worn by the public. It is also said that some commoners in Nantes wore earrings made in the shape of guillotines (the method of the king's and queen's death), and jewelry fashioned as "liberty caps" was said to be abundant, as were copper pieces proclaiming "Liberté, Egalité, ou La Mort" (Liberty, Equality, or Death).

NOTES

1. Some historians include the reigns of George IV (1762–1830) and his brother, William IV (1765–1837), in this time frame.

2. The period between 1910 and 1952 (the reigns of King George V [1865–1936] and George VI [1895–1952]) may also be referred to as "Georgian" in certain contexts; however, for our purposes here, we use "Georgian" to mean the era of the British kings who ruled during the eighteenth and nineteenth centuries.

Glass Jewelry

> There is nothing that is wisdom's equal, neither gold nor costly glass. (Job 28:17, *CEV,* paraphrased)

Just exactly when the ancients first used glass in their daily lives is a matter of speculation among scholars. Most agree that before learning to manufacture glass, our ancestors discovered glass in nature, both in long, slender tubes known as fulgurites (caused when lightning strikes sand) and as the result of the heat of a volcanic eruption, creating what today is called obsidian. Samples of obsidian jewelry dating back thousands of years have been found at many ancient archaeological sites.

When, where, and how humans first learned to make glass is uncertain. Samples of a glass-type glaze have been discovered on ceramic vessels dating back as far as 5,000 years; the first-known glass vessels date to about 1,500 years later, in the Mesopotamian region and in Egypt. Both Egypt and Syria were glassmaking centers for hundreds of years before the Common Era. The invention of the blowpipe about 30 B.C.E. along the eastern Mediterranean coast made glass production faster and a lot easier. Above all, blown glass was much cheaper, which made it available to everyday folks for the first time. During the first four centuries of the Common Era, glassmaking flourished in all areas where Rome had influence.

Glass made by human hands appears to have first been used by jewelrycrafters to create beads sometime around 3000–2500 B.C.E. Using soda ash, silica, and some sort of stabilizing agent, such as limestone, early glasscrafters in Egypt and India used their glass works to imitate precious stones, such as lapis lazuli and turquoise. Later, as the technology spread, the Phoenicians (in what is now Lebanon) began making glass beads both for local use and exportation as early as 1200 B.C.E. Glass beads have also been found in sites dating to 900 B.C.E. in Austria, in Switzerland (600–100 B.C.E.), and among the ancient Celts (200–100 B.C.E.), indicating a widespread appreciation for the beauty and quality of fine glasswork.

The second major stage in early glass production, particularly with regard to glass beads used in jewelry, came about during the rise of Islamic influence in the Middle East between 700 and 1400 C.E. Nearly all Islamic beads dating to this

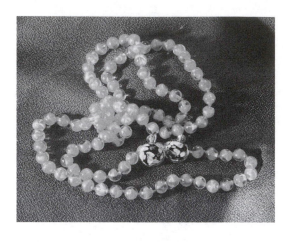

Glass beads and earrings of the 1960s. Copyright © 2007 by Anthony F. Chiffolo.

era are glass and are distinguished by their methods of decoration using multiple colors, prescribed patterns and styles, and the glassblowing techniques of trailing, feathering, dragging, and folding.

The third stage in early glass production, unparalleled then as today, took place during the Venetian era when Italian glassmaking was removed to the island of Murano in the late thirteenth century. Venetian glassmakers were among the finest and most studied as well as learned practitioners in glassmaking techniques. They revived many old ways of making glass beads, particularly the hollow-cane-drawn method, which produced (and continues to produce) some of the best glass beads known to history.

From the fourteenth century on, glass beads show up in all parts of the world, both native-made and imported, from the Americas (see **Native American Jewelry**) to China to Iceland. These beads are the backbone of the history of jewelry in many locations.

But just as not all glass was used for beadmaking, all glass jewelry was not in the shape of beads either. In the eighteenth century, Frenchman Georges-Frederic Strass (1701–1773), who understood better than anyone of his day the potential of English handblown leaded glass to stand in for expensive diamonds, created a special lead glass that could be handcut to look just like a diamond. Called paste, his technique was employed by jewelers of the day, using glass to imitate all sorts of precious gemstones (see **Costume Jewelry**). In nineteenth-century Germany, Daniel Swarovski (1862–1956) found a way to cut glass crystal to such perfection that it resembled fine diamonds. In the twentieth century, Frederick Carder (1863–1963), a Steuben artisan, introduced to the glass and jewelry markets many types of rare-colored art glass, including jade, aurene, alabaster, and cintra glass.[1] Since then, glass has become a major component of all jewelrymaking. Some other major categories of glass jewelrymaking include:

> *Favrile glass:* Favrile, from the Old English *fabrile* (handcrafted), was a creation of Louis Comfort Tiffany (1848–1933) in what he described as

"a composition of various glasses, worked together while hot." Tiffany's intent was to produce a glass with an iridescence reminiscent of butterfly wings, the necks of peacocks and pigeons, and the wings of certain kinds of beetles. Favrile glass is also distinguished by its unusual shapes and turns. As a type of art glass, it is one of the most highly sought after and expensive in the world. Favrile glass can be found in much of the Arts and Crafts movement jewelry of the late nineteenth and early twentieth centuries.

Furnace glass: Furnace glass is created using large decorated canes that have been built up out of smaller canes, one on top of the other, during the glassblowing process. The canes are then encased in clear glass, and beads are extruded, which have twisted and striped patterns. However, no air is blown into the glass, so it appears thick, much like the glass in some paperweights. The process requires a large-scale glass furnace and an annealing kiln to complete the final crafted product. Furnace glass is the stuff of many older glass beads, particularly Italian specimens.

Gablonz: Gablonz glass is named for the region in what is the German/Czech/Austrian area of Bohemia (Perlen Aus Gablonz), where highly decorated glass beads have been made since (lampworking) techniques were developed during the Biedermeier period of fashion (1815–1860) in France and Germany. These beautiful beads contain within them pyramids, cones, feathers, and flowers and are highly sought after by collectors and jewelrycrafters for inclusion in their works of art. The beads, all handpressed, often appear in rosaries of the late nineteenth century and early twentieth.

Givre: Givre, from the French, meaning "lightly frosted," refers to a stone or a bead made of clear glass that has been fused with color patterns around a transparent core. The term is often used with certain types of rhinestones. Givre beads are found in many French and German necklaces, earrings, and bracelets, particularly costume pieces of the 1920s–1960s.

Lampworked glass (aka *flamework glass*): Lampworking is a craft term for the process of melting and forming raw glass into specific shapes using a high-temperature torch. In this process, a 3000+ degree oxygen/propane torch is employed to melt borosilicate glass rods; intricate color workings are produced by adding common metals, metal oxides, and precious metals to achieve the desired effects. Lampworking has been popular since the nineteenth century but is very labor-intensive.

Millefiori: Millefiori (Italian for a "thousand flowers) are rods (or canes) of multicolored glass that have been fused together to create intricate geometric and floral designs. The process has been known since the early days of the Roman Empire, but it was perfected in Murano, Italy, more than a thousand years later. Millefiori pieces are made today as they have been for nearly 800 years of glassmaking and jewelrycrafting: A glass rod is covered with layers of colored glass and heated, then fused several times; the fused rods are then cut into small discs and placed into a mosaic pattern within a metal framing. All is then heated yet again, ground, and polished to perfection. Millefiori pieces are popular as pendants or in buttons and beads for jewelrycrafting.

Peking (Beijing) glass: Even though glass was probably made in China as long ago as 300 B.C.E., most Chinese glass dates to after 1662 C.E. Peking glass is one of those later commodities and refers to a kind of cameo glass that first became popular in China in the eighteenth century. Early Peking glass was created to imitate porcelain; later a technique was developed using overlaid layers that are partially carved away, creating a kind of cameo effect. (Peking glass is sometimes called cameo glass for this reason.) This layered glass is still made in the old manner today and is popular in the making of snuff bottles and beads.

Vauxhall glass: In the eighteenth century, Vauxhall was the site of one of England's largest glassworks factories. Jewelry made with glass from the factory (though most likely not produced on-site) came to be known as Vauxhall glass. Vauxhall pins, tiaras, earrings, and necklaces often featured clear, deep-black, or burgundy glass, usually with a mirrored backing. Now, as when they were first made, Vauxhall pieces are collectors' gems.

For discussions of other types of glass jewelry, see the entries on **Sea and Shore**, **Diamond Look-alikes**, and **Costume Jewelry**.

☞   DID YOU KNOW?

Some of the most beautiful glass in the world was used in the making of the heads of hatpins during the late nineteenth century. Peacock eye glass, a Bohemian glass that incorporated silver foil and a cobalt dot to conjure the image of the eye of the male peacock's tailfeathers, was extremely popular during the Victorian and Edwardian eras and today is highly valued among collectors. Art glass hatpin heads were also popular and are distinguished by the hand-blown materials that were pressed or blown into a mold. But some of the most unusual and colorful samples of hatpin heads are those made of Carnival glass, an iridescent pressed pattern glass that was produced in the late nineteenth and early twentieth centuries. Carnival glass gets its name from an unlikely turn of events in glasscrafting history, namely so much was made, as manufacturers were so sure it would be a great hit in every U.S. household, that overproduction flooded the market. Carnival glass did not catch the imagination of everyday consumers; therefore, it was given away as premiums at carnivals and fairs. In the twenty-first century, Carnival glass has found a new appreciation among collectors, and pieces now sell for hundreds of dollars.

NOTE

1. Jade glass is a nearly opaque blue, green, or yellow glass that Carder introduced in the 1920s. Carder introduced aurene glass in 1904; by spraying clear glass with stannous chloride or lead chloride and reheating it, he was able to produce a murky, translucent glass with an iridescent surface. Alabaster glass was created much in the same way in the 1920s. Cintra glass was another Carder creation, formed by picking up chips of colored

glass with the end of a blow pipe and casing them in a thin layer of colorless glass. All have since made their way into jewelrycrafting, particularly in beadmaking and the three-dimensional floral designs of pins and necklaces.

Gold

Periodic table symbol: Au

Atomic number: 79

Origin of name: from Old English/Germanic word (*gulth, ghol*) meaning "yellow, green" or possibly "bright" (periodic table name origin from Latin, *aurum*)

Important historical background information: known since prehistoric times

Geographical location of element: in antiquity, Egypt, Nubia, Black Sea area, Central America, Colombia, Peru; in modern times, South Africa,[1] Canada, the United States (particularly South Dakota and Nevada), Russia (Siberia), India, Australia, Chile, Argentina; found primarily in quartz deposits but also in pyrite, chalcopyrite, galena, sphalerite, arseno-pyrite, stibnite, pyrrhotite, petzite, calaverite, sylvanite, muthmannite, nagyagite, and krennerite

Gold is the child of Zeus, neither moth nor rust devoureth it. (Pinder, ca. 500 B.C.E.)

Gold is a precious, shiny, dense, yellow transition metal. It is the most malleable and ductile metal known to humankind and is without a doubt one of the most popular of all jewelry and coinage metals. Gold is the monetary standard used by the International Monetary Fund (IMF) and the Bank for International Settlements (BIS) in all their transactions. Because gold is a soft metal, it must be alloyed with other metals (copper and silver, for instance) to be workable and useful.

When gold is sold in the form of coinage or jewelry, it is measured by weight in karats (see **Karats**), with pure gold being 24k, and 22k, 18k, 14k, and 10k as normative standards (although British gold is sometimes marked 9k and 15k); gold-filled jewelry is usually 12k. Gold is used in a wide variety of applications, including (but not limited to) photographic, medical, computer, embroidery, spacecraft, dental, jet engine, communications, as well as in making awards and honors. Gold is available for purchase in many forms, including wire, foil, coin, and bars.

Gold has been highly valued since before recorded history. From the time it was discovered, it has exemplified royalty, purity, and wealth. As proof of these symbolic values, the funerary mask of King Tutankhamen (reigned 1333–1324 B.C.E.) of Egypt was pure gold. The earliest known coinage, from the ancient kingdom of Lydia (in what is now modern Turkey), circa 650 B.C.E., was made of gold (see **Coin Jewelry**).

Gold jewelry was common in nearly every ancient civilization, from the Sumerians to the Egyptians and other African nations, the Greeks and Romans, the Etruscans, the Scandinavian peoples, the Celts, and Native American civilizations. It was, most always, a precious metal, which means it was adornment for rulers and the rich. In the Common Era, the patrons of jewelers were the courts and the Church, and most jewelry was made in either monasteries or imperial workshops. About the thirteenth century c.e. in Europe, all of that changed with the establishment of goldsmith "guilds," an indication that jewelrycrafting, even with precious metals, was growing beyond the doors of religious and state hierarchies.

The Spanish exploitation of gold from the Americas meant that in Europe and other venues where the Spanish traded, gold became more plentiful—in fact, practically ordinary. By this time, persons of moderate means probably owned some gold jewelry or coins. But it was the nineteenth-century gold rushes in the United States and its territories, along with the discovery of gold in South Africa and Australia soon after, that marked the turning point in gold production and gold ownership. As a result, today gold is a universally available metal, and though desirable, it is no longer the most precious of metals in jewelrycrafting (platinum has taken on that honor).

Yet for some, only gold will do (in any color). For instance, Chinese and Indian brides wear 24k gold jewelry on their wedding day as a good luck charm symbolizing a lifetime of happiness and good fortune.

And the best place to buy it? Some would say Italy, which today is at the forefront of the gold jewelry industry. Of course, there are fine gold jewelers all around the world. Often, the sites close to the major gold deposit areas can offer the best deals. In other words, make a trip to where the product originates, and one is rarely disappointed. And how much to pay? Pricing is usually based on four factors: karatage, design, gram weight, and the work that has gone into the piece. The karat marking and the gram weight (if that information is available) will let the buyer know how much gold is in the piece; yet two other factors need

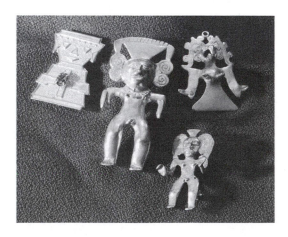

Gold jewelry in the style of the pre-Columbian era in the Americas. Copyright © 2007 by Anthony F. Chiffolo.

to be considered, especially because the amount of gold is no indication of the fineness of the craft. Obviously, the better the design and execution, the greater the value of the piece.

And what of color? Though gold appears in many colors (black or ruby, in fact, when finely divided, and in some forms purple),[2] 24k (or pure) gold has just one look, and that is *very* yellow. All the other colors we see in gold jewelry are alloys of gold with silver, copper, zinc, nickel, or some other metal. What is known as yellow gold is more gold than yellow, due to mixing it with a secondary metal so that it holds its form. Rose gold (or pink or red gold), which was very popular at the end of the Victorian era (see **Victorian Jewelry**), is made by adding more copper and removing silver additives. White gold is fashioned by increasing alloys of silver, zinc, and nickel. Green gold (which is hard to find) is created by mixing pure yellow gold with pure silver.

It's always best to purchase valuable pieces from a reputable dealer. Some stores or factories have goldsmiths on staff who are skilled in working with precious metals. Goldsmiths can file, solder, forge, cast, and polish gold, a trade they learned usually by apprenticeship via a knowledge base that has been handed down for centuries, since the time of the guilds of the Middle Ages.

☞   DID YOU KNOW?

Sure, gold is precious, but just how much gold is how much? It is a well-known fact that a lump of pure gold the size of a matchbox can be flattened into a sheet the size of a tennis court; but of course, then one would be afraid to play on it! Or to look at it the other way around, it has been said that if one took all the gold in the world that has ever been refined, it would form a single cube just 66 feet square (on all sides). Not that any of us would ever have the opportunity to pull off such a feat. In fact, it was illegal in the United States to own large quantities of gold (other than coins and jewelry) from 1933 to 1975. Which kind of makes sense, since 75 percent of all gold now in existence was refined in the last 95 years. There may be "gold in 'dem thar hills,'" but except for a few nuggets here and there, we're never going to be holding a lot of it in our laps without some government agency ready to stake its claim for the general well-being of the world's economy!

NOTES

1. South Africa has long been the number one gold-producing country, accounting for 79 percent of the world's production in 1970 (see "Gold" at http://en.wikipedia.org/wiki/Gold).

2. See "Gold" at http://en.wikipedia.org/wiki/Gold

Gothic and Neo-Gothic Jewelry

Period: fourteenth–sixteenth centuries

Birthplace: medieval Europe

Origins: courts and playgrounds of the wealthy

Influences: chivalry, chaste worship of women, sumptuary laws, heraldry

When modern enthusiasts speak of Gothic jewelry, their referents are most likely tied to the late nineteenth century and the Victorian tales of Dracula, creepy mansions, and the horror genre, with visions of heavy, dark furniture and dimly lit rooms. However, the nineteenth-century epoch is properly called Neo-Gothic or Gothic Revival, the true Gothic era having passed into time at the end of the sixteenth century.

Rings, pendants, necklaces, pins, hat badges, belt clasps, and other ornamentation were an important part of the dress code for Gothic men and women. Men often wore chains around their neck or over their shoulders as a demonstration of allegiance to their liege or to some political faction, or sometimes as a symbol of high office. Despite laws that forbid the exposure of a woman's neck and shoulders, jewelry fashioned to highlight these "sensuous" body parts was very popular. One need only to look at the portraits of famous women of the day—the Duchess of Burgundy (1457–1482), Isabella of Portugal (1451–1504), Margaret of Bavaria (1376–1434), to name just a few—to understand the perceived importance of both owning and wearing fine jewelry to complement one's personal and public appearance.[1]

The Gothic era was known for several unique innovations in jewelrymaking. Chief among them was the enameling technique used by French and Burgundian goldsmiths known as *basse-taille* ("bas-relief") enameling (see **Enameling**), which "consisted of cutting away a design or figural composition in low relief on a sheet of silver or gold and flooding the area with colored translucent enamel. Since the highest point of the relief is below the surface of the surrounding metal, the enamel lies in varying thickness over the whole area. Because the enamel is translucent, not only does the composition of the low relief show through, but the light is reflected back from the silver or gold through the varying thicknesses of the enamel, thereby adding a brilliant tonal quality to the enamels and creating an impression of three-dimensional modeling ranging from the bright highlights of the enameling to the rich tones of the deep recesses of the engraved relief."[2]

Also popular in this era was the technique called *émail en ronde bosse* ("in the round"), or what today might be called encrusted enameling (see Enameling). This consisted of creating a miniature sculpture out of gold, either rounded or with high relief, then covering it with multicolored or alternating layers of enamel.

A second major contribution of the Gothic era to the history of jewelrymaking was the improved methods of diamond cutting, led by lapidaries in the Netherlands. Gothic artisans introduced new ways of cutting a diamond, for instance. Until the late 1300s, most diamonds were table-cut, a process by which the tip of the stone was merely ground off to give it shape. Gothic lapidaries discovered that faceting diamonds and other precious stones allowed them to catch the light, making them flashier and hence more desirable to the buyer. Soon, gold and precious stones became the apex of fashion. '

A third characteristic that defined Gothic jewelry and jewelrymaking was the ubiquity and popularity of rings of all shapes and sizes and of every conceivable design and material. During the Gothic period, it was not unusual for those who could afford them to wear several bands on each hand, often with more than one ring per finger, sometimes even on the thumbs. Seal and signet rings were usual fare, especially among the wealthier landowning commoners, as a means by which to identify and legitimize their land and other dealings.

The Gothic era is also the advent (and some would say, the zenith) of the craft of cameo and intaglio cuts in shell and precious stones. This was due in great part to a late Gothic resurgence of interest in all things classical, a movement that would soon be renamed and characterized as part of the "Age of Enlightenment."

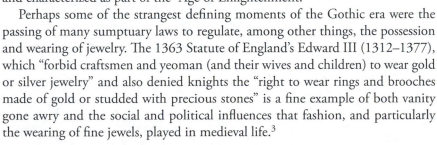

Eleanor of Aquitaine (1122–1204), Queen of France and England. Note her Gothic crown and brooch, her belt, and the Gothic cross on her book. Used by permission of Tom Tierney from his book *Great Empresses and Queens Paper Dolls,* published by Dover Publications, 1982.

Perhaps some of the strangest defining moments of the Gothic era were the passing of many sumptuary laws to regulate, among other things, the possession and wearing of jewelry. The 1363 Statute of England's Edward III (1312–1377), which "forbid craftsmen and yeoman (and their wives and children) to wear gold or silver jewelry" and also denied knights the "right to wear rings and brooches made of gold or studded with precious stones" is a fine example of both vanity gone awry and the social and political influences that fashion, and particularly the wearing of fine jewels, played in medieval life.[3]

☞ DID YOU KNOW?

One of the most popular jewelry items of the Gothic period was the *enseigne*, a brooch, badge, or pendant worn on a hat as a decoration. These pieces were meant to convey to the observer some message about the wearer of the hat, having been crafted to display a heraldic coat of arms, a motto or allegiance, initials of the owner, or at times, mythological, allegorical, religious, or secular themes.

NOTES

1. It appears that earrings were not *en vogue* for ladies during the Gothic era, due to headgear and hairstyles that ostensibly hid a good part of the ears.

2. Boullianne, Michelle M., "Gothic Period Jewelry" at http://www.ostgardr.org/costume/mouche.gothic.jewelry.html

3. Ibid.

Grading (Diamonds)

Why do diamond grades begin with the letter "D" (as opposed to A, B, C)? Perhaps to most effectively drive home that diamonds are in a class by themselves. (The Diamond Registry, New York)

If one is about to examine a diamond to assess its worth, it's important to keep in mind the considerations of jewelers and gemologists alike, namely clarity, color, cut, and carat weight. Known in diamond grading as the 4Cs, each is an important factor that helps to determine the value of a stone.

Let's start with carat weight. One of the first questions buyers and admirers ask about a stone is "how big is it?" The answer is usually given in carats; yet carat is not a measure of size but of weight. Oddly enough, few would ask "how much does it weigh?"; yet weight is exactly what a carat measurement is. In diamond grading, one carat is equal to 100 "points." Therefore, a diamond that measures 50 points is one-half carat in weight (sometimes listed as .50ct). In the metric system, five carats is equal to one gram. In rings and other jewelry that have multiple

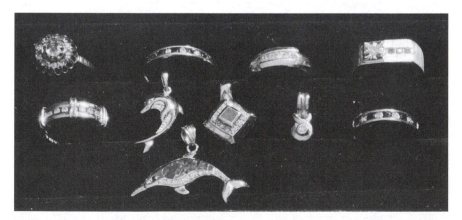

Diamonds come in all shapes and sizes, and are found in nearly every type of jewelry product imaginable. Yet all stones are not created equal, even when they appear to be the same size. If purchasing a diamond, it's good to learn how they are graded. Copyright © 2007 by Anthony F. Chiffolo.

stones, one will often encounter a number followed by TCW, which stands for "total carat weight." This is not the weight of the jewelry piece itself, but the weight of the diamonds *outside* of their settings—an important distinguishing factor and a bit of essential wisdom to keep in mind when having a stone evaluated by a jeweler. The only true way to be sure of carat weight is to remove the stone from its setting. Although there are caliper settings and measurements that can approximate weight without removal, they are not accurate and should not be depended upon for true diamond value.

Next on the list is clarity. The clarity of a diamond is dependent upon the number, type, position, size, and color of its internal characteristics and surface features. Known as inclusions (internal) and blemishes (external), these irregularities can range from "flawless" to "heavily included." A diamond grader counts, evaluates, and measures (using a 10x [at least] magnifier) the flaws of the stone, taking note of the pieces of other materials (such as carbon bits, or bubbles, or "feathers," or "clouds") that became trapped in the diamond as it was being formed by nature. The grader then gives the diamond a rating accordingly: pure

CLARITY GRADE	DESCRIPTION
FL - flawless	No internal or finished flaws. The highest grade for clarity (extremely rare)
IF - internally flawless	No internal flaws (extremely rare)
VVS1-VVS2 - very very slightly included	Very difficult to find inclusions under 10X magnification
VS1-VS2 - very slightly included	Difficult to find under 10X magnification, impossible to see inclusions with the naked eye
SI1-SI2-SI3 - slightly included	Easy to find inclusions under 10X magnification, may be able to see inclusions with the naked eye
I1-I2-I3 - included	Inclusions that can be visible to the naked eye

The scale for clarity grading ranges from FL (flawless), to I-3 (many imperfections or inclusions that are easily visible to the naked eye). This chart demonstrates different variations of clarity among stones of differing qualities. Courtesy of Prime Style, www.primestyle.com

D	E	F	G	H	I	J	K	L	M	N	O	P	Q	R	S	T	U	V	W	X	Y	Z
Colorless			Near Colorless				Faint Yellow			Very Light Yellow				Light Yellow						

Most diamonds look white, but there are many subtle shades. Diamonds with no hint of color at all are very rare and are called colorless. Grading laboratories use a color scale that ranges from D (completely colorless) to Z (strong yellow). Diamonds ranging from D to F in color have virtually no color tone and are the most valuable. Diamonds in the range of G to J are almost colorless and are less expensive. Diamonds of K color and lower are often used in jewelrycrafting but have little overall value. Courtesy of Prime Style, www.primestyle.com.

(noted as such); VVS-1 or VVS-2 (very, very small inclusions); VS-1 or VS-2 (very small inclusions); S-1 or S-2 (small inclusions), and I-1, I-2, or I-3 (included). Obviously, the fewer problems, the greater the value of the diamond.

But it takes more than just good weight and top clarity to own a diamond of value. One has to consider its color also. Diamonds ideally should be colorless, yet colored diamonds can be quite valuable in their own right (depending, of course, on other 4C factors). Diamonds are rated by color from "D/E/F" (colorless) to "G/H/I/J" (near colorless) to "K/L/M/N" (faint yellow) to "O/P/Q/N/R" (very light yellow) to "R/S/T" (light yellow) to "U/V/W" (yellow), and ending in "X/Y/Z" (light-fancy type). The farther left of each color group and scale, the more valuable the piece (generally speaking). Sometimes jewelers/gemologists use a colorimeter to grade diamonds, but trained graders make the best decisions with the naked eye under good, natural north daylight.

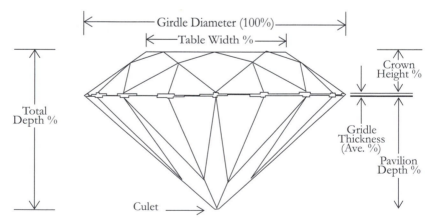

A well-cut diamond is composed of facets with the correct angles, which are perfectly placed to maximize the diamond's brilliance. "Very good" cut diamonds are exceptionally proportioned, high-quality stones that reflect back up to 90 percent of the light entering the diamond. The "ideal" cut diamonds refer to the very best of round diamonds. "Good" rated diamonds are well-cut stones because of their ability to reflect light. Diamonds with less than good proportion are rated "fair" or "poor" and are generally less expensive. Courtesy of Prime Style, www.primestyle.com

Finally, there is what diamond merchants refer to as the "forgotten C": Cut (see **Cuts**). A cut is what gives a diamond its brilliance and sparkle. Cuts are likewise graded from 1+/1 (excellent) to 2/3 (good) to 4 (average) to 5/6 (commercial) to 7/8 (irregular). Yet this scale is the stuff of diamond merchants, in all reality. The truth is, when choosing a diamond, if one is not impressed with the way it sparkles when the light hits it, it's time to move on to another stone!

☞ DID YOU KNOW?

When it comes to diamonds, it's all about numbers it seems, including dates and years and percentages. Here are a few interesting diamond facts:

- The 4Cs for grading diamonds were first introduced to the diamond industry in 1939.
- The largest gem-quality diamond in the rough ever found was the Cullinan diamond (South Africa, in 1905), which weighed in at 3,106.75 carats.
- 80 percent of the world's diamonds are not suitable for jewelry.
- Most diamonds are between one billion and three billion years old.
- A large South African diamond, found in 1988, weighed in at 599 carats. It was cut into several stones, the largest of which is called the Centenary. It weighs 273 carats and is the largest, modern-cut, top-color, and flawless diamond in the world! Value: at least US$100 million.

Hair Adornments

In combs, barrettes, bandeaux and other accessories there are many varieties, and a judicious selection is of no small importance in the general effect of the hairdressing. Too ornate or too numerous ones are in bad taste and detract from, rather than add to, the beauty of the coiffure. The large hairpins of shell with the tops inlaid with gold filigree or set with brilliants are very attractive and modest ornaments. Two or three of these may be used at the sides of the coiffure and prove of very effective service as well as decoration. (*The Delineator*, 1911)

Through the centuries, many jewelry items have been designed to highlight the hair of both men and women. It is often said when commenting on someone's beauty that "their hair is their best feature." If so, why not "accentuate the positive" as the old maxim goes, and adorn those precious locks with further beauty, using one of the following "hairpieces"?

AIGRETTE

An aigrette is a simple but elegant hair ornament, usually a small plume of feathers (resembling an egret plume; hence the name) or a spray of glitter, often with a large jewel or buckle as an accent. Aigrettes as a fashion item replaced the *enseigne* (a badge placed on a hat or cap popular during the Renaissance era). They were worn in the hair attached on a headband or placed as is and were very popular with the flapper set in the 1920s.

BARRETTES

A barrette is a hair clasp (also called a hair slide in England); it was frequently made of fine materials, such as gold or silver, but in recent times most often of plastic. Barrettes were traditionally worn by size, with the smaller ones in the front and the larger on the sides or back of the head. Barrettes have become a customary part of head wardrobe for women, who when fashion demands it tend toward barrettes that are decorated with glitter, rhinestones, or some other flashy material.

HAIR COMBS

Hair combs are jewelry pieces that women wear as adornment; they are sometimes utilitarian, but are mostly decorative. The earliest combs were probably made of bone, ivory, and wood. One of the first producers of combs in the American colonies was Enoch Noyes (1743–1828), who in 1759, along with his partner William Cleland, launched an entire cottage industry of combmaking using cattle horn. Located in the area around West Newbury and Leominster in Massachusetts, they became so successful that by 1793 there were as many as 70 hornsmiths making horn combs.[1]

As times and fashions changed, combs of tortoiseshell, silver, brass, and tin became popular, especially during the Victorian era. Of particular distinction were combs made from the feathers of the Chinese kingfisher. Their lovely, bluish-turquoise colors were ideal for the elegant designs of many combs; yet the demand for kingfisher combs was so great that the bird was hunted to the point of near extinction.

In Africa, most combs are made of local types of wood, as they have been for centuries. For the collector, this means hundreds of opportunities to learn about the flora and woodworking abilities of African crafters. The same, of course, is true on nearly every continent, since combs are ubiquitous as hair adornments in the world of modern fashion.

HAIRPINS

Though rarely thought of as jewelry, decorative hairpins have been a part of fashion since hair adornments first became popular. Hairpins come in two types: one-point and two-point. The one-point (or single-stemmed) hairpin in use since classical times, was often made of wood or bone, and was very often highly decorated. The ancient Etruscans and Romans were fond of making one-point hairpins with fruit motifs; the Anglo-Saxons were said to favor birds and gemstones (especially garnets) for their versions. In Asia, these pins (sometimes

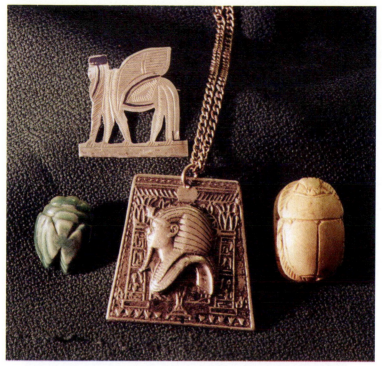

Post-Victorian Egyptian revival jewelry. Copyright © 2007 by Anthony F. Chiffolo.

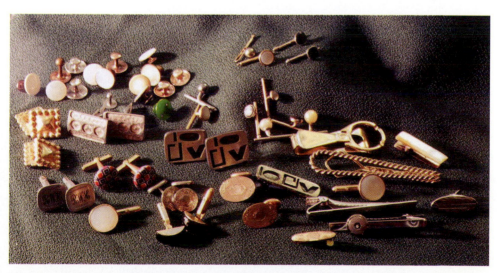

Men's necessaries, from cufflinks to tiebars. Copyright © 2007 by Anthony F. Chiffolo.

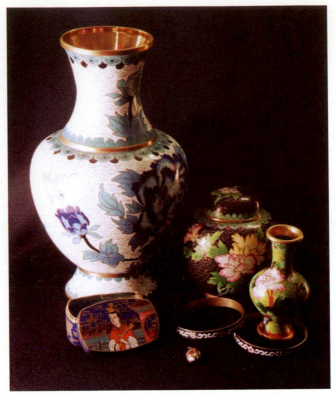

Cloissoné and champlevé adornments and treasures. Copyright © 2007 by Anthony F. Chiffolo.

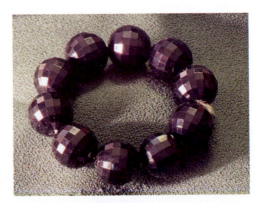

Faceted French jet stretch bracelet. Copyright © 2007 by Anthony F. Chiffolo.

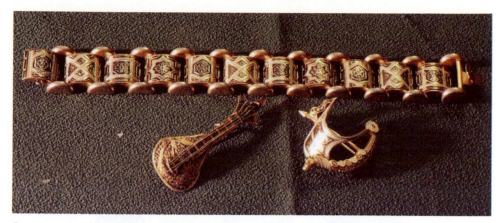

Damascene jewelry, a favorite souvenir from Spain. Copyright © 2007 by Anthony F. Chiffolo.

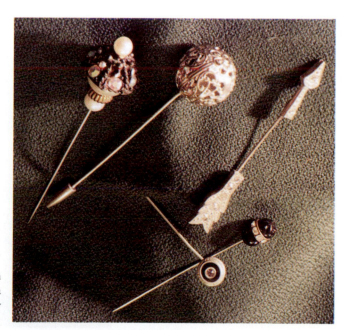

Men's stickpins for use with a tie, cravat, or to dress up a lapel. Copyright © 2007 by Anthony F. Chiffolo.

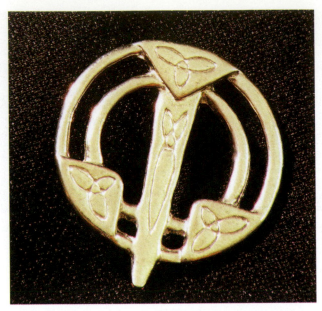

Typical Celtic kilt pin. Copyright © 2007 by Anthony F. Chiffolo.

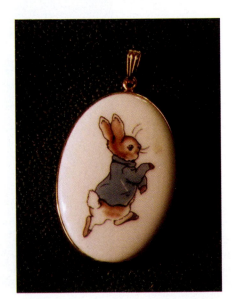

A Beatrix Potter character fine porcelain pendant by Wedgwood. Copyright © 2007 by Anthony F. Chiffolo.

called hairsticks) were often long and worn in pairs, crossed and rising high above the head. During the Renaissance era, extremely fancy and richly decorated one-point pins were *en vogue,* especially among the wealthy; called bodkins, they were immortalized by Shakespeare in his epic *Hamlet.* Two-point hairpins were quite different in both style and utility. Early on they were a kind of U-shaped implement with identical shanks that met at the head in a crosspiece, sometimes touching, sometimes not. They are recorded in use in Asia as early as the third century c.e.; however, these early models had shanks that were very sharp and extremely fragile. As time passed they became sturdier and more durable. Double-point hairpins that come together at a mid-piece and at the ends are today known as bobby pins. Pins that do not touch are called French hairpins, chignons, or hairpicks. South Korea and the People's Republic of China are the top producers of both one- and two-point hairpins today.

Another type of hair adornment of this genre is the T-pin, or wig-pin, a small pin with a very sharp point designed to penetrate the wig scalp, often chrome-plated so that it does not rust when the wig is washed and styled.

In the twentieth century, hairpins in the United States took on a whole new look. Rice and Hochester Makers of New York offered a very popular product known as the Tortoise Brand hairpin, which during the 1920s was available in shell, amber, and black, selling for $.25 per dozen. During this same era, Swartchild & Co. of Chicago advertised "the Neverslip Hairpin," designed to attach an eyeglass chain to the head so that one would always know the whereabouts of eyeglasses that tended to otherwise stray. During the late 1930s and early 1940s, hairpins could be had for $.10 on a card that sported 24 pins. In the 1950s, soft curls were all the rage, and it was not unusual to see a woman with an entire head of hairpins holding each curl in place. The use of plastic curlers to set hair in the 1950s required hairpins (and lots of them) that could stay in place overnight.

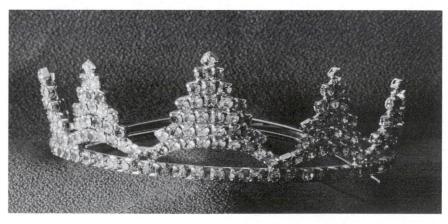

The tiara is a popular hair adornment—and not just for royalty! Copyright © 2007 by Anthony F. Chiffolo.

Today hairpins are as popular as ever, often decorated with crystals and painted butterflies. The bridal industry has hairpins to match a wedding gown or add a splash of elegance to upswept hair. All in all, women can now keep their hair in place and be fashionable at the same moment, a true instance of the best that jewelry has to offer.

TIARAS

Tiaras (also known as diadems) are jeweled headdresses that were often worn by royalty in bygone days. Yet tiaras have a long history going back thousands of years and today are worn by princesses and commoners alike.

The first-known tiaras show up in Egyptian hieroglyphs depicting the rules of pharaohs and priests more than 3,000 years ago. Pre-Common-era Celtic tribes decorated their heads with tiaras made of bronze. The ancient Greeks and Romans were fond of tiaras, which were usually simple bands of cloth worn about the forehead. One might say that the laurel crowns popularly awarded to classical-era athletes were a kind of tiara; later, imitative crowns made of gold and silver were worn by the emperors as symbols of their imperial station. The empress Josephine set European fashion afire in the nineteenth century C.E. with her *templer*, a kind of band with a pendant jewel at midsection designed to rest on the forehead or at the temples (hence its name). Templers were very popular all through the Victorian, Art Nouveau, and Art Deco periods.

In modern times, tiaras have evolved to a place where they are different from crowns or diadems, which are usually fully round and most often adjustable. Modern tiaras must either be sized for the wearer or positioned on the head in a way that best fits.

The base materials of a tiara are quite simple: Thick-gauge metal wires (often gold or silver) are soldered together, then heated so that they are soft enough to bind smaller jewelry parts to them. They are often coated with a base metal so that the look is uniform. Small arms (usually of filigree), which are to hold gemstones or rhinestones, are soldered to the framework in a matching alloy substance. The framework is then chemically cleaned and polished so that the gems can be at last set into their wire compartments, known as bezels. Finally, an inner band of stuffed velvet or some other cloth is added to cushion the weight of the tiara against the scalp.

Some current fashion commentators have written about the "return of the tiara," yet it really has never gone out of fashion. Tiaras are quite popular in bridal wear (at bridal showers for the bride-to-be, and at weddings for the bride and flower girl), as well as for *quinceañeras* (the Latina's fifteenth-year traditional birthday party), Sweet-16 parties, pageants, New Year's parties, and among doll collectors as well.

☞   DID YOU KNOW?

Perhaps the most famous tiara in the world (and the most copied) is the Cambridge Lover's Knot tiara set with brilliant and rose cut diamonds and pearls, which was given to Princess Diana (1961–1997) by Queen Elizabeth II (1926–) on the occasion of *her* wedding to Prince Charles (1948–) in 1981 (though she found it too heavy to wear on her nuptial day), who had in turn been given it by her grandmother, Queen Mary (1867–1953), who used gems received as wedding gifts to copy a tiara owned by *her* grandmother. (This gives new meaning to "hand-me-downs"!) It is a very old design, perhaps created by the famous Munich court jeweler Caspar Rieländer, in 1825. Originally there were 38 pearls, 19 hanging down and 19 shooting straight up above each lover's knot, which were detachable. It has been altered over the generations (diamonds removed, put back in, removed, etc.), but the design remains classic. Given its history, provenance, and beautiful jewels, the tiara is considered priceless. Copies for future brides, however, made of Swarovski crystal and faux pearls, can be had for under $200.[2]

NOTES

1. Bachman, Mary, "Collecting Combs as Decorations for the Hair" at www. oldandsold.com/articles/article042.shtml

2. Source: "Lover's Knot Tiara" at http://www.royal-magazin.de/lovers-knots/loversknots.htm

Hatpins

Well, you know the old saying—walk softly and carry a long hatpin. (*The Year of the Horse* by Eric Hatch [b. 1901])

When one thinks of jewelry, the category of hatpins[1] is most likely not the first item that comes to mind. But hatpins were a major fashion accessory from the early 1600s in Europe to the early part of the twentieth century. In England, for instance, there is evidence of a seventeenth-century Gloucestershire manufacturer who employed nearly 1,500 people in his factory producing nothing but hatpins. But the Industrial Revolution of the nineteenth century gave birth to the establishment of a regularized business in hatpins on a large scale.

In England, the prominent jeweler and silversmith Charles Horner (1837–1896) of Halifax was one of the leading manufacturers of good quality, mass-produced hatpins and pin holders. The English center of the manufacture and trade in hatpins was Birmingham, but it could not keep up with the demand. As one might imagine, the desire by British ladies for hatpins necessitated the need for importing what could not be produced fast enough locally, and Britain turned to France, always a key fashion center, to fill its orders. Alarmed at the effect these imports were having on the British trade economy, Parliament

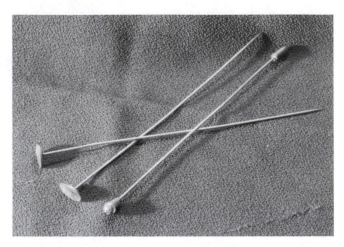

With the look of a lethal weapon, the Victorian hatpin held a formidable presence in many a nineteenth-century woman's boudoir. Copyright © 2007 by Anthony F. Chiffolo.

passed an act that restricted the sale of hatpins to just two days per year, in early January.

☞   **DID YOU KNOW?**

Because British consumers of the late nineteenth century were restricted in their purchases of hatpins to just two days in January, Victorian women saved every cent they could manage to squirrel away to take advantage of these January sales events. Some wordsmiths point out that this practice gave rise to the term "pin money." An alternate origin is that Queen Victoria (1819–1901) taxed her subjects at the beginning of each year to pay for the imported French pins she herself desired. In either case, it's a "point" well taken!

NOTE

1. Not to be confused with hat pins (two words), a badge worn by men on their headgear, especially in Scotland.

Jewelry Metals and Alloys

Among those who devote themselves to the transmutation of metals, however, there can be no such thing as mediocrity of attainment. A man who studies this Art, must have either everything or nothing . . . the Transmutation of Metals, from an imperfect to a perfect state, is a real and true achievement. (Philalethes [1770–1847], *Metamorphosis of Metals*)

In the art of jewelrycrafting, a large variety of metals and their alloys[1] are used to create the desired look and feel of a particular piece. Some are very rare and precious metals, while others are mass-produced and very cheap. A very few jewelry metals are quite beautiful, but very toxic, while just as few are quite unattractive in their natural state, yet when smelted and reworked are both eye-catching and worn by some daring soul on nearly every part of their body. The top ten metals and alloys used in jewelrymaking are gold, silver, platinum, copper, rhodium, nickel, titanium, tungsten, palladium, brass, and pewter. Though "second tier" in importance, the following small group of metals and alloys also play an important part in jewelrycrafting.

ALUMINUM

Periodic table number 30, symbol Al. From the Latin, *alumen* ("alum," the metal base). Aluminum is a dull and ductile silvery metal that is lightweight, nontoxic, nonmagnetic, and nonsparking, with superb corrosion resistance. The use of aluminum worldwide exceeds that of any other metal, save iron. It is the most abundant element in the earth's crust. It has been known since the time of the ancient Greeks and Romans, who used aluminum salts for dyeing and for dressing wounds. Its "discovery" as a modern-day metal depends on how one understands the term; yet most almanacs credit the Danish physicist and chemist Hans Christian Ørsted (1777–1851) with the find in 1825. Aluminum has been produced commercially only in the last 100 years. The major producers of aluminum today are the People's Republic of China (the number one producer), South Africa, New Zealand, Canada, Russia, Suriname, Iceland, and parts of the Middle East. In the modern world, aluminum finds its greatest usage in the electrical industry, mirror making, the space program, transportation, packaging, construction, durable goods, machinery, the recording industry (CDs), glassmaking, fuel, and medicine.

Aluminum has become a metal of choice for many jewelrymakers. Its attraction is that it is malleable (second only to gold), ubiquitous, and relatively inexpensive; it can also be anodized in a variety of colors. It is frequently alloyed with titanium and tungsten. Crafters can purchase it in various formats, including foil, sheet, wire, rod, and tube. Chains made of aluminum are a top-market jewelry item, and watch manufacturers are paying special attention to aluminum for their customers who want durability, a bit of flash, yet a timepiece that is not heavy on the wrist. Since the early 1990s, the LGBTQ community has boosted the aluminum jewelry market with its demand for colorful, alternative metal pieces.

ANTIMONY

Periodic table number 51; symbol Sb. From the Middle Latin, *antimonium,* based on an obscure Arabic word. Antimony's symbol is an abbreviation of the Latin *stibium.* Antimony is a silvery-white metalloid. It is found in more than 100 mineral species, yet it is not very abundant. Antimony has been known since ancient times, its usage going back at least 5,000 years. The ancient Egyptians

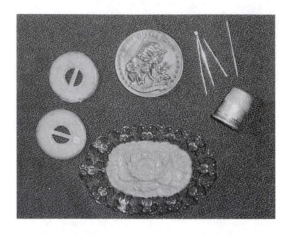

Jewelry and accessories are made from all sorts of mixed metals, including lead, steel, antimony, bronze, and aluminum, as seen in these samples from grandma's sewing basket. Copyright © 2007 by Anthony F. Chiffolo.

used a black-powder form of antimony (called *kohl*), which was water-soluble, as a type of mascara to paint above and below the eyes. Today, more than 80 percent of the world's antimony is produced in the People's Republic of China; Bolivia, South Africa, and Tajikistan are also significant producers. In the modern world, antimony is primarily used as a fire retardant but is also used in the production of paints, enamels, and ceramics, in the electronics and rubber industries, in medicine, and in making matches and bullets.

As an alloy, antimony has been very important in jewelrymaking. It is a major component of Britannia metal, used in older pieces of jewelry, particularly those from England in the Victorian era, and in white metal pieces going back as much as 200 years. Antimony is also used in silver soldering to add strength and was frequently used by Zuni artisans in their work from decades ago. Antimony is a primary element in pewter jewelry, of which there are many pieces on the market, both old and new.

Crafters can purchase antimony in various formats, including cast cake, granules, ingots, pieces, powder, shot, or single crystals.

BRONZE

Bronze is a metal whose primary component is copper, alloyed most usually with tin, although it may also contain phosphorus, manganese, aluminum, beryllium, and silicon.[2] Bronze was a very important metal in past millennia (so much so that historians refer to an era known as the Bronze Age). The earliest usage of bronze dates back more than 6,000 years in Susa (modern-day Iran), Mesopotamia (modern-day Iraq), and Luristan (modern-day Iran). Because tin and copper rarely occur together in the earth's crust, making bronze was usually dependent on trade. Most tin in Europe came from Great Britain, so it became a bronze center also.

Bronze is a very commonly used metal. In ancient times, nearly any item that required strength (weapons, farm tools, building materials) was made of bronze. In the modern world, bronze is used in castings for sculpture, turbine engines, fan and propeller blades, coins, springs, musical instruments (cymbals, bells, and saxophones), screws, wires, and nails.

In jewelrymaking, bronze has not been a favorite metal due to its weight. Nevertheless, many examples of bronze jewelry have been found at ancient Byzantine sites and at other sites throughout the Middle East, Scandinavia, and Asia.[3] In fact, in almost any civilization where bronze was made, bronze jewelry has been encountered. Today there are many makers of bronze jewelry. One French jewelry designer, Hervé Van der Straeten (1966–), has made a name for himself working solely in gilded bronze.

Those wishing to craft in bronze can purchase it in sheets, wire, beads, granules, powder, paste, plugs, and in other formats as well. The jewelry tools for working in bronze would be the same as those of copper brass.

CADMIUM

Periodic table number 48, symbol Cd. From the Latin *cadmia,* and Greek *kadmeia* ("calamine"). Cadmium is a rare, soft, blue-grey-white, ductile transition metal. Even in small quantities, it is extremely toxic. Its "discovery" is credited to the German chemist Friedrich Strohmeyer (1776–1835) in 1817. Germany was the major producer of cadmium for the next 100 years. Today, it is mined and refined in the People's Republic of China, Japan, and South Korea (the three largest producers) as well as in Mexico, the Netherlands, India, England, Peru, Germany, and the United States. Fifteen other countries produce small amounts of cadmium. In the modern world, cadmium has found its greatest usage in paint pigments, glassmaking, photography, television sets, dyeing, batteries, and nuclear engineering.

Cadmium is a major component of the jewelrycrafting industry. It is often alloyed with silver or gold to create solder, thus making it essential to the entire jewelry metals industry. Of course, as cadmium is used to make batteries, it is commonly found in most quartz watches. Cadmium is also important to the process of electroplating and is thus critical to the coating and lasting durability of silver-based products. Cadmium is often alloyed with gold, silver, and zinc to create green gold. Crafters can purchase cadmium in many formats, including foil, granules, pellets, powder, rod, shot, sticks, sheets, and wire.

LEAD

Periodic table number 82, symbol Pb. From the Germanic and Old English word *lot* ("weight, plummet"). Lead's symbol is from the Latin *plumbum,* which is where we get our modern word, "plumbing." Lead is a bluish-white to dull-gray heavy and malleable metal. It is extremely resistant to corrosion but highly toxic. It has been known and used for more than 7,000 years by many ancient civilizations, most notably by the Romans, who used it for piping water.

Today, lead is produced by many countries, the chief among them being the People's Republic of China, the United States, Kazakhstan, Australia, Canada, Mexico, Peru, and the United Kingdom. In the modern world, lead is used in the transportation, firearms, painting, glass, electronics, construction, roofing, and fishing industries. Its primary use, however, is in car batteries.

Lead is a major presence in the jewelrycrafting industry as well. It is often alloyed to make solder, and is one of the prime metals used in pewter. Both stained glass and Zuni silver jewelry have contained lead in the past, though modern crafters advise against its usage due to lead's known toxicity. In recent years, tons of children's costume jewelry has been recalled due to high amounts of lead, which has proven to be both dangerous and deadly. Anyone working with lead to create jewelry should be aware of its drawbacks. Crafters who wish to work with lead can purchase it in a variety of formats, including foil, granules, ingots, powder, rod, sheet, shot, and wire.

MERCURY

Periodic table number 80; symbol Hg. From the Latin *Mercurius* ("Mercury," Roman god of merchants; akin to "merchandise"). Mercury's symbol is from the Latinized-Greek *hydrargyrum* ("silvery water"). Mercury, sometimes called "quicksilver," is a heavy, silver-colored transition metal and is the only common metal that is liquid at ordinary temperatures.[4] It has been known for at least 4,000 years and was used by diverse civilizations for a wide variety of reasons. The ancient Greeks used mercury in ointments; the Romans for cosmetics. In Asia, it was a kind of health additive, as it was thought to be good for the body and to prolong life. By at least 500 B.C.E., mercury was already being used as an amalgam to help create other metals. At one time, a good portion of the world's mercury came from Peru, Italy, Slovenia, the United States, and Mexico; however, due to overproduction and usage, these sources are now completely mined out. Today, mercury is produced primarily by Spain, the People's Republic of China, Tajikistan, and Kyrgyzstan. In the modern world, mercury is used for dentistry, measurements (thermometers and barometers), medicine, electrochemistry, lighting, and nuclear power.

In the jewelry industry, mercury has long been used to refine silver and gold ores. It was most often alloyed with silver, gold, copper, and tin to make jewelry and other "flashy" items. In recent years, Mexican craftspersons have made a pendant filled with colored mercury that is often worn around the neck on a beaded chain or leather cord. While quite beautiful and aesthetically alluring, it is dangerous to one's health and the environment if broken.

STEEL

Steel is a metal alloy, made up primarily of iron and carbon. It has been known certainly since the third century B.C.E., and the first steel products were probably produced in what are now Sri Lanka, India, and the People's Republic China, all about the same time, using a crucible method, whereby wrought iron, carbon, and glass were melted together to form a new metal. First known as *pulad* by the Persians, and *wootz* by Europeans who traded for it, the word came into the English language from the Germanic languages meaning "something that could stand, place, be firm," in reference, no doubt, to steel's hardness once forged. Steelmaking was a product of English and Swedish ingenuity for most of the Middle Ages through the Renaissance in Europe. It was an Englishman, Henry Bessemer (1813–1898) of Sheffield, England, who developed a method to mass-produce steel in 1855. Since that time, steel has been a major force of the metal commodities market. The majority of steel produced today comes from the People's Republic of China, Japan, the United States, Russia, South Korea, Germany, India, Ukraine, and Brazil.

There are many types of steel, depending on the alloy used and the forging process. Today, steel is used primarily in building construction, sword and razor manufacturing, canning, transportation, the space program, and medicine—in fact, as the steel industry is fond of saying, "steel is everywhere in our lives."[5]

In jewelrymaking, steel as we understand it is rather new on the scene. Thanks to the invention of stainless steel, with its cutting-edge possibilities and the ability to be cleaned in such a way that it is virtually germ-free, steel has become a metal of choice for body-piercing enthusiasts and practitioners. Body jewelry of every type and for every part of the corpus can be purchased made of steel. Stainless steel has recently made great inroads into the men's jewelry market, especially for those who like alternative, durable metals (much like those who prefer titanium and tungsten). Stainless steel has also for many years now been popular with watchmakers, who use it for their casings and band parts.

TIN

Periodic table number 50; symbol Sn. From the Anglo-Saxon, *tin*. Tin's symbol is an abbreviation of the Latin *stannum*. Tin is a highly malleable, ductile, silvery-white metal that is practically noncorrosive and is therefore used as an alloy to coat other metals, such as zinc or steel. When alloyed, it creates some of the most important and vital industrial metals on the world market, including bronze, solder, and white metal. It has been known for nearly 6,000 years; its mining probably began in Cornwall and Devon in Great Britain, though the pure form of the metal was not in use till circa 600 B.C.E. Today, tin is mined throughout the world, with the greatest production centers in Southeast Asia and significant deposits in Tasmania. Tin is used in the printing business and in the making of glass windows, organ pipes, and superconductors.

Being that tin is primarily used as an alloy, it is a very important element in jewelrycrafting. Pieces made of bronze, or solder, or with a white metal base—all have a tin component. Yet nonalloyed tin jewelry is also available. For instance, several companies have been set up in recent years to produce tin jewelry from the South Crofty mines in Cornwall, England, where tin was mined for nearly 4,000 years; the mine closed in 1998. Tin earrings, brooches, pendants, and cufflinks are available on-site or through the Internet. Some creative jewelers are also showing both agate and quartz jewelry that has chemically induced tin inclusions, which are quite spectacular. There are also many artisans worldwide who make jewelry from scrap tin, including those living in some of the poorest areas of the world (in Bhopal, for instance).

Crafters will find tin available for purchase in various formats, including (but not limited to) bars, foil, granules, ingots, powder, shot, sticks, and wire. Tin-oxide polish is also found in many "beginners" jewelrymaking kits.

ZINC

Periodic table number 30; symbol Zn. From the German, *Zink*. Zinc is a lustrous, bluish-white element that is the fourth most common metal in use today (only iron, copper, and aluminum have a higher production rate). Zinc is the twenty-third most abundant element in the earth's crust. It has been known for more than 3,000 years, with evidence of its usage at sites dating back to ancient India and Israel, Gaul, and prehistoric Transylvania. Its "discovery" as a modern-day metal, though greatly disputed, is credited to the German Andreas Margraff (1709–1782) in 1746. Today, zinc is mined throughout the world, with the greatest production centers located in Australia, Belgium, Canada, the People's Republic of China, Ireland, Peru, Sweden, and the United States. Zinc is an essential element for sustaining all animal and plant life. In the modern world, zinc finds its greatest usage as a metal alloy, although it is also a component in the automobile industry, in batteries and pipes for pipe organs, in paint, rubber, and sunscreen manufacturing, and in the medical and health fields. Since 1982, it has been the primary metal in making U.S. pennies.

Zinc is also an essential element in jewelrymaking. Crafters can purchase it in various formats, including dust, foil, sheets, powder, pieces, shot, granules, and wire. It is often combined with copper, nickel, and lead to make nickel silver, a common alloy in Native American jewelry. It is also one of the primary metals used in solder, jewelry castings, and findings, and to illuminate watch dials and faces. Perhaps its greatest contribution is its presence in brass—often as much as 45 percent, combining with copper and/or other metals for colors that approach the look and feel of gold. Zinc is also alloyed to make bronze and Britannia metal, both of which are used in jewelrycrafting.

☞   DID YOU KNOW?

Ever heard of carroting? No, it's not a way to dig up, cook, or otherwise use carrots. In the eighteenth and nineteenth centuries, carroting was a process by which animal skins were prepared to make felt hats. The only problem was that carroting involved using mercury in a solution that was highly toxic. The vapors from carroting were so strong that they caused mercury poisoning in many hat-makers, which gave rise to the origin of the phrase "mad as a hatter."[6]

NOTES

1. Some other metals and elements used in jewelrymaking, but in small quantities, include beryllium, manganese, iron, and carbon.

2. In antiquity, arsenic was also a component.

3. See the article on "Metsamor" at http://www.tacentral.com/history/metsamor.htm

4. See "Mercury" at http://www.webelements.com/webelements/elements/text/Hg/key.html

5. See "Steel in Your Life" at http://www.steel.org/AM/Template.cfm?Section=Steel_in_Your_Life

6. Source: "Mercury" at http://en.wikipedia.org/wiki/Mercury_(element)

Karats

Twelve karats? That's only half gold.
Cheap rings leave a girl like me cold.
But twelve-carat rocks,
Will sure rock my socks
A diamond that size and I'm sold!
(Victor Kandampully in *The Omnificent English Dictionary in Limerick Form*)

In Biblical times, precious commodities were sold and measured according to their equivalent weight in carob seeds of the pods of Middle Eastern locust trees.[1] Carob seeds were used because of their reputation for having a uniform weight, but their uniformity has been proven to be untrue, because there is as much variation in carob-seed weights as there are with other seeds. For thousands of years, each nation had its own weight standard for trading; standardization in measuring the weight of precious metals and gemstones, particularly gold, is a recent phenomenon.

Today, gold is almost universally measured in karats (expressed by the abbreviation K or k), where 24k is pure gold. Any karat value that is below 24k indicates that the gold has been mixed with some other alloy, usually copper, nickel, zinc, or silver. The more alloy that is added, the stronger the resulting metal, which allows for a greater scratch resistance and fewer possibilities of damage; however, adding more alloys reduces the resale value of the metal, since there is less gold content. Adding alloys also determines the color of the gold product.

The most popular karatage for jewelry worldwide is 14k, which means it has .585 out of 1000 percent gold (that is why Italian jewelry, for instance, is marked .585). However, gold is sold all over the world in 8k (Germany), 9k (England), 10k (U.S. minimum), 15k (England), 16k (rare), 18k (European and designer), 21.5k (usually fine coinage), 22k (India), and 24k (the People's Republic of China, Hong Kong, Taiwan) portions also.[2]

Most gold jewelry for resale is clearly stamped with its karat content. This is usually indicated by hallmarks, a system that originated in England in the fourteenth century C.E., whereby the name of the maker, town, regent, weight, and so forth are stamped onto the jewelry item; or, as in the United States, jewelry is

Karat	Dec. Parts	Karat	Dec. Parts
10	.4167	18	.7500
11	.4583	19	.7917
12	5000	20	.8333
13	.5417	21	.8750
13 1/2	.5625	21.6	.9000
14	.5833	22	.9167
15	.6250	23	.9583
16	.6667	23 3/4	9900
17	.7083	24	1.0000
17 1/2	.7292		

The fineness of gold karats (in decimal parts fine gold).

stamped either with the karat value (10k, 14k), or content is shown by number percentages (.585, .750, .999), a more common practice in Europe and Asia. In any case, one should be wary of purchasing jewelry that is unstamped, and buying from a reputable retailer is always advisable, since fraudulent stamping is unfortunately now commonplace.

Other marks one might encounter on gold jewelry are as follows:

YG or *KY:* Yellow Gold

WG or *KW:* White Gold

GP, KGP, RGP: Gold-plated. Gold-plated items have a very thin layer of gold that has been applied to the surface of the item. This also means that there is some other type of base metal underneath.

GF, KGF: Gold-filled. Gold-filled items have a layer of 10k or a higher amount of gold that has been mechanically applied to one or more surfaces of the base metal, then rolled out and drawn to a certain thickness.

EGF: Electroplated gold-filled

Gold that is laid over silver is called "vermeil" or "gold wash."

☞ DID YOU KNOW?

All the gold ever mined would form a cube that measures only 19 meters (62.43 feet) on each side. The cube, for example, would easily fit under the Eiffel Tower in Paris.[3]

NOTES

1. Karat (or carat) is a Middle English word, from the Old French, from the medieval Latin *quarâtus* (carob bean), from the Arabic *qirât*, a bean pod or a weight of four grains, from the Greek *keration*, a weight, which is also the diminutive form of *keras*, a horn.

2. 24k gold, known in some Asian countries as *chuk kam*, is usually marked .999.

3. See the article "Gold Karats" at http://gold.goldenmine.com/goldkarats.htm

Mexican Silver Jewelry

Period: 1931 to present
Birthplace: Taxco, Mexico
Origins: Aztec, Mixtec, Mayan civilizations
Influences: Spanish colonization; historic Native American/Mexican motifs

Perhaps some of the most culturally fascinating and esthetically beautiful contributions to the modern jewelry industry are the pieces that come from Taxco, a small colonial-style city situated between Acapulco and Mexico City in the mountains of the State of Guerrero. Long known and appreciated for its silver mines, Taxco was "rediscovered," some say, when an associate professor of architecture by the name of William Spratling (1900–1967) of Tulane University in New Orleans made his first visit to the pueblo to study Mexico and its culture. Charmed by its rich history and a wealth of artistic talent among its regional indigenous peoples, Spratling moved to Taxco in 1929. Several years later the U.S. Ambassador to Mexico, Dwight Morrow (1873–1931), commented to Spratling how unfortunate it was that Taxco was so rich in silver with a history of silvercrafts design, yet it had never become a center of silvercrafts production. Seemingly from that moment forward, the artistic and economic history of Taxco changed in monumental ways.

In the artisans of Taxco, William Spratling recognized the potential for revitalizing the craft of silversmithing. Using some of his own designs influenced by Aztec and Mixtec motifs, Spratling convinced two goldsmiths from nearby Iguala (Artemio Navarrette and Alfonso Mondragon) to develop an apprentice system of training young silversmiths in his workshop, called *Las Delicias Taller*[1] (named after the street where it was located), to create impressive individualistic designs reflective of their personal talents and their own rich cultural history, giving jewelry marked *Hecho en Taxco* (Made in Taxco) an internationally, distinctive identity. Many of Spratling's students, among whom Héctor Aguilar (1905–1986), the Castillo brothers, Salvador Teran, Antonio Pineda (1919–), and Rafael Melendez (d. 1968) are some of the best known, went on to found their own *talleres*. Today, silver jewelry made by these Taxco artisans commands high prices, often in the thousands of dollars.

Perhaps because of his architectural background and his extensive international travel experience, Spratling's works (and those of his students) were a product of the best of the design era. With overlapping Art Deco and pre-Columbian tones, linear shapes, and simple patterns, the jewelry of the Taxco talleres took on a kind of Cubist viewpoint. The use of heavy-gauge and nearly pure silver gave depth to the color and texture of their jewelry and a lot of strength to their finished product. Today the artisans of Taxco produce sterling rings, necklaces, bracelets, and earrings that are often instantly recognizable as the work of fine artisans and worthy of adding to one's personal collection.

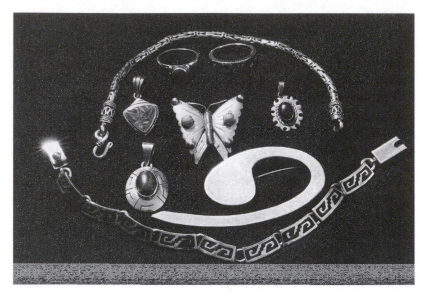

Silver jewelry made in Mexico, DF and in Taxco, the silver jewelry capital of the world. Copyright © 2007 by Anthony F. Chiffolo.

By 1939, several of Spratling's students had moved on and opened their own workshops: Héctor Aguilar, the manager of Las Delicias, left to establish *Taller Borda;* and the Castillo family—Antonio, Margot, Chato, Coco, and cousins Salvador and Mimi Teran—opened *Los Castillo Taller.* Both workshops continued the high-quality work that was learned under Spratling's tutelage, yet each branched out to create works in silver that made their own design claims. For Aguilar and his group, the design themes centered on pre-Columbian sculpture, as well as manuscript paintings and imprints from hundred-year-old clay seals. Often he mixed copper and silver in his jewelry, giving it a look that appealed to both men and women. For Los Castillo, the married-metals approach was also evident in their early work, but it proved to be too expensive and time-consuming to continue. Los Castillo also experimented with "divorced" objects: feathers with silver, blued steel, silver-encrusted onyx, and the like.

In the late 1940s, Margot Castillo left the taller founded by her husband, Antonio, and opened her own studio, again with a unique approach to jewelrycrafting. Having come to Mexico via San Francisco, Margot was influenced by Japanese art and by the Art Deco movement; hence her designs reflect her interests and passions. Margot was especially well known for the use of champlevé, a hands-on, silver-over-enamel process that is extremely labor-intensive, and requires a steady hand. Due to worker disputes, her studio was forced to close in the mid-1970s, yet her work seems to transcend time and is highly regarded and well collected.

Of all the Taxco jewelry designers, no one has received more accolades for his work than Antonio Pineda. A product of the Las Delicias Taller as well as other studios, Pineda opened his doors in 1941 after studying art in Mexico City. Influenced by the Modernists, he consequently produced large-scale jewelry, often with semiprecious and precious stones, that requires a certain confidence to wear. His jewelry, like his sculpture, is always eye-opening and evocative but with clean lines, smooth surfaces, and a rugged sensuality. Any Pineda work that appears on the market today causes great interest.

Other Taxco artisans that merit serious attention include Sigi Pineda, Margaret vonVorhees Carr, Matilde Poulat, Enrique Ledesma, and Hubert Harmon.

For those interested in Mexican jewelry by the artisans mentioned here, it is important to be able to identify their pseudohallmarks. According to antiques experts Ralph and Terry Kovel, "from the 1940s to 1979, Mexican sterling was stamped with an eagle mark indicating sterling quality, and sometimes with a designer mark or 'Taxco, Hecho in Mexico.' After 1979, the Mexican government required that each piece be marked with the word 'Mexico,' the numbers '925,' or the word 'Sterling,' and a two-letter plus three-number code indicating the workshop."[2] Some sample marks of Taxco designers are as follows:

Selected Maker's Marks

William Spratling (1900-1967): American, founded a workshop in Taxco in 1931. His fine designs and apprenticeship program launched the Mexican silver craft industry. After he died, the workshop was bought by Alberto Ulrich and continues in business.

Hector Aguilar (1940-1966): Managed the Spratling shop in 1939, then started his own shop. He created silver jewelry for major American department stores. The shop closed in 1966.

Antonio (b. 1919): Antonio Pineda Gomez established a workshop in 1941 after working for Spratling. Pieces are marked "Antonio."

LOS CASTILLO **Los Castillo** (1930-present): The Castillo brothers were trained by Spratling, then founded one of Taxco's largest workshops.

Margot de Taxco (1948-1985): American, came to Mexico in 1937. Married silvermaker Antonio Castillo, then divorced him and established her own shop in Mexico City in 1948. Some of her original molds are being used today.

Matl (1934-1960): Tradename used by Mathilde Poulat and her nephew Ricardo Salas. When Mathilde died, Salas continued to make jewelry in her style and signed them "Matl Salas."

Sterling pseudohallmarks can help identify the maker of fine Mexican jewelry and aid in determining its value. Permission provided by Ralph and Terry Kovel, Kovels.com. Kovels on Antiques & Collectibles, Vol. 32- Number 10, June 2006.

☞ DID YOU KNOW?

Taxco is not the only city in Mexico that can claim culturally significant jewelry design. A few years before William Spratling arrived in Mexico, a U.S. designer by the name of Frederick Davis (1880–1961) and his partner, Rene d'Harnoncourt (1901–1968),[3] contracted with several silversmiths in Mexico City (known as Mexico, DF [Distrito Federal]) to provide him with silver jewelry, which from 1925–1933 he signed F.D., and from 1933–circa 1950, Sanborn's. Though perhaps not as well known today as works by the Taxco artisans, Davis's jewelry, especially early pieces, are treasured by collectors and are often valued on the high end of the silver jewelry market.

NOTES

1. *Taller* is the Spanish word for "workshop," though in essence Spratling's workshops were more design studios and later small factories where the jewelry was actually fabricated.

2. Kovel, Ralph and Terry Kovel, "Mexican Silver," *Kovels on Antiques and Collectibles,* vol. 32, number 10, June 2006, 114.

3. D'Harnoncourt went on to become the director of the Museum of Modern Art in New York City.

Mourning Jewelry

> Hair is at once the most delicate and lasting of our materials, and survives us, like love. It is so light, so gentle, so escaping from the idea of death, that with a lock of hair belonging to a child or friend, we may almost look up to heaven and compare notes with the angelic nature—may almost say, "I have a piece of thee here, not unworthy of thy being now." (Leigh Hunt in a May 1855 article in *Godey's* magazine)

Jewelry has been made and worn for all occasions and a multiplicity of reasons. In cultures where it was proper to both mourn the dead and important to outwardly demonstrate reverence for loss and respect for the deceased, mourning jewelry was not only "popular," but a necessity. Jewelrycrafters of the era were therefore faced with new challenges, such as creating effigies of a loved one or using their skills to weave human hair—often stolen in a final moment before the corpse was to be laid in the ground—into a cross, or a pin, or earrings.[1]

At no time in history was the manufacture of mourning jewelry more in play than in the Victorian era (1837–1901). Queen Victoria (1819–1901), who lost her consort, Prince Albert, in 1861, went into a prolonged state of public mourning, taking on a very dour disposition and dressing in black for the rest of her life. Perhaps in sympathy at first, then out of respect, women all throughout England, the British Empire, and in countries once connected to Great Britain followed her example, and at the time of death and for years after their own personal loss wore emblems of their separation from loved ones and expressed their grief in the form of mourning jewelry.

(It was not only women who expressed their loss in such public ways. Husbands also often acknowledged their grief by wearing a ring that was specially cast and engraved with the name of their wives in gold, on a black background. The inscription, which usually included the dates of their years together, or the date of their wedding, or perhaps the time of her death, was not written on the interior of the ring, as was usual for married couples. In this tradition, the writing was on the exterior of the band, for all to see, remember, and pay respect. One might say it was a symbolic extension of "wearing your heart upon your sleeve.")

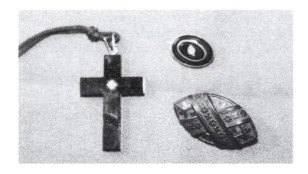

Mourning jewelry of the Victorian era: An obsidian cross, a French jet pin, and an English jet brooch. Copyright © 2007 by Anthony F. Chiffolo.

In England, any black stone was appropriate fare. Onyx was ideal, even deep purple amethyst and black coral. The most popular mourning jewelry material was jet, of which there were two types. English jet (also known as "gagate") is a cut and polished coal, prevalent in Whitby in the northern part of the British Isles. During Victorian times, it was sometimes shaped or carved into cameos, often as a facsimile portrait of the deceased. French jet is cut and faceted black glass; it first appeared in the 1860s and can be seen in many beads that are a staple of nineteenth-century jewelry.

The French and Austrians, for their part, made a rather unique contribution to funerary practices of this period. It became customary, upon the death of one's spouse, to cut a lock of hair and to place it, along with the deceased wedding ring (or some other significant piece of jewelry), in a glass-sided box with a velvet pincushion interior, fixed in such a way that the contents could be viewed without opening the container. Known as "jewelry caskets," these elegant boxes were set on a table next to the portrait of a loved one or displayed on a mantlepiece or nightstand where they were constantly on view. Jewelry caskets were an essential part of proper etiquette in their remembrance of the dead.

Yet another unique innovation had a major effect on jewelrymaking of the Victorian period: photography. The invention of the camera and the ability to reproduce miniature likenesses on paper, glass, or even porcelain meant that jewelers were now asked to create pins, lockets, stickpins, and watchcases that included a picture of the deceased.

☞ DID YOU KNOW?

When Queen Victoria died in 1901, her eldest son, Edward (1841–1910), himself 70, came to the throne. Wearied by such a long state of mourning, it is said that he set out to launch a new course in fashion. Mindful of his mother's grief at the loss of her consort, but wishing to lift the 40-year pall it had created, Edward looked back in history to a happier time of gaiety and celebration, and as a deliberate choice styled the fashions of his court after those of Marie Antoinette (1755–1793), the eighteenth-century French wife of Louis XVI (1754–1793). This meant that black was still acceptable, but to lighten the mood, clear crystal was added, and it became all the rage. Hence the Edwardian period of jewelry as fashion came to be defined by the combination of jet and cut crystal in necklaces, earrings, and bracelets; marcasite in everything; cut steel against black satin as shoe ornaments; and all manner of black-and-white elegance.

NOTE

1. Hair jewelry was popular from early on in the Victorian era; the hair, however, was not only taken from those near death, but also from those very much alive, who donated it from each cut for the hair jewelryweaver's purpose. Animal hair (such as horse hair) was also a popular source.

Native American Jewelry

Period: Prehistory to present day, though most extant jewelry dates to the sixteenth century forward; high point of jewelry market began in late nineteenth century

Birthplace: North America[1]

Origins: Nomadic tribes of the United States, Mexico, and Canada; modern Native American jewelry began in the U.S. Southwest

Influences: nature's flora and fauna; shamanistic ceremonies and religious beliefs; trade with Spanish and other Europeans; unique tribal culture and traditions

The jewelrymaking and -wearing tradition among Native Americans is as ancient as the nations themselves. As long ago as 5000 B.C.E., beads of shell (*heishi*), bone, stone, seeds, and copper were fashioned and strung as jewelry by Native Americans. With the arrival of Europeans to American shores, glass beads were traded and incorporated into the craftmaking of the native tribes. The Senecas, Neutrals, and Iroquois were among the earliest to trade glass beads with the French and Spanish via Italy and rework them into fine handicraft. Most popular for trade purposes were necklaces strewn on twisted sinew; later, cheap leather was used for some amulets and other pendants. The Algonquins and Iroquois were especially fond of wampum, an Algonquin-derived term that refers to small beads made from shells. The beads of greatest value were those made from dark purple, black, and white quahog clamshells; both tribes used the beads as trade items with European settlers, trappers, and explorers.

Native Americans of the U.S. Southwest, among them the Navaho, Zuni, and Hopi peoples, were well known for their jewelrycrafting; in the early times of their trade, silver, coral, shell, and turquoise were the materials of choice, especially for adornments of the body and hair, worn primarily for ceremonies. Each native group had a distinctive jewelrymaking theme, most often based upon its physical surroundings (location), the natural world of its habitations (flora and fauna), and the ability and willingness to engage in trade with visitors from the "Old World" countries.

Some of the oldest Native American jewelry discoveries of the Southwest United States, dating back hundreds of years, have included mounds with beaded necklaces (a symbol of prestige), *ketoh*, or bow guards, and conch shells from the Pacific Ocean. Within these jewelry mounds turquoise has been found mixed with both coral and conch in significant quantities, which is notable in that it demonstrates that those skilled in crafting jewelry traded it with other tribes and peoples.

The Navaho seem to have been the primary force in the jewelrymaking trade among Native Americans of the Southwest. They first appear in the culture and history of the region sometime between the fourteenth and sixteenth centuries C.E., and being nomadic in nature, helped to spread their knowledge of the other trade to other local natives. They were probably the first to use silver in combination with available materials to make *concha* (shell) belts, bracelets, bow guards, tobacco flasks, and necklaces, creating a unique market among those who were looking for products of beauty, durability, and superb crafting. Rings, earrings, pins, hair ornaments, buckles, and the ubiquitous bolo evolved from these first-crafted items. Navajo jewelry is distinguished by its crescent and other geometric designs depicting buffalo, bears, snakes and spiders, squash blossoms, butterflies, and *kokopelli*, the spirit dancer and flute player who is the embodiment of all that moves and lives in the natural world.

Toward the end of the nineteenth century, the Navajo/Black Sheep artisan Atsidi Sani (1830–1870) began to teach others the jewelrymaking trade, helping to create a kind of cottage industry among Native American peoples. He first passed on his broad knowledge and trading experience to his sons, who in turn passed it on to a Zuni craftsman known as Lanyade sometime in the early 1870s. Since prehistoric times, Lanyade's own tribeskin were known to be excellent lapidaries, and he was no exception, with particular skill in metalworking, making

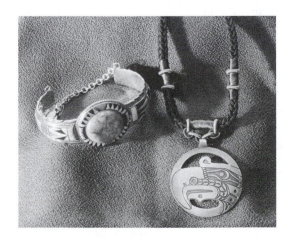

Native American bracelets and pendant display a rich diversity of style and culture. Copyright © 2007 by Anthony F. Chiffolo.

items in copper, brass, and iron. Hence, though influenced by Navajo artisans, the Zuni came to develop their own style of jewelry, incorporating fine and channel inlay into the pieces they produced for trade.

Encouraged by the appreciation of his work, Lanyade began to sell and trade jewelry to the people of the pueblos around him. While visiting a Hopi reservation, he passed on his skills to a tribesman named Sikyatala, who in turn introduced a whole generation of Hopi to the jewelrycrafting trade. For Hopi artisans, the development of a particular style of jewelry was more intentional and less a matter of evolution. In 1938, the Museum of North Arizona in Flagstaff initiated a program with the intent to produce jewelry that would be understood as exclusively and expressly "Hopi." Working with Hopi silversmiths Paul Saufkie (1898–1993) and Fred Kabote, this "guild" formulated an overlay technique using heavy-gauge silver sheets and solder, decorated with bird-motif designs adapted from pottery shards found in Pueblo ruins dating back to the fifteenth and sixteenth centuries C.E.. They also used *kachina* (ancestral spirits) symbols as well as animal and clan motifs to create jewelry that was clearly distinctive.

In the twentieth century, the demand for Native American crafts was extensive. This expanded market called for higher production and a wider material base, which has led to the presence of other finery—such as lapis lazuli, opal, abalone, mother-of-pearl, amber, and gold—in present-day Native American jewelry. Today, Native American jewelry is among the finest in the world and is highly prized in Western and European society.

☞ DID YOU KNOW?

As of the 2004 U.S. census, Native American nations with more than 50,000 members are the Cherokee, Navajo, Choctaw, Blackfeet, Chippewa, Muscogee (Creek), Apache, and Lumbee; the Cherokee are the largest group with a population of nearly 698,000 out of 4.3 million people who self-identify as Native Americans. Interestingly enough, just three of these nations—the Navajo, Zuni, and Hopi—produce three-fourths of the Native American jewelry sold. Each tribe has its own style of jewelrycrafting. Navajo jewelry is usually made of cast or hand-worked silver with notable turquoise settings. Zuni jewelry is known for its more intricate patterns that feature small pieces of coral, jet, and turquoise, often framed in silver. The Hopi are renowned for their beautiful silver overlays, which use little or no turquoise.[2]

NOTES

1. Native American jewelry usually refers to jewelry made by native peoples in North America, including the Inuit tribes of Canada and Alaska. The jewelry of other "American" civilizations, such as those in Mesoamerica, including the Mayans, Aztecs, Toltecs, and Incas, are described under separate entries of this book.

2. Source: U.S. Census Bureau.

Necessaries

Buy what thou hast no need of, and ere long thou shalt sell thy necessaries.
(*Poor Richard's Almanack*)

Just what a necessary is (or was) depends on whom one asks or what source one is using. It is such an important term in the discussion of justice, for example, that there are many laws on the books that seek to define "a necessary." Divorce courts have deemed that in many instances, cars, furs, and yes, even jewelry are the necessaries of life, and once having owned them, certain parties may even be entitled to them for as long as they live. That jewelry itself, in the broadest sense of the term, can be deemed a necessary is intriguing; that other jeweled items or items of jewelry are defined as necessaries keeps the tongues of the arbiters of fashion a-wagging. What is called a necessary in the history of jewelry has changed over several centuries and continues to change as fads become fashions and fashions fade.

Historically speaking, a necessary (or *nécessaire*) is another word for an *étui*, a tiny, decorative case that was sometimes worn on a chatelaine (see below). The étui dates back to the 1720s, when it was used to carry "necessary" items, such as pencils and sewing scissors.[1] Later, chatelaines themselves became known as "necessaries" when they were worn by a servant or lady of the house. Many of the necessaries of the past 200 years have survived the fickleness of fashion and the test of time. Among them are the following.

CHATELAINES

A chatelaine is a series of long chains with a decorative clasp or hook from which many items are hung; these items may be conceits or necessaries and were usually between five and nine in number. Early on, chatelaines were worn at the waist, attached to a belt or girdle; in later years they were simply pinned to a dress or hung from a button through a large ring at the top of the chain. Their large central piece held long, extended chains from which hung a variety of household items: Scissors, sewing cases, knives, notepads, perfume bottles, watches, glove buttoners, ear spoons, and keys were some of the necessaries of the eighteenth and nineteenth centuries. In the twentieth century, small hand mirrors, penknives, change purses, pillboxes, cigarette cases, and address books were typical necessaries. The chatelaines, and sometimes the implements themselves, were made from gold, silver, silverplate, stamped metal, and cut steel. Very short chatelaines were known as *chatelettes* and often had a swivel at the end of the chain from which one could hang a watch. (In later jewelry fashion, this became the infamous watch fob and chain that every well-dressed gentleman carried.) Longer chains were sometimes referred to as macaroni.

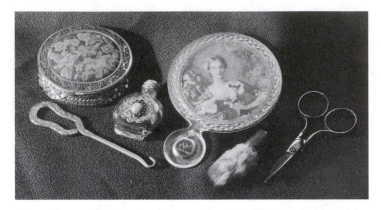

For a woman of fashion, many things were "necessary." Copyright © 2007 by Anthony F. Chiffolo.

Chatelaines were a very important fashion item from the seventeenth century through the early part of the twentieth century, though their use declined greatly after 1830. By the mid-nineteenth century, chatelaines had become more of a decoration (or a conceit) and were considered "costume jewelry." It is said that the introduction of diminutive rhinestone-covered plastic evening purses during the Art Deco period ended the reign of the chatelaine forever. Many fashion critics and historians claim that the charm bracelet was the replacement for the once ubiquitous chatelaine.

One could posit that the modern affinity among men of all ages for carrying a large key chain to which a Swiss Army penknife (containing all that the modern man might find "necessary") is attached is the twenty-first-century version of the chatelaine, giving credence to the maxim "there is nothing new under the sun"!

COMPACTS

The time was that a woman would not have thought of leaving home without her compact. It held everything she needed to "powder her nose," and in compressed form at that! To be sure, powdering your nose 50–75 years ago wasn't just merely practical, it was an event. If that be so, then the bigger the compact, the more important the nose! Or so it seemed. Compacts started out as discrete items, like the "Boodle Boxes" made by Prozonni in the early years of the twentieth century. They held a little rouge, a sponge, and a bit of face powder in an oval case that slipped easily into an evening bag or small mesh purse. The watchmaker Elgin-American even had a compact that looked like a lapel watch. By the 1920s, larger compacts were on the scene, thanks in great part to Hollywood's glamorization of the flapper and the entrée of major jewelry firms into the fray (such as Cartier). These large compacts, now a fashion item that did not need to be hidden, were known as "flapjacks," aptly named as they were big and flat like a pancake (hence "pancake makeup"?), often with a diameter as wide as 6 inches.

Of course, it did not take long for other fragrance and jewelry firms to bring prefilled compacts to market. Coty, Yardley, and Bourjois, for instance, were among the first in the trend of commercial compacts "ready to go" with everything a woman might require. Some compacts included a mirror, lipstick holder—even coins for the ladies' room. Whiting & Davis, Volupté, and Stratton continued to make the more decorative cases, which the user could fill with her own choice of cosmetics. Wisely, all marketers of compacts were up on the latest design trends. To their creativity and foresight we owe many thanks for the thousands of wonderful compact treasures that are highly collected today: compacts with Asian and Egyptian motifs, Art Nouveau nymphs and gracious goddesses, Art Deco geometric forms; compacts with exquisite borders of gold and silver tones surrounding sylvan gardens; and African animal prints.

By the 1930s, women owned an average of eight compacts each, which probably included a least one with a Mickey and Minnie Mouse cartoon character on its lid.[2] Volupté introduced a Scarlett O'Hara compact in 1939, and it was very common to find the painting of a classical Renaissance artist on a compact cover. Compacts were a Depression-era luxury, with prices from 20 cents to over US$1 for Elgin-American's cloisonné creations.

Compacts were also sold as souvenirs; it was not unusual during World War II for soldiers overseas to send their sweethearts back home a compact as a remembrance, both of enduring love and places visited. And despite wartime restrictions on metal and petroleum, some patriotic compacts were manufactured and sold well. Following the war, costume jewelry and handbag designers (like Whiting & Davis) came out with compacts that were a part of an accessory suite: Removable lipstick applicators combined with rouge and powder and eye makeup appeared in the best of stores at the fashion counters.

In the 1950s, as travel by car, train, boat, and plane became more commonplace, souvenir compacts featuring the likes of Mt. Rushmore, the Golden Gate Bridge, Hollywood, and the Florida Everglades were very available. By the 1960s, pop-art and op-art compacts made the rounds, but the plethora of cheap plastic throwaway versions that were then available made the heavier and clunkier compacts passé.

Today, compacts are a relic of the past; yet because of their beauty and functionality, they have a great collecting audience. Like most collectibles, the more unusual the compact, the greater its appeal to collectors. Hatpins with compacts built into the head, or figural compacts in the shape of a piano or a chair, are every afficionado's dream. And they can be had for as little as US$1 at tag sales, or US$200–$300 on eBay, depending on what one is looking for. Just be careful of some of that vintage rouge—it doesn't come off so easily!

MATCH SAFES

Match safes (or *vestas*, as they are known in England)[3] are small metal boxes or tins fashioned to carry the "strike anywhere" sulfur-coated matches that were ubiquitous during the mid-nineteenth century. Called "safes" because matchsticks were dangerous to carry and had the potential to ignite if heated or handled in the wrong way, these boxes were small enough to be carried in a gentleman's vest or pants pocket, and they quickly became a necessary of the day (after all, the match, invented by John Walker [1781–1859] of England, is said to be one of the greatest inventions of the nineteenth century). Many match safes were modified snuff boxes to which had been added a striking surface; when new, they were usually made of sterling, or nickel-plated brass, but quite a number can be found that were fabricated out of wood, ivory, mother-of-pearl, tortoise-shell, vegetable ivory, leather, bone, or some kind of thermoplastics (celluloid or Bakelite) and were set with diamonds, rubies, or other semiprecious and precious stones. A number of safes incorporated additional "necessaries," such as cigar cutters, coin holders, corkscrews, stamp holders, whistles, and knives.

Undoubtedly, the distinguishing feature of pocket match safes was their strike area. These notched or ribbed surfaces were located on the bottom or sides of the box; some had emery or sandpaper inserts; others had a striker that had been worked into the design or that automatically ignited the match upon removal.

Advertisers, especially tobacco and fuel companies, were quick to stamp or emboss match safes, particularly those made of celluloid, with information about their product or business or, in some cases, an important event (the World's Fair, for instance). Whitehead and Hoag of Newark, NJ, patented the celluloid process and became a prolific manufacturer of match safes, helping to make them one of the most popular men's jewelry items of the late-Victorian and Edwardian eras.

The necessity of match safes was eliminated with the invention of both the safety matchbook and the pocket lighter in the early part of the twentieth century. However, match safes continue to be popular with collectors; the International Match Safe Association (IMSA) has a wide and large membership, which has helped to increase collecting interest.

SHIRT ACCESSORIES

Though some might argue that men's dress accessories are more correctly classified as conceits, the truth is that "shirt with tie" has become such a staple for the well-dressed man that it's difficult to remember a time that the two did not appear together. This fashion pairing necessitated several revisions to the way in which a man's wardrobe was assembled.

The addition of collars to a man's blouse/shirt in fifteenth-century Europe meant that some type of fastener was needed to keep it in place. Collar buttons were the answer, and they were as fancy as any button could be, made of gold, or brass, or decorated porcelain. But it was the invention of the detachable collar in the sleepy little city of Troy, New York, by one Hannah Lord Montague (1794–1878) in 1827 that gave collar buttons and cufflinks their raison d'être among U.S. males. Mrs. Montague, weary of the perspiration stains on her husband's shirt collars and cuffs, invented removable versions that could be separately washed and starched. From that point to the mid-twentieth century, nearly every man in the United States owned a series of collar buttons, or studs, and links for cuffs.[4] (The military has continued the practice for much of its dress regalia, and the clergy still use collar buttons to keep their rounded linen or plastic "dog" collars in place.)

In formal wear, stud buttons for the entire shirtfront, and cufflinks, are still the norm. They come in every conceivable material, though onyx or mother-of-pearl is the most popular for "proper" occasions.

If one subscribes to the research of the costume historians, neckties have been around since about 200 B.C.E.[5] They were worn in pre-Common Era China, in ancient Rome, and in seventeenth-century Croatia (hence the possible origin of the French cravat, or "necktie"). The British helped to make "sporting a tie" a national way of dress, and in the United States, bandanas, bolos, and plantation ties (thin ribbons) were common fashion on the road and on the farm. It was the French designer Jean Patou (1880–1936) in the 1920s who invented the modern men's tie, made from silks usually reserved for fine women's clothing. Since then, ties have been de rigueur for the well-dressed man. Yet to keep the well-dressed man well dressed, some sort of pin or clasp was necessary so that what had been wrapped about the neck and tied could stay in place. In the seventeenth century, ties were secured by fancy brooches, often with cut gemstones to complement their color and fabric. These brooches were gradually replaced by the gentleman's stickpin, which looked much like a hatpin yet was very often designed with some sort of "manly theme" in mind: Horseshoes, sports equipment, and wild fauna were common motifs. The twentieth century saw the tie clip (or clasp), tie pin (or tack), and tie bar become a major part of men's fashion wear, often sold in sets with cufflinks and/or collar buttons. Some of the major manufacturers of men's dress accessories are Swank, Kramer of New York, Forzieri, Hickok, and Anson. These companies also feature brass removable collar stays (made of other materials as well), which can be inserted to keep button-down shirts looking crisp after laundering.

THIMBLES

Probably very few people would ever think of thimbles as a jewelry item, except for those who collect and make them. Thimbles have been a jewelry economy for thousands of years, since about the time of the introduction of thread and textiles circa 3000 B.C.E. Thimbles made of bone and wood were discovered in the ruins of Pompeii, dating to 79 C.E. and have long been considered more than just a bell-shaped implement designed to protect the top of the finger when sewing. Thimbles were a prize possession and have been made of nearly every type of material that was strong enough to stand up to the blunt end of a needle: at first in leather, and later in bone, wood, or ivory. Eventually thimbles were made of bronze and iron; and once fine sewing handiwork became the craft of ladies of elegance, gold, silver, brass, pewter, steel, copper, plastic, and porcelain varieties appeared on the scene. During the Renaissance and thereafter, thimbles were bought from mercers or toy and trinket sellers. Records show that Queen Elizabeth I (1533–1603) gave a thimble lavishly encrusted with precious stones to one of her ladies-in-waiting. Today, thimbles made of china by Wedgwood, jasperware, and Meissen, along with sterling hallmarked versions, are among the most collectible.

Collectors are especially proud to own thimbles that are fancifully decorated with coral, bloodstone, or turquoise insets or coated with enamel or cloisonné. Thimbles have been "a necessary" for centuries, often as part of an entire sewing retinue hanging from a chatelaine.

A simple numeral on the rim of the thimble is what indicates finger size.

☞   DID YOU KNOW?

Fabergé's Labor of Love: A Case of Cherchez la Femme

Constance Bond

In the early 1960s, a collection of exquisite cigarette cases was bequeathed to the Musée des Arts Décoratifs in Paris. The gift of a somewhat mysterious elderly man named Charles Antoine Roger Luzarche d'Azay, who had been a French secret service officer early in the century, they were hallmarked and dated: 18 of them had been custom-made in Fabergé workshops between 1901 and 1915, mostly as New Year's gifts.

But from whom? It was a classic case of *cherchez la femme*, as museum curators, linguists, and other experts studied the variety of esoteric and seemingly private symbols incorporated into the cases' designs: crescent moons, intertwined serpents, lists of French military campaigns, cryptic Arabic inscriptions, an elephant with a diamond-studded diadem that was actually a secret compartment containing a portrait of a woman. And, perhaps most intriguing, a map of the Nile Valley in three shades of gold, with eight places marked by precious stones, including a ruby for Port Said, a sapphire for the Suez, a diamond for Cairo.

Efforts were made to learn more about M. Luzarche d'Azay, including trips to his hometown and requests to the Ministry of War for details on his service history. But very little could be discovered about him. Then, three years ago, spurred by an exhibit of the cigarette cases in France, friends of the officer came forward. M. Luzarche d'Azay, they revealed, had been deeply in love with the beautiful but, unfortunately, married French aristocrat, Princess Cécile Murat.

With that information, as well as the fruits of scholarly digging, Géza von Habsburg, who curated the Fabergé show in France, has put together some big pieces of the puzzle. Clearly, he says, the secret service officer worked undercover in the Near East, probably including Egypt. But von Habsburg continues to pursue this "case of the cigarette cases," which he regards as one of the most fascinating in Fabergé history. He asks, for example: Was the map of Egypt "connected with Luzarche d'Azay's spying activities or, more romantically, do the gems mark the secret trysting places of two lovers?" We may never know; but as he continues the search for photographs or letters, the cases speak eloquently enough for themselves.[6]

NOTES

1. Col, Jeananda, "Étui" at http://www.allaboutjewels.com/jewel/glossary/indexe.shtml

2. "Collectable Compacts: Style, Fun and Function" at http://www.myantiquemall.com/AQstories/compacts/Compacts.html

3. Vesta was the Roman goddess of the home hearth and fireplace, which gives us some insight into the origin of the name.

4. This is not to imply that women did not have and wear detachable collars and use collar buttons also; however, the fashion trend of white shirts for business ("white-collar workers") meant that men, by far, owned more studs and cufflinks than did women.

5. Johnson, David, "2000 Years of the Necktie" at http://www.infoplease.com/spot/tie1.html

6. Source: Bond, Constance, "Fabergé's Labor of Love: A Case of Cherchez la Femme," *Smithsonian Magazine*, March 1996.

Necklaces

Gloves as sweet as damask roses;
Masks for faces and for noses;
Bugle-bracelet, necklace-amber,
Perfume for a lady's chamber;
Gold quoifs and stomachers . . .
(William Shakespeare [1564–1616], *The Winter's Tale*, Act IV, Scene III)

A necklace is a piece of jewelry that is worn around the neck. It is a universal form of adornment found in nearly all ancient cultures. Early civilizations constructed necklaces out of every type of material, from metal to shell, seed pod to animal teeth, leaves to colorful precious stones. In northwestern China, archaeologists excavating a site near the city of Yinchuan have discovered some 100 pieces of ostrich eggshells that had been polished and drilled, leading scientists to assume that they may have been pieces of an ancient necklace dating back 20,000 years![1] But that's nothing new. According to Pei Shuwen, Associate Research Professor with the Institute of Vertebrate Paleontology and Paleoanthropology of the Chinese Academy of Sciences, "Early societies in Africa used shells to make necklaces as early as 100,000 years ago."[2] This would seem to indicate that necklaces are most likely one of the oldest known forms of jewelry/adornment.

In ancient Assyrian art, the Mother Goddess is depicted offering a necklace (perhaps one she has made?) before the Tree of Life. Among the ancient Egyptians, necklaces and collars were part of daily wear: the *usekh*, made of numerous rows of beads of varied materials, and the *shebiu*, with thick, biconical beads, were among the most popular styles. Common folk often wore just a simple single-string necklace made of glass beads or faience;[3] royalty were more elaborate in their expression, often appearing at court and battle in magnificent pectorals[4] inlaid with turquoise, carnelian, and lapis lazuli.

In ancient Persia and Central Asia, pectorals shaped like a chain with a cameo in the center were common among members of the upper class and in artwork that represented the gods. Recent excavations of sites inhabited by the Yelang people of southwest China have uncovered jade necklaces that date back to circa 300 B.C.E.[5] The ancient Phoenicians wore necklaces made of glass beads, due to their access to the sandy shores of the coasts along which they sailed (it takes a lot of silica, found in sand, to make glass). Phoenician jewelrymakers had learned to fuse varieties of colored glass into rods that they cut and ground to expose beautiful patterns; they also developed a process whereby they dragged glass of one color against another using wire to create intricate designs.[6]

During the Mauryan and Sunga eras of India's history (321–72 B.C.E.), both men and women wore necklaces. They were of two kinds: a short, broad, and flat necklace made of gold and inlaid with gemstones called a *Kantha*; and a longer necklace made of chains or beads of three-to-seven strings with an amulet at the center of each string called a *lambanam*.[7]

The ancient Greeks were fond of necklaces made of gold. In Rhodes, jewelers crafted gold plaques into pectorals, embossed with animals and likenesses of the gods. Elsewhere in Greece rosettes cut from stamped units of sheet metal were strung together using a *chenier*[8] to form a necklace from which hung gold pendants, most often in the shape of acorns, flower buds, and pomegranates. Also popular were necklaces that featured rows of pendants hung from a finely meshed gold filigree strap. This style was copied by first-century C.E. Etruscans, who hung stamped pendants of sirens, centaurs, and local deities on fine woven chains; of particular note was the *bulla*, a kind of hollow receptacle in which an amulet was placed. These were worn by men, women, and children to help keep them safe from unknown evils (see **Amulets**).

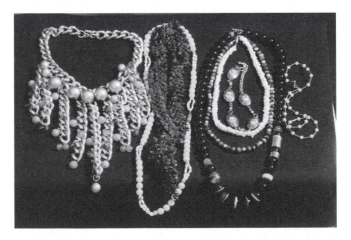

Necklaces come in all shapes and sizes, frills or no-frills! Copyright © 2007 by Anthony F. Chiffolo.

During the Hellenistic era (fourth–first centuries B.C.E.), gemstones began to be incorporated in Roman and Greek jewelry. Since the necklaces were a bit weightier, a design change was necessary to allow for both comfort and style. The Hellenistic answer was the collet, a round band of metal wrapped about a gemstone to keep it in place. Necklaces with a series of linked collets became part of Hellenistic fashion and hundreds of years later showed up as a component of Byzantine jewelry.

In the pre-Common Era Celtic world, a unique form of neckwear appeared. Known as the *torc* (or torque), it was an incomplete circle of thick ingot metal that had enough flexibility to either fit over the wearer's head or slip onto the neck below jaw level. (The torc may have originated in Asia, where a similar instrument had been designed as a means of carrying pierced coinage; torcs from Central Asia and Persia were a sign of army rank.[9]) Finely decorated tubular torcs made of gold, silver, and bronze were being worn by Celtic men at the dawn of the Common Era.

During the Dark Ages in Europe there is not much evidence of a continuation of neck adornment, with the exception, perhaps, of some necklaces made of glass. Amber necklaces and pendants, probably from the Baltic, appear among some Anglo-Saxon groups from the fourth century C.E. In the Americas, Mayan peoples of ninth-century Mesoamerica prized body adornment. Their necklaces, made of jade, shell, jaguar teeth and claws, and obsidian, were worn by both men and women. Pottery statues from 800 C.E. show women with large beaded necklaces also.[10] Aztec artifacts recovered from the great temple at Teocali, Mexico, include an elaborate mother-of-pearl necklace of more than 200 separate pieces, with golden and greenstone beads. The Incas in Peru and Chile were making necklaces with small sheets of gold fanned out to make spectacular collars. Later, when the Spanish arrived, they would continue their work in platinum and silver, sometimes adding precious gemstones as well.

Necklaces were not in vogue during the latter part of the Middle Ages due to the fashion of high neckwear; however, with time came change in styles and attitudes, and by the fifteenth century, necklaces and chains and collars were seen again, especially in the courts of Europe and among the wealthy. Christian devotional pendants (like the Tau cross), many of exquisite form and substance, were also popular, particularly with women. By the sixteenth century, plain gold chains were seen around the necks of both men and women, as well as pendants with the wearer's (or a loved one's) initials. The 1600s was the century of the pearl necklace and the era of cut and polished stones carefully linked and placed on chain collars. One innovation of the period was the lavaliere, a pendant necklace with a dangling stone, named for Duchess Louise de La Vallière (1644–1710), the mistress of the French king Louis XIV (1638–1715). The 1700s in Europe was dominated by diamonds, diamonds, and more diamonds; and for most of the century, the emphasis was more on the cut of the stone (colored stones as well) than on what held them in place around the neck.

In the Americas, in what is now the U.S. Southwest, natives had been making beads for necklaces since before the arrival of Columbus. The fine grinding of turquoise, coral, and shell beads into *heishi* necklaces was long established, as was the soaking and piercing of porcupine quills. Wood, bone, and seed beaded necklaces were also common. Through trade with the Spanish and others, natives acquired Venetian glass and Czech glass "seed" beads that, because of their beauty, quickly found their way into native crafting. Navajo, Hopi, and Pueblo artists learned silversmithing from the Spanish in the early 1800s, which gave form to uniquely native neckwear such as the squash blossom necklace, with its crescent-shaped pendant and silver and turquoise florets.

In Europe, the nineteenth century was a time of great and quick-moving change in jewelry trends. At the start of the century, necklaces were rather heavy and ostentatious, perhaps because many were made by machine. But by the 1840s, lighter fare was offered in the way of fine gold chains, seed pearls, slides on a chain, and a more naturalistic approach. Of course, the main jewelry trendsetter was Queen Victoria (1819–1901). Her love of cameos, Italian mosaics, coral, ivory and amber pendants, and silver necklaces meant that most of Europe, the Commonwealth, and England's former colonies (literally half the world) dressed as she and members of her court did. Her daughter-in-law, Alexandra of Denmark (1844–1925), also set a new trend by appearing in public wearing a choker to hide an ugly scar. Soon, scars or no scars, chokers were the rage, and no well-dressed woman would be seen in public without a choker above the collar of her blouse. And the discovery of precious metals and jewels in the tombs of North African kings and queens at the end of the century brought about an Egyptian and Assyrian revival in jewelrycrafting that had women all over the world buying reproduction necklaces and collars to emulate and imitate King Tut (reigned 1333–1324 B.C.E.) and Cleopatra (69–30 B.C.E.).

The twentieth century was like no other when it came to neckwear. It seemed as though fashions changed with every decade. At the early part of the century, crystal and French jet necklaces were the fashion of the Edwadrdian era (see **Edwardian Jewelry**). Following World War I, the flapper era, with its short hair and shorter hemlines, required long, long strands of pearl and glass beads, knotted at just the right length to complete an outfit. The Great Depression launched the costume jewelry (see **Costume Jewelry**) business in a way that could not have been anticipated. Soon, jewelry that looked good but cost a lot less than the real McCoy was available to everyone. That included necklaces and pendants and chains and collars. Hollywood movies, and later, television, set trends thereafter. The necklaces of the 1950s tended toward the simple: One chain, one pearl or gemstone was considered pure, demure, and attractive.

The New Beat Generation of the 1960s changed all that. The "Bohemian" look was in, with longer hair and a return, once again, to natural products. Ethnic African and native beads, puka shell collars, flowers and bright colors, unisex chains, and—well, "just about anything goes" seemed to be the order of the day. Since then, there has been no turning back. "Necklaces" are as popular as ever; in fact, so much so that most wearers don't take them off to swim, shower, or play sports.

☞ DID YOU KNOW?

In the last 50 years, if one were to give an award for the most fascinating moment or trend in jewelry neckwear, the prize would undoubtedly go to the twenty-first-century pendant urn offered by companies with names such as Urn Express and Ashes to Ashes. Through these vendors (and in lots of other places) one can purchase a keepsake pendant in the shape of an urn (or whatever one fancies) into which the ashes (known in the business as "cremains") of a loved one (including a favorite pet) have been deposited. Mind you, not all the ashes, but at least some of them. In this way, one can literally have the deceased "close to heart." For those who want something a little more elegant, cremains (which contain a lot of carbon) can also be fashioned, under high pressure, into a diamond that can be worn around the neck or in a ring. Available from companies like LifeGem, funerary items are fast becoming one of the hottest jewelry trends of the twenty-first century.

NOTES

1. See "Ancient Chinese May Have Worn Necklaces 20,000 Years Ago," *China View Magazine* (December 14, 2005) at http://www.stonepages.com/news/archives/001639.html

2. See "Ancient Chinese May Have Worn Necklaces 20,000 Years Ago," *Xinhua* (December 15, 2005) at http://english.people.com.cn/200512/15/eng20051215_228143. html Excavations in what was once Algeria (1930) have also turned up drilled shells that were thought to be part of necklaces, dating back 100,000 years.

3. Faience was a decorating and finishing process used on ceramics; in ancient Egyptian jewelrymaking, particularly with beads, a lead-based glaze was combined with tin oxide to give the beads a beautiful and lasting translucent sheen.

4. Pectorals were one of the most distinctive forms of Egyptian jewelry, that is to say, "breast ornamentation," worn by members of the royal court. They usually had the shape of a fairly large openwork frame that covered the upper half of the torso and were decorated with symbols representing the activities of the ruler, with intricate metalwork and stunning gems.

5. "Ancient Archaeological Sites Newly Discovered" at http://www.chinapage.com/archeology/ancient-site.html

6. Mason, Anita and Diane Packer, "Necklaces," in *An Illustrated Dictionary of Jewelry.* New York: Harper and Row, 1973, 254.

7. "Mauryan and Sunga Periods [321–72 B.C.E.]—Ancient Indian Costume" at http://www.4to40.com/discoverindia/index.asp?article=discoverindia_mauryansungaperiod

8. A *chenier* is a short piece of metal tubing that was cut for hinging one portion of jewelry to another.

9. See "Ancient Chinese Jewelry" at http://www.chinatownconnection.com/ancient-chinese-jewelry.htm

10. Mesoamerican Gallery at the University of Pennsylvania Museum of Archaeology and Anthropology, "Adornment and Concepts of Beauty" at http://www.museum.upenn.edu/new/exhibits/galleries/mesoamericaframedoc1.html

Nickel

Periodic table symbol: Ni

Atomic Number: 28

Origin of name: rooted in the German *kupfernickel* ("false copper")

Important historical background information: "discovered" in 1751 by Swedish chemist Baron Axel Fredrik Cronstedt (1722–1765)

Geographical location of element: Canada, Russia (Siberia), Cuba, Australia, New Caledonia, Turkey, Indonesia; occurs with sulfur in millerite, arsenic in niccolite, arsenic and sulfur in nickel glance; most often obtained from pentlandite; also found as a major constituent in most meteorites, as well as in volcanoes and on the ocean floor

Nickel is a hard, malleable, and ductile silvery-white metal of the iron group of elements. It is one of five ferromagnetic minerals (the others being iron, cobalt, gadolinium, and dysprosium) and is primarily used as an alloy metal, combining with copper, chromium, silver, gold, lead, cobalt, and aluminum to form harder and more durable substances that are resistant to corrosion, such as nickel steel and nickel cast iron. It is the fifth most common element in the Earth.[1] In industry, nickel finds its greatest use in the making of stainless steel. However, it is also important in the manufacture of magnets, coins, glass plating, plumbing and electrical works, kitchenware, aircraft components, razor blades, ceramics, batteries, and in jewelrycrafting, where it is very popular due to its ability to take on a high polish. Many jewelry findings and clasps are made of nickel, as it is relatively cheap but strong (often the clasps last long after what they are clasping has fallen apart!). Besides jewelry, nickel is a major fabric of fashion design and is the metal of choice for belts, buttons, clothing hooks, hairpins, zippers, eyeglasses, and watches. Sometimes called "the hidden metal," it can be found virtually everywhere.

The use of nickel goes back thousands of years, perhaps as early as 3500 B.C.E.; some ancient Syrian bronze statues contain at least 2 percent nickel, which shows that nickel was alloyed at a very early stage in the history of metalsmithing. In the nineteenth century, men's watches, casings, and watch fob chains were often made of nickel, as it was durable and its grayish but shiny appearance was considered "manly." In fact, nickel appears in a very large percentage of jewelry for men and women that was made before 1980, before the concept of allergy-free metals became a common concern of jewelrycrafters and vendors. Until then, nearly all yellow-gold jewelry of 14k (or less) and almost all white-gold jewelry contained enough nickel to cause an allergic reaction in those who were so predisposed. Even sterling jewelry that was manufactured nickel-free was most often coated with nickel. Despite these potential health drawbacks, nickel has been for a long period (and to some extent is still) a popular choice for body jewelry and piercings

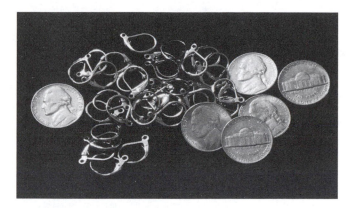

Nickel pierced loops are a common finding used in jewelry production.
Copyright © 2007 by Anthony F. Chiffolo.

(although *all* nickel jewelry is currently banned in Europe).[2] Today, much of what is being sold as Celtic, Wiccan, or pagan jewelry contains nickel, or is often heavily nickel-plated. For those into modern "Goth" or "Gothic" jewelry, nickel-plated accessories such as chains, cuffs, chain mail, and collars are very popular.[3]

Those who work with nickel can find it available in foil, sheet, wire, spheres, flakes, powder, rods, mesh, and what are known as "evaporation slugs," a liquid state that when exposed to a high heat or light source leaves behind a deposit of the metal. Jewelrycrafters working with nickel use many of the same tools used with all fine metals that can take a high polish: cutters, trimmers, pliers, files, burnishers, soldering guns, abrasives, smelters, grinding stones, as well as other power and hand tools.

☞ DID YOU KNOW?

Ask any U.S. school kid, and they can tell you that a nickel equals five cents, right? Right! But that was not always the case. "Nickel" (or "nicks") was originally the term applied to the Indian one-cent coins in usage from 1859 through the end of the Civil War, as they were made from a cupro-nickel alloy. Following the war, three-cent coins came on to the scene and were also called nickels. With the introduction of the so-called five-cent "shield-nickel" in 1866, the word nickel became synonymous with 5¢. Which in itself is quite strange, as most nickels contain very little nickel—mostly copper (75 percent). But if we called them "coppers," folks might think we were referring to police officers, who got their nickname ("cops") from the copper buttons that used to adorn the fronts of their uniforms.

NOTES

1. Only iron, magnesium, oxygen, and silicon are found in greater abundance.
2. See "White gold compositions without nickel and palladium" at http://www.uspatentserver.com/686/6863746.html
3. See for instance "Chainmail & More" at http://www.sblades.com/collars.php

Palladium

Periodic table symbol: Pd

Atomic Number: 46

Origin of name: from the Greek *Pallas,* named after an asteroid that appeared in the skies two years prior to its "discovery"

Important historical background information: "discovered" in 1803 by W. H. Wollaston (1766–1828) in London

Geographical location of element: Ural Mountains, Australia, Ethiopia, South and North America; also found in nickel-copper deposits located in South Africa and Ontario

Palladium is a rare, silver-white metal; it is part of the platinum group of metals: rhodium, ruthenium, palladium, osmium, iridium, and platinum, which it resembles closely in its chemical makeup. Palladium has many uses—in the switching systems of telecommunications networks, in dental tools, in surgical instruments, in electrical contacts and aircraft spark plugs—and is an essential element in the creation of cold fusion. But its primary usage is in jewelrycrafting as a coating over other precious metals (it does not tarnish), in the making of watch springs, and in coinage.

Palladium is most often alloyed with gold or platinum. When mixed with gold, it increases gold's melting point, gives it more strength and hardness, and turns yellow gold to white. When combined with platinum, it functions in much the same way. The platinum/palladium mix is well suited to the making of chains as it is easily cast, welded, and soldered, making it quite popular with chain manufacturers in Japan and the People's Republic of China, who favor the look and durability.

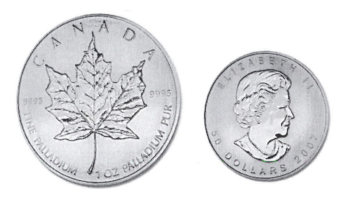

A Canadian $50 palladium coin.

One of the common forms of palladium, known as *precium*, is used in jewelry-crafting almost exclusively for school rings, which tend to take on a lot of wear. Precium is a palladium/silver alloy (25 percent palladium; 62–75 percent silver and other materials); it was developed by Handy and Hardman (precious metals manufacturers) especially for use by jewelers in casting and the working of fine metals.

Jewelrycrafters can purchase palladium in many forms, including evaporation slugs, foil, granule, powder, shot, sheet, sponge, and wire. It is, however, quite expensive, partially due to stockpiling by major corporations who use it in manufacturing.[1]

☞ DID YOU KNOW?

As rare an element as it is, palladium is used today by some countries in minting their coinage. The kingdom of Tonga began issuing palladium coins in 1967, including the famous and much-collected Tonga palladium *Hau*. Since that time, a number of other countries have issued palladium coins, including Canada, the Soviet Union, France, Russia, China, Australia, and Slovakia, though most have been special commemoratives.

NOTE

1. For example, in 2000, Ford Motor Company created a price bubble in palladium by stockpiling large amounts of it in the fear that supplies from Russia might be interrupted due to sanctions or trade restrictions. When prices fell in early 2001, Ford lost nearly US$1 billion.

Pewter

> *Composition:* Primarily an alloy of tin and copper. There are three grades of pewter: fine, trifle, and lay,[1] each with varying degrees of tin, the latter two with differing amounts of lead; modern pewter is alloyed with copper, silver, antimony and/or bismuth
>
> *Origin of name:* probably a variation of *spelter* (in French, *peautre*)
>
> *Important historical background information:* the second alloy known to humankind;[2] common from the Middle Ages through 1850, it all but disappeared only to be revived as an art product in the late twentieth century
>
> *Primary usage:* tableware, housewares, decorative objects, coins, collectible figurines, pendants and other jewelry items

Pewter is a white, shiny, malleable metal alloy that is very similar in appearance to silver.[3] A combination of tin and copper (and sometimes other alloys such as lead, antimony, and bismuth), it has been in use for thousands of years. It was probably first made in the Bronze Age (2000–500 B.C.E.), though perhaps not intentionally.[4] Egyptian tombs have yielded pewter items as well, and it appears to have been in ancient China and Japan also. The discovery in British archaeological sites of ancient Roman pewter artifacts, such as coins, seals of office, and utensils, is a tribute to the durability of this versatile metal. Pewter was also known in East Asia. It first appears in Western recorded history circa 1074 C.E., when an ecclesiastical synod allowed its use as a substitute for gold and silver in church appointments, for example, chalices, candlesticks, altar crosses, patens, and the like. By the end of the thirteenth century, a pewter trade was well established in major cities such as Paris and Bruges; from there it spread to Augsburg, Nuremberg, Moos, Poitiers, and other trade centers.

Pewter was originally crafted into housewares for the wealthy, but as it became more affordable, pewter pieces began to show up in local taverns and inns. By the end of the seventeenth century, its use in Europe was nearly universal. Pewter made its way to the Americas about the same time, primarily as a finished product; yet most imported pewter was later melted down for ammunition during the Revolutionary War. Following the war it found some industry in the newly established United States. However, pewter's ultimate undoing as a desirable product was undoubtedly the growing trend to set the table with glass, china, and pottery housewares, all of which were often more showy, better decorated, lighter to handle, and just as cheap. Indeed, by the mid part of the nineteenth century, pewter had taken on the stigma of vulgarity, and the pewter trade nearly died out. Despite these challenges, England continued to be the center of pewter production and by the 1930s managed to reinvent the market for pewterwares by continuing to forge a fine product for a reasonable price.[5] Today pewter is once again popular in North America, Europe, and in many countries, particularly among collectors of figurines and chess sets and Celtic reproductions and with

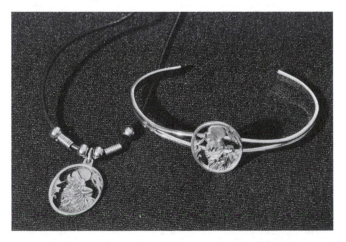

Pewter jewelry is especially favored by those who want a quality look for a fair price. Copyright © 2007 by Anthony F. Chiffolo.

medievalists. In the twenty-first century, the largest producer of pewter is Royal Selangor in Malaysia.[6]

For those interested in working with pewter, it can be cast, cut, formed, fused, and spun. The tools of the trade, depending on the format used, might include a lathe, a welder, solder, wax, plaster of Paris, a crucible, pliers, snips, an anvil, hammers, clay sculpting tools, a dremel, a stylus, chucks, spinner's soap, sanding cloths, a hobby knife, files, epoxy putty, a blowtorch, and a variety of other hand and power tools. Pewter, like most metals, can be purchased in a variety of formats, including wire, mesh, sheets, and foil, and is available from most craft stores or Web sites.

Pewter can be very easily cast into intricate objects, which has made it ideal for jewelrymaking. Like other alloys, it has been used in jewelrycrafting for as long as people have adorned themselves with precious metals. In the mystical realm, pewter jewelry is said to reduce headaches when placed on the forehead, and when placed on the chest, to help with lung ailments.

In the modern market, pewter jewelry is most popular among those who fancy Celtic and medieval reproductions and "ethnic" creations; it is also extremely popular with the "Goth" (twentieth-century neo-Gothic) and Wiccan communities.

Much pewter jewelry that is currently on the market is made in the People's Republic of China and contains some lead; therefore it is important to shop around, know one's source, and seek out dealers who are selling only "lead-free" pieces, just to be safe.

☞ DID YOU KNOW?

In the Middle Ages, people who were fairly well-off ate from pewter vessels. However, because the pewter made at the time had a high lead content, meals with a great amount of acid would often cause the lead to leach into the food, causing lead poisoning. The primary culprit appeared to be tomatoes, making them unwelcome on the dinner table for nearly the next four hundred years!

NOTES

1. See "Pewter" at http://en.wikipedia.org/wiki/Pewter

2. See "About the Pewtercraft" at http://www.threefeatherspewter.com/pewter craft.htm

3. It is, in point of fact, often referred to as "antique silver."

4. Because pewter and bronze are related alloys (pewter is mostly tin with a bit of copper; bronze is mostly copper with a bit of tin), historians have speculated that pewter came to be when someone reversed the recipe, adding a bit too much tin when they should have been pouring copper.

5. See Boyle, Beth Maxwell, "Pewter History" at http://www.ramshornstudio.com/pewter.htm

6. Sly, Peter, "Pewter History" at http://www.pec.on.ca/pewter/history.htm

Pins and Brooches

> Then she ran into the kitchen, and cooked the king's soup; and as soon as the cook was gone, she put the golden brooch into the dish. (From *Cat-Skin*, a fairy tale by the Brothers Grimm)

Most people know them merely as "pins," yet the appellation can cause much confusion (since there are many types and kinds of pins). Perhaps "brooch" (or "broach," from the Old French meaning "long needle") is a more precise term to describe the decorative jewelry item that has been worn by both men and women for thousands of years as both an adornment and a clothes fastener.

The wearing of brooches dates back to at least the Bronze Age.[1] Ancient brooches are referred to as *fibuale* and were called such because they resembled the outer leg bone (in Latin, *fibula*) in a shape that is much like that of the modern safety pin. Though decorative by nature, their primary function seems to have been to hold clothing together, such as the folds of a wraparound skirt (in Scotland) or a shawl or toga portion (in Rome). Fibulae that have survived from this period are highly sought after and as such are very expensive, even those made of the crudest of materials.

Fibulae gradually gave way to an improved product; their clunky construction proved too unreliable as a fastener. According to some sources, it was Athenian women in the era of the Roman Empire who developed smaller, more delicate fasteners that soon were coveted by most of the upper classes of European society. In Europe, these brooches remained the major clothing fastener from the third century C.E. until nearly the beginning of the fourteenth century. (In India, brooches made of gold and ivory were part of native costume as early as the Kushan period [130 B.C.E. to 185 C.E.]). Brooches are recorded in the costume history of many European groups. Up until the twelfth century C.E., Irish chieftains and men of rank wore a smock-like tunic called a *leine,* over which was worn a large woolen cloak, or mantle, that was fastened on the breast with a metal brooch or pin.[2] Scottish women of this era wore similar dress, with the mantle fastened by a silver brooch.[3] Viking women utilized pairs of oval bronze brooches, sometimes called tortoise brooches (due to their shape), which served to hold their dresses up.[4] These brooches were of two basic types: the penannular, which had a gapped ring, and the pseudo-penannular, which had a closed ring.

As styles and fashions changed, and the realities of hard work and daily living set in, brooches made little sense as a clothing fastener, especially for the common classes living in colder climes who needed tight-fitting and heavy clothing to keep them warm. Brooches, with their sharp points and rusting

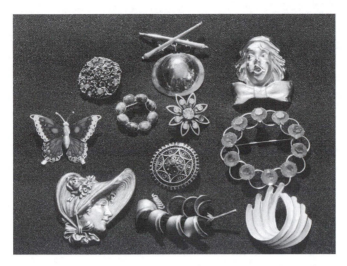

Every pin has a personality all its own. Copyright © 2007 by Anthony F. Chiffolo.

metals, were not useful. European workers instead made eyelets for their pants and shirts and laced their garments tightly with string or leather cord.

In 1849, Walter Hunt (1796–1859), a U.S. inventor, created what he called the "miracle fastener," known today as the safety pin. These pins were used much in the same way as buttons, and they were decorated with emblems, coats of arms, gemstones, and glass, set in silver, copper, or brass. Most modern pins follow on this theme, and late-nineteenth-century jewelers introduced a wide variety of them, which set the stage for what is being worn today.

In modern parlance, the term "brooch" has nearly disappeared. Some reference books make a clear distinction between a brooch and a pin; yet almost all brooches fit into the category of "pins" (from the Latin *spina*, or "thorn"). Still, the term "pin" encompasses so much more. Pin can refer to the safety type, or to a stickpin, hatpin, bar pin, sweater pin, lapel pin, sash pin, tie tac, hairpin, veil pin, cuff pin, badge, emblem, or an assorted variety of items that have a point.

Some of the most famous antique jewelry pieces that have survived the ravages of time have been brooches, including the ninth-century Anglo-Saxon Fuller brooch (see below); the Harford Farm Brooch, which bears an inscription written in runic language; the mid-ninth-century Anglo-Saxon Strickland Brooch; the eleventh-century English Pitney Brooch; the eleventh-century English silver disc brooch of Ædwen; and the eleventh-century Viking Brooch in the Urnes style.

☞ DID YOU KNOW?

One of the most famous brooches in history is the ninth-century Anglo-Saxon "Fuller brooch." It is a large disc (about 11.4 cm.) that is made of hammered sheet silver that has been inlaid with niello (see **Enameling**). Its center roundel depicts one of the earliest known representations of the five human senses. The outer border sports 16 smaller medallions, each with a human or nature motif. What makes the pin so unusual is that it has survived for nearly 1,200 years in near-perfect condition, making it most likely the only surviving piece of nonreligious Anglo-Saxon metalwork to be handed down through generations (versus buried) since it was first made. The curator of the British Museum, Sir Hercules Read (1857–1929), proclaimed it a fake and had it taken off display and sold for silver-meltdown cost to a Captain A.W. F. Fuller (1882–1961). Later discoveries of similarly crafted pieces led to the determination that it was indeed the real thing and nearly priceless! In 1952, Capt. Fuller donated it back to the British Museum with the caveat that it bear his name.[5]

NOTES

1. See "Brooch" at http://eb.wikipedia.org/wiki/Brooch
2. Coakley, F., "Costume" at http://www.isle-of-man.com/manxnotebook/history/dress/dress.htm
3. Riley, M. E., and Kass McGann, "The Evolution of the Kilt" at http://72.14.209.104/search?q=cache:YSF1DZL_PKoJ:www.reconstructinghistory.com/scottish/medievalscot.html+HISTORY+OF+BROOCHES&hl=en&gl=us&ct=clnk&cd=6
4. Coakley, F., "Costume."
5. Source: http://dictionary.laborlawtalk.com/Fuller_brooch

Plastics

> While today we think of plastics as cheap, for the first three-quarters of the twentieth century they were a high-priced luxury item. Even in the 1950s, plastic products were three to four times more expensive than wood or enameled metal. They were a premium, an extravagance, and the most stylish decadence. (Wilson Art International, "Plastics")

Many jewelry items, particularly beads, bangle bracelets, earrings, and necklaces are made of a material that looks like it might be plastic. Plastic, as we understand it, is a broad term that includes many types and kinds of articles, from Styrofoam to Saran Wrap to Velcro, "rubber-like" substances to "steel-strong" pieces that resemble glass but are clearly "other."

Since the early nineteenth century, hand-made "plastics" (though they were not called such) have played a major role in the fashion and jewelry world.

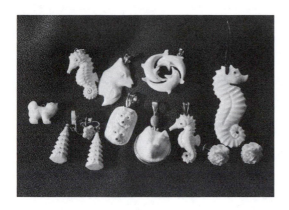

Is it ivory, bone, scrimshaw, or a plastic product? Only the most discerning eye can tell. Copyright © 2007 by Anthony F. Chiffolo.

Natural plastic-like materials, such as amber and tortoiseshell, have been used in jewelrymaking since before recorded history. Some types held up well; others did not. Hence, collectors of antique and vintage jewelry are always on the lookout for items made of:

Amber: Though not a plastic, amber is a yellowish-brown natural fossil resin that began as a pine tree excretion millions of years ago. Its color varies from pale yellow to red to black. Much of the world's amber is from the Baltic Sea region, Eastern England, and the Netherlands, but significant deposits have been discovered in the Dominican Republic, Myanmar, and Australia. Amber is one of the most "forged" jewelry materials in history. To test "real amber" from the many fakes on the market, place the piece in seawater: Real amber will float, imitation amber will sink.

Bakelite: Bakelite is a dense, phenolic resin invented by the Belgian scientist Leo Hendrix Baekeland (1863–1944) in 1907.[1] It is composed of carbolic acid and formaldehyde and was first used to imitate amber. Bakelite pieces are made in a mold and are sometimes carved (such as the ever-popular Apple Juice bracelets); it was also not uncommon to lay one color on top of another in the melding process, creating a type of swirl effect. Carved and swirled pieces tend to fetch more on the resale market, as do bracelets and earrings that feature polka dots. It is often difficult to determine if a piece is truly Bakelite; some collectors claim that it has a particularly gasoline-like smell when it is rubbed (but so does *celluloid*); others claim that when rubbed on clothing, it will cause static electricity (but so will plastic). Some say that Bakelite has a purple hue when put under a black light; others prefer a "hot-pin" test (not a good idea, as it ruins the piece). It is best to buy from a reputable dealer, as Bakelite is no longer being made.

Celluloid: Celluloid is a plastic-like material made from cellulose, a plant derivative; it is composed mainly of soluble guncotton and camphor. Celluloid was invented in 1869 by the U.S. chemist John Wesley Hyatt (1837–1920) as a substitute for ivory in billiard balls. Originally known as xylonite, celluloid is highly flammable and easily damaged by moisture. Jewelry made of celluloid is often fragile, and older pieces when poorly handled tend to self-combust. Celluloid jewelry pieces are lightweight and often ivory-colored. If one owns a celluloid item, it is important to store it well (between pieces of cotton, perhaps) and keep it away from climates with high humidity.

Ebonite: Also known as vulcanite, ebonite is a hard, darkly polished early plastic product created by adding sulfur to vulcanized rubber. It is easily molded and was commonly used in the nineteenth century to make combs, hair ornaments, buttons, and mourning jewelry. Ebonite is often confused with gutta percha (see below).

Gutta percha: Gutta percha is a resin from the Isonandra gutta tree; it is often found in jewelry from the mid- to late nineteenth century. It is rubbery when soft but very solid otherwise. Gutta percha was later used for electric cable insulation and for fillings in dentistry.

Ivory fiberloid: A type of synthetic ivory made from plant materials. Also known as French ivory, ivoride, ivorine, genuine French ivory, or tortine. Vegetable ivory is another ivory-like product made from the seed of the South American ivory palm. It was often used in smaller items, like dice and jewelry. Items made of true ivory, as with those made of Bakelite, are difficult to discern with the naked eye. Many "experts" have been easily fooled, so it is always best to consult a knowledgeable collector.

Lucite: Lucite is a lightweight, transparent, thermoplastic resin developed in 1937 by the DuPont company. (A thermoplastic is one that melts under heat, such as acrylic and nylon.) Lucite jewelry comes in many shapes and colors, from brightly decorated bows to carved bangles and odd-shaped finger rings. Lucite jewelry is still being made today, although the older pieces are what collectors want and treasure. One very popular collectible is called confetti lucite; it is transparent but with glitter or other small pieces of material within.

Wax-bead: Wax is a common ingredient in many pieces of jewelry of the last 200–300 years. It was especially popular in the making of faux pearls, which have a bead as their base and then are covered with a wax luster. Unfortunately, these beads have a tendency to peel and/or turn yellow. Wax pearls were particularly popular during the late Victorian era through the 1930s, during which they were used as hair and dress decorations and jewelry.

There are many other plastics and thermoplastics (such as resin, acrylic, vinyl, nylon, lacquer) on the market today from which jewelry is made. But let the buyer beware: Plastics come in all shapes, ages, and varieties and are very versatile. It takes a good eye and a lot of research to know what's what when valuing "plastic" jewelry.

☞ DID YOU KNOW?

Just when you thought it was safe to go back in the water comes shrinkable plastic jewelry! One of the most recent craft innovations, shrinkable plastics are clear or opaque sheets of ultra-thin plastic that "melt" to one-fourth their original size when baked in the oven. Using colored permanent markers or acrylic paints, scissors, a hole punch, some fine sandpaper, a little glue, and clear nail polish to add a lasting varnish, "loads of fun and lots of original jewelry" is now the motto at kids parties and adult get-togethers alike. One can purchase entire kits (Shrinky Dinks, for instance) or cut-up any No. 6 recyclable plastic container and heat it in a 250-degree oven for four or five minutes. Check out the Internet or a local craft store for more variations on this theme.

NOTE

1. Bakelite is sometimes called catalin; though similar, catalin is not the same as Bakelite.

Platinum

Periodic table symbol: Pt

Atomic Number: 78

Origin of name: from *platina* (Sp., "little silver")

Important historical background information: Charles Wood (1702–1774) independently isolated platinum in 1741, but it was known in Europe and the Americas long before

Geographical location of element: South Africa;[1] also Ontario, Colombia, Ural mountains, Western U.S. states; also found in nickel and copper ores and in meteorites

Platinum, "the only metal fit for a King" (according to Louis XVI [1754–1793] of France), is a rare, grey-white transition metal that is both malleable and ductile.[2] It was first designated a "precious metal" by the Swedish scientist Theophil Scheffer (1710–1759) in 1751; it is 30 times rarer than gold. Platinum is used primarily for jewelry, but it is also a critical component in dentistry and is a key element in electrical contacts, laboratory equipment, medical implants, chemotherapeutic drugs, and automobile emissions-control devices.

The history of platinum is long but checkered with identification uncertainties, as platinum did not always show up in pure form. We know from Egyptian burial sites that gold containing traces of platinum was being imported from Nubia as early as 1200 B.C.E. to make jewelry, and that the sarcophagus of Shepenupet, the high priestess of Thebes circa 700 B.C.E., features gold and platinum hieroglyphics; however, it is uncertain if either civilization understood what platinum was or how precious it is. The Incas (circa 100 B.C.E.), who were gifted metalsmiths, used platinum in their jewelry and adornments and may have had a better idea as to its unique properties. When the Spanish arrived in the Americas in the late sixteenth century, they found platinum to be a nuisance, mixed in as it was with their precious gold, calling it *platina* ("little silver") and thereby designating it an inferior metal.

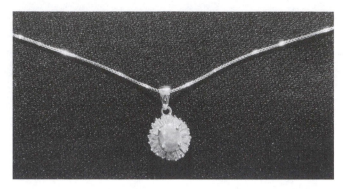

A stunning opal pendant in an elegant platinum setting. Copyright © 2007 by Anthony F. Chiffolo.

In 1803, the British scientist W. H. Wollaston (1766–1828) was the first to discover a process to make platinum malleable; from that time forward, platinum was used commercially. Jewelers Peter Carl Fabergé (1846–1920) and Louis Cartier (1875–1942) demonstrated to an ever-interested public that platinum was an ideal metal for precious things—Fabergé when creating his famous Easter eggs for the czar of Russia, Cartier when selling platinum jewelry for the first time on a commercial scale, demonstrating its hidden quality of bringing brilliance to diamond settings. Soon after, platinum jewelry was all the rage, but due to its high cost, it remained out of range for all but the very rich. But the very rich were willing to comply: In 1937, the Duke and Duchess of Windsor exchanged platinum wedding rings; in 1967 Elvis and Priscilla Presley did the same; in 2000, Michael Douglas and Catherine Zeta-Jones were married with rings made of platinum.

Platinum jewelrycrafters today can purchase the rare metal in various formats, including foil, gauze, insulated wire, mesh, powder, sponge, sheets, wire, and "evaporation slugs," a platinum liquid state that when exposed to a high heat or light source leaves behind a deposit of the metal. Platinum jewelrymakers use many high-tech machines today to produce their work, including rolling mills, turning machines, burnishers, hand and hydraulic presses, bangle tube cutters, strip metal cutters, lathes, and more mundane hand tools, such as pliers, wooden or plastic hammers, and tweezers.

Most platinum jewelry is 95 percent pure platinum; to be workable and strong, platinum is often combined with iridium, palladium, ruthenium, or some other alloy. To be assured that the product one is looking at is made of platinum, ensure it carries the mark ".950 Plat" or "Plat."

☞ DID YOU KNOW?

Soon after the French Revolution of the late eighteenth century, the jeweler to King Louis XVI (1754–1793), Marc-Étienne Janety (1739–1820), returned to his native country when asked to create the prototype for a standard metric kilogram that was to be made from platinum (due to its durability, there was little corruptibility as the years wore on). This platinum-iridium cylinder is housed at the Bureau International des Poids et Mesures in Sèvres, France, along with another platinum-iridium bar that is the prototype for the meter (measured for standard's sake with two marks on an ingot bar). Janety's precision and skill have landed him in our math books, which just goes to prove that jewelers can do more than just make pretty baubles, and that there is a science to jewelrymaking![3]

NOTES

1. South Africa is the largest producer of platinum in the world.
2. According to the Precious Platinum Web site (http://www.preciousplatinum.com/output/Page26.asp), platinum is so rare that if all that exists in the world were poured into an Olympic-sized swimming pool, the liquid would scarcely cover one's ankles (by comparison, gold would fill more than three pools).
3. Source: "Platinum" at http://en.wikipedia.org/wiki/Platinum

Porcelain and Pottery Jewelry

Does not the potter have power over the clay, from the same lump to make one vessel for honor and another for dishonor? (Romans 9:21, *NKJV*)

Jewelry is made of just about every material known to humankind, so it should be no surprise that porcelain and pottery would be among the materials listed for jewelrycrafting. Because of their delicate nature, however, working with porcelain and pottery in jewelrymaking requires extra care to prevent chipping and breaking in ways that do not challenge jewelers who use other types of materials. In the same vein and for many of the same reasons, good porcelain/pottery jewelry has become quite expensive because of the rarity of encountering antique pieces that are in good condition; newer pieces command a higher price because of the costs of handling to ensure the delivery of a flaw-free commodity.

In the United States, from the early 1800s to about 1920, thousands of women purchased porcelain "blanks" and hand-painted their own jewelry items: buttons, hatpin heads, oval and rounded pendants, and pins with scenic designs or portraits of women were popular. Today, porcelain jewelry is made by many craftspeople who have all the basics at hand: the plaster, the glaze, the kiln, the paints, and the know-how. Porcelain jewelry has been made the same way for hundreds of years; some of the trade's top producers are:

AYNSLEY

Aynsley is an English fine-china-making company founded as a pottery business in 1775 by master potter John Aynsley (1752–1829). Located in Longton, England, Aynsley has made porcelain pieces of distinction using local Staffordshire clay for several hundred years. John Aynsley II (1823–1907) changed the focus of the company in the nineteenth century and opened a new factory in Stoke-on-Kent with the goal of creating a fine bone china. Using 50 percent "calcined bone ash" in the porcelain to make a product that was very strong, translucent, and exceptionally white, Aynsley caught the attention of Queen Victoria (1819–1901) herself and was given a royal commission, helping to establish the lofty reputation that the company still enjoys to this day.

Aynsley jewelry is distinctive. Hand-painted, multicolored, three-dimensional flower pins with a brass backing arrive in an exquisite blue silk box with a white silk interior. Thimbles, stickpins, and other small jewelry items made by Aynsley have captured the popular imagination and have become a staple of the English souvenir and travel collectibles' market.

DELFT

Delftware is a type of tin-glazed pottery, often blue and white, that is most commonly identified with the Netherlands.[1] Its origins go back to the early seventeenth century, when the Dutch East India Company began importing Chinese porcelain to Holland. As only the rich could afford the imports, Dutch potters began to imitate the Chinese work, and by the mid-seventeenth century, the town of Delft had become firmly established as one of Europe's major pottery centers.

Delftware is created using a series of glazes: first a tin-based white glaze (aka faience) is applied, then a metal-oxide decoration, followed by a lead-based clear overcoat, which leaves the surface of the work glossy. Delftware is distinguished by native Dutch scenes, such as windmills, flowers, landscapes, and fishing boats.

Delft jewelry is often set in .800 or .835 silver (the standards for the Benelux countries, Austria and Germany), usually with superb filigree workings and granulation. Necklaces, pendants, earrings, pins, bracelets, charms, rings, and cufflinks are the most common products, though today Delftware is used to create nearly every imaginable jewelry item and jewelry accessory.

LIMOGES

Limoges is a hard-paste porcelain that has been produced in and around the French city of the same name for more than 200 years. The soil in this area is rich in kaolin (a limestone-colored element that provides the white hue and elasticity needed to shape a piece), quartz (a degreasing agent that decreases the possibility of deformities when kiln-baking), and feldspar (the active ingredient in Limoges glazes, which gives it a translucent quality). These raw materials are crushed and mixed (along with other materials), and the clay, once filtered and sifted, results in a product that lends itself quite easily to the production of beautiful jewelry, translating into high prices on the collectibles market. The quality of the work, the elegant materials, and the delicacy of Limoges jewelry push prices for a fine piece to well over US$100.

Many pieces of Limoges jewelry are hand-painted (most particularly antique samples). Limoges rings, pendants, bracelets, necklaces, pins, cufflinks, and earrings are the most common jewelry items, and Limoges thimbles, belt buckles, hair ornaments, and hand mirrors are among the most common accessories on the market today. In the United States, the jewelry designer Ian St. Geilar is known for the use of Limoges in his jewelry creations.

WEDGWOOD

Wedgwood, a fine English pottery is named for Josiah Wedgwood, the son and grandson of British potters, who was born in 1730 at Burslem, Stoke, in the Staffordshire area of England.[2] His years as an apprentice in the family business served him well in the production of the wares that bear his name. An aspiring scientist of sorts, Wedgwood was more interested in the techniques of pottery crafting than the business of manufacturing; it was this focus that brought about the creation of two of Wedgwood's earliest successes: basaltware and jasperware. Black basalt, named after the Egyptian rock, appeared in 1768, and it found moderate interest among British consumers. Jasperware, which Wedgwood had been working on since the early 1760s, finally came to market once he discovered that local deposits of barium sulphate could be used to create the look, form, and substance of the dense, white stoneware (easily tinted to feature colors) thought acceptable to potential buyers. Wedgwood was not disappointed: jasperware was a great success and continues to this day to be the most recognizable of all Wedgwood wares.

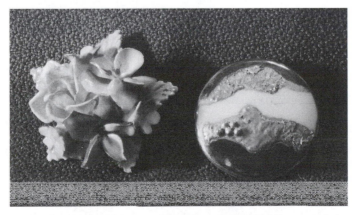

A pair of 1960s porcelain pins. The flower pin on the left was made by Aynsley. Copyright © 2007 by Anthony F. Chiffolo.

It should not be surprising to learn, therefore, that many cameos from the late eighteenth century had a jasperware background. During the Art Nouveau period, Wedgwood brooches that featured figures from classical mythology in bas-relief were extremely popular. Today, Wedgwood makes jewelry both in the classical jasperware and basaltware, as well as in their more traditional Queensware porcelain, which features a creamy background not unlike that of Limoges. Wedgwood earrings, rings, pendants, bracelets, and necklaces are most usual, but brooches, particularly those in cameo form, are among the finest creations Wedgwood produces. For men, tie clips, belt buckles, watch accessories, and rings are among Wedgwood's offerings. In recent years, Beatrix Potter Peter Rabbit jewelry has been produced by Wedgwood, to great acclaim among collectors.

☞   DID YOU KNOW?

• Aynsley flower pieces, known as "florals," are actually arranged in bouquets by floral designers that have been hired by Aynsley in order to ensure a realistic look to the finished product.

- Delftware is not popular amongst Dutch citizens, having lost most of its appeal due to mass production for the tourist market.
- At present, all clay used in making Delftware is imported from other countries.
- The adjective used to describe the Limoges region of France, *limousine*, is the origin of our English word for a fine luxury car.
- Blue is the first color that Josiah Wedgwood used in making jasperware, and it is still the most collected color nearly 250 years later.
- It is said that Josiah Wedgwood was the inventor of the time clock, a device by which workers could "punch in and out" to record the actual hours they had labored during the work week, thus guaranteeing the payout of fair wages for a job well done.
- Josiah Wedgwood was the grandfather of British naturalist Charles Darwin (1809–1882).

NOTES

1. Neither the pottery patterns nor the potters who made Delft pottery were native to Holland: Most were Italian potters who emigrated to Belgium to escape religious persecution and from there made their way to Rotterdam and Haarlem. However, Delftware has also been produced in England since the 1700s. It was originally called galleyware but renamed to compete with the popular Dutch product. Not all Delft pottery is blue and white; many Delft items are made of red clay, or in a kind of Imari pattern that features a number of colors and the use of gold trim.

2. Wedgwood died in 1790.

Retro Jewelry

Period: 1939–1952

Birthplace: United States

Origins: war-time America

Influences: Hollywood fashions of the 1940s; whatever the Duchess of Windsor (1896–1986) was wearing; American pop culture

With Europe at war in the late 1930s, jewelry production in the United States came into its own. Many European designers and craftspersons emigrated to the West and opened up shop in New York, Philadelphia, Baltimore, Chicago, St. Louis, San Francisco, and other major U.S. cities. Jewelry took on a decidedly "American look," with all the familiar themes of the past, but with one exception: Big and bold was "in." Large stones, rose gold, rhodium plating, the "chunky look," synthetics, and all things yellow and blue—topaz, citrine, aquamarine, turquoise—were the rage of fashion. As the United States entered World War II, Hollywood sought to divert the masses with what they did not have: plenty of anything. Costume jewelry enjoyed its greatest moment as jewelry houses sought to replicate finery on the cheap.

In the early years of the Retro period, patriotic themes were prevalent. Jewelry with flags, eagles, military insignias, and red and blue synthetic stones could be found in every jewelry and department store, from the finest Fifth Avenue shop to the five-and-dime. Glorification of the heavy machinery that undergirded the war effort showed up in jewelry design, from zippers to rivets to pipes to brick-work. Charm bracelets, fur clips, and screwback and clip earrings were what every well-dressed woman was wearing. And because supplies were short, and everything was being used to fight the enemy, inexpensive jewelry allowed one to live vicariously: No lace for bows—how about a bow pin? No money for flowers— how about a bracelet of small daisies? No ribbons or ruffles to add some pizzazz to a skirt—dress it up wearing a ribboned and ruffled necklace. Little food for a Thanksgiving meal—cornucopia earrings (very popular!) expressed the mood.

Once the war was over and many servicemen returned home to their long-suffering girlfriends and fiancées, marriage was on everyone's mind. The economy of these times had a direct bearing on a woman's engagement ring. "Illusion settings," whereby a stone was made to look much bigger than it was thanks to elaborately carved, square white-gold mountings, which gave the diamonds a much larger appearance, were the answer to many a soldier's prayer and wallet. As they were fond of saying, "that's a lot of bang for the buck!" And then the baby boom was off and running.

With so little money to go around, even for the wealthy, costume jewelry made a big splash during the Retro era. Many designers who had been in business for

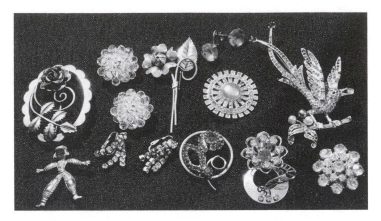

Retro pins and earrings: A smart look that never seems to go out of style.
Copyright © 2007 by Anthony F. Chiffolo.

decades found a new market by producing an affordable product with a "good look" to it. Designers such as CoroCraft, Trifari, Napier, Monet, Regency, Weiss, Hobé, Whiting and Davis, Florenza, Vendome, DeRosa, Hagler, Danecraft, VanDell, and Kreisler, to name but a few, were extremely popular with all buyers. This was the era of "frozen movement" in jewelry design, that is to say, designs that looked so authentic one had to touch them in order to be sure they weren't the real thing. It was also the epoch of the "jelly belly," pins or other jewelry that had clear, transparent Lucite middles.

For men, the top designers of the Retro period were Pulsar (watches), Swank, Anson, Paul Smith, and Carl Art, as well as Hickok (cufflinks and tie accessories) and all things Western (including Native American).

"Retro" is a rather new term in the history of jewelry, as it was not known by this name during the days following the end of World War II. Due to the rising dominance of American folk culture in the late 1940s, there is a rather seamless segue into what fashion design now labels the Post-Deco period, and the two styles tend to overlap greatly.

☞   **DID YOU KNOW?**

"The origin of 'Jelly Belly' jewelry lies in the historical archives of Trifari. During World War II, Trifari converted some of their factories to produce Lucite windshields and turrets for U.S. fighter planes. These windshields had to be flawless, so any large Plexiglas sheets that were even lightly marred were thrown on a scrap heap, deemed unusable for the Army Air Corps. Trifari's most famous jewelry designer, Alfred Philippe, looked at the growing stack of discarded Plexiglas and had a stroke of genius. He had the company jewelers cut up the Lucite windshields into small cabochons, fitted them into some whimsical jewelry designs, and voila! . . . Jelly Bellies were born!"[1]

NOTE

1. "Trifari Jelly Belly Sterling Vermeil Angelfish Fur Clip" at http://www.cooljools.com/images/TrifariJellyBellyAngelFish.htm

Rhodium

Periodic table symbol: Rh

Atomic Number: 45

Origin of name: from the Greek *rhodon* (rose), due to the color of one of its chloride compound structures

Important historical background information: "discovered" in 1804 by W. H. Wollaston (1766–1828) in London

Geographical location of element: major deposits in the north of Siberia (Russia), in Ontario (Canada), and in Transvaal (South Africa); other mineral deposits that contain rhodium, resulting from the erosion of primary deposits, in Russia, Colombia, and Alaska

Rhodium is a very rare, silvery-white metal with a high reflectance; it is a member of the platinum group (that includes platinum, rhodium, ruthenium, palladium, osmium, and iridium), with both a higher melting point and a lower density than platinum. It is extremely durable and looks a lot like chrome in appearance. Rhodium is the most expensive of all the precious metals, about US$6,200 per troy ounce in May of 2006, making it about six times as costly as gold (by weight).

Rhodium is used primarily as an alloying agent to harden both platinum and palladium. The rhodium alloy that is created is a major component in furnace

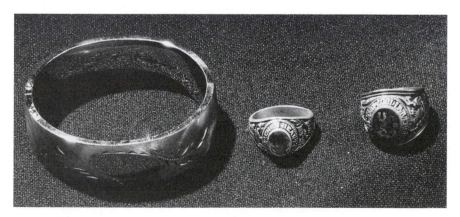

Rhodium is a favorite "outer skin" for class rings, but it lends a brilliant tarnish-free polish on bracelets and other jewelry as well. Copyright © 2007 by Anthony F. Chiffolo.

windings, glass fiber bushings, aircraft spark plugs, and other high-heat-bearing parts, as well as for spotlight reflectors and pen nibs. Plated rhodium is used for optical instruments and was a hugely popular finish for cigarette lighters, particularly those made by Ronson during the Art Deco period.

In jewelrymaking, rhodium is used for decorations and to help give white gold an extra sheen (white gold is naturally a light-grey color). Jewelrycrafters like rhodium because it is virtually tarnish proof and is practically immune from attack by acids. Jewelry buyers like a rhodium finish on white gold as it makes the metal hypoallergenic, allowing those who suffer from allergies to white gold to wear their wedding rings. Although the rhodium plating does tend to wear off after hard usage, it is easily (though not cheaply) reapplied and will last for up to 18 months without significant wear.

☞   **DID YOU KNOW?**

Rhodium has been used for honors, or to symbolize wealth, when more commonly used metals such as silver, gold, or platinum are deemed insufficient. In 1979 the *Guinness Book of World Records* gave Paul McCartney a rhodium-plated disc for being history's all-time best-selling songwriter and recording artist. Guinness has also noted items such as the world's "Most Expensive Pen" or "Most Expensive Board Game" as containing rhodium.[1]

NOTE

1. Source: "Rhodium" at http://en.wikipedia.org/wiki/Rhodium

Rings

I had to dare a little bit. Who am I kidding. I had to dare a lot.
Don't wear one ring, wear five or six.
People ask how I can play with all those rings, and I reply,
"Very well, thank you." (Entertainer and pianist extraordinaire Liberace [1919–1987])

Rings are probably the most purchased and often-worn item of jewelry in the world, and so it has been for many millennia. They have been worn on every finger and thumb (sometimes all at once), on the toes, through the nose and nipples and other body parts, on top of gloved hands, around the neck on a chain, sewn to garments, threaded through the cords of hats, and attached to legal documents. Rings have been used as body adornment and as a fashion statement; they have more importantly been used to confer high office, to apply signatures on official documents, to carry perfumes and poisons, to preserve the bones of the saints, to attack enemies, and to indicate social rank.

In Judaism, it is the exchange of rings in the wedding ceremony that seals the vows. Rings are, more than any other jewelry item, highly charged with personal significance.

As a decorative item to adorn the body, rings have been around for just about as long as metal wire could be manipulated to create a circle or coil. The ancient Egyptians were known to wear rings with scarabs attached as early as 5,000 years ago, though they were primarily used as amulets and signets to inscribe important documents. The Greeks were fond of signet rings also, often set with a gemstone in some kind of bezel, though they did create and wear much finger jewelry that was merely decorative, such as the ever-popular snake-design rings of the era of Alexander the Great (fourth century B.C.E.).

In ancient Rome, the wearing of rings was highly regulated by imperial design and social class. Early Roman rings were made of iron and worn by men; families of distinction (patricians) might own a gold ring that was worn by the head of the household to later be passed on to the male heir. By 200 B.C.E., soldiers and important political figures were awarded gold rings by the powers that be in tribute to their service of country; and in the years leading up to the Caesars, actors and other common folk in government favor were gifted rings for having pleased the crowds. With the dawn of the Roman Empire came a great influx of gold, and jewelry became more popular and cheap enough and the social lines blurred enough that at some point nearly every man in ancient Rome wore not one, not two, but as many as eight rings covering both hands. The middle finger on each hand was left bare. Many of these rings were set with gemstones or finely worked glass (see **Costume Jewelry**) or with coins bearing the likeness of the Emperor and/or his wife; often these rings were decorated with niello (see **Enameling**).

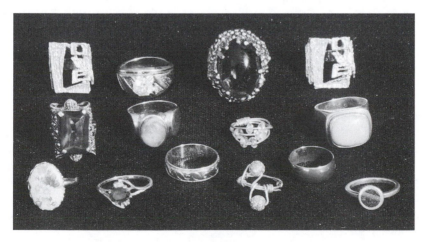

Rings for every finger (and thumb), for men and women alike! Copyright © 2007 by Anthony F. Chiffolo.

The story of Roman rings is, in short order, the birth of some of the most important jewelry trends in all of recorded history.[1] It was during the Roman period that the betrothal ring first comes on the scene. At the betrothal, the father or guardian of the bride-to-be would make a promise to a suitor, then gave his ring as a pledge to follow through on marriage at some future date. Known as the *anulus pronubis,* it was at first made of iron and did not incorporate a gemstone. In later years, it was gold, more ornate, and might even be inscribed. Another ring of this period was the *fede* (Latin for "loyal, true") ring, shaped like two clasped hands (the modern version is the claddagh). Fede rings have continued to be popular to the present day as a symbol of friendship and commitment. A third important ring of the Roman empire was the key ring, sometimes worn on a chain, but often worn on the finger. This ring is the precursor to the modern circlet that holds house, office, and car keys. A fourth important ring of this era was the poison ring, a ring with a hidden compartment that contained a bezel on a hinge to hide perfumes, relics, messages, and yes, even poison. Poison rings were popular from antiquity through the end of the Middle Ages and Renaissance. And finally, many Roman rings of the early part of the first millennium C.E. were worn as amulets (see **Amulets**).

Throughout Asia, some of the earliest archaeological discoveries, such as those at Oxus, show that rings played an important part in Asian body adornment as well. Many of the rings unearthed were seal rings with anthropomorphic or zoomorphic designs (bull, deer, lions, and panthers, for instance). There was quite a sophistication to the jeweler's methods, as not only were the rings capable of making a sign or mark in wax or ink, but the bands had been worked by hand and were either ribbed, smooth, covered in spheres, or ridged.[2] Burial research shows that most rings were worn on the left hand only, and mostly by women, in contrast to European traditions.

In Africa, Badarian artifacts dating from the fifth century B.C.E. reveal that Egypt was a ring-wearing culture. Graves containing beads, bone needles, copper pins, combs, mirrors, bracelets, ivory finger rings, and nose and ear studs have been uncovered at various Badari digs in Northern Africa.[3]

Throughout Europe from the time of the Middle Ages until the dawn of the Renaissance, rings were a popular jewelry item. The Celts and Teutonic tribes were fond of rings, especially the signet variety. Sometimes the rings contained a gemstone; more often than not, the stone, most likely a garnet, was uncut and unpolished. By the thirteenth century, rings took on a nearly ubiquitous stirrup shape (a Roman throwback), and gems were generally cabochon cut.[4] In the late fifteenth century, a new style introduced a bezel in the shape of a quatrefoil, an extremely popular design throughout the Renaissance era.[5] For the next several hundred years, rings took on a lighter look, with less attention given to large stones and more attention given to smaller and more colorful gems that created floral-like patterns.[6]

There were innovations, however. The practice of passing out mourning rings at funerals came about in the seventeenth century and continued well until the late nineteenth century. For men and well-paying royalty, scientific rings fitted with watch mechanisms or mathematical/astronomical instruments, reflecting the inventions of the day, were also popular. The discovery of diamonds in South Africa in the nineteenth century changed how rings were made and stones were cut, as well as how jewelry was worn and who could afford it.

Today, finger rings are worn by nearly everyone, including infants and young children, and they are made from every conceivable element available to humankind, from plastic to gemstone, from animal parts to sea creatures, from old silver spoons to recycled jewelry bits, from cloth to the hardest steel. They often carry social significance, such as wedding rings, or celebrate a rite of passage, such as school rings; they are used as an expression of love and friendship or by mothers to celebrate the birth of their children; worn as a pendant around the neck, they may honor a lost love or loved one; they are used by fraternal groups and sororities to indicate membership and by second- and third-generation immigrants to honor their native country. With body jewelry, the wearing of nose rings, nipple rings, genital rings, navel rings, eyebrow rings, and multiple earrings is meant to convey independence, noncompliance with traditional mores and values, sexual self-identity, classical beauty, and native or ethnic identification.

☞ DID YOU KNOW?

The wearing of rings on the toes is as old as the hills, they say. Certainly this is true in India, where it is a symbol of being married. Known as *bichiya,* toe rings are usually ornately fashioned of silver (it is considered improper that they be made of gold) and worn in pairs on the second toe of both feet. In other cultures, the wearing of toe rings is relatively new. At first considered by the jewelry industry to be a passing fad, they are now a fashion staple, with entire stores featuring only toe rings opening in U.S. malls and on the Internet. Toe rings are available in every size, shape, and material that one could ever imagine. They are finding a particular audience with brides as adornment for their wedding day.

NOTES

1. For a detailed look at this history, see Anita Mason and Diane Packer, "Rings," *An Illustrated Dictionary of Jewellery,* 310ff.

2. See "Ancient Chinese Jewelry" at http://www.chinatownconnection.com/ancient-chinese-jewelry.htm

3. See "Pre-history Africa & the Badarian Culture" at http://www.homestead.com/wysinger/badarians.html

4. A cabochon cut is one with a smooth rounded top surface. It is the oldest style of stone cutting and was the only style of cutting stones until lapidary advancements in the late Middle Ages.

5. A quatrefoil shape is four overlapping circles, somewhat like a four-leaf clover.

6. These rings were known by the name *Giardinetti,* after their miniature garden-like settings.

Sea and Shore

All art is autobiographical; the pearl is the oyster's autobiography. (Italian filmmaker and director Federico Fellini [1920–1993])

The ocean and its shores were natural habitats for the first jewelrycrafters of history to find the materials to create their wares. For thousands and thousands of years, native gatherers and divers have employed the best that the tides of seas, rivers, and lakes washed ashore or hid in their depths for jewelry production.[1] Today, despite many advancements in technology, for the challenges of an eroding landscape, and overfarming and overfishing, many of the same techniques and tools that have been in place for millennia are still used to bring us some of the finest "natural" jewelry of fashion and design. In addition to the conch shell, famous as the material of cameos (see **Cameos**), many other types of sea creatures and their body parts have been made into jewelry, some in small shapes (puka shell), some in larger (cowries), some plucked off the shore itself (shark's teeth), others the result of careful diving (paua).[2] All have made their way, despite incredible odds but in all their finery, to jewelry stores and craft shows around the world. Some of the most desired jewelry of both sea and shore include the following.

ABALONE

Abalone (*Haliotidae*, fam. *haliotis*) is a gastropod found primarily in the Pacific Ocean (some are found in South African waters), of the same family as clams, oysters, and mussels. They are prized for their muscle tissue, which is a delicacy in many parts of the world. The abalone used in jewelrymaking is the iridescent inner-shell lining made of alternating layers of calcium carbonate and conchiolin.

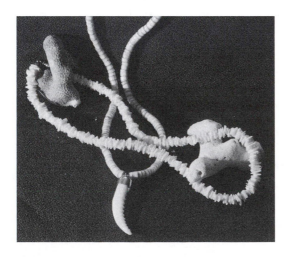

Puka shell necklaces, still popular today, drape portions of coral thousands of years old, torn from the reef by a raging sea. Copyright © 2007 by Anthony F. Chiffolo.

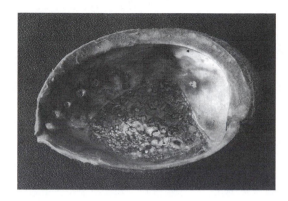

Rainbow-colored nacre from an abalone mollusk. Copyright © 2007 by Anthony F. Chiffolo.

Though it is often confused with mother-of-pearl, which is an oyster product, abalone is extensively employed in the creations of Native American peoples, who acclaim its beautiful luster and the way that it complements and sets off both silver and turquoise. In the Japanese market the pearls from abalone are called *Awabi*.

CORAL

Perhaps one of the oldest substances in nature to be used in jewelry (some say for as long as 25,000 years), gemstone corals are the skeletal deposits of the living gastrovascular marine organism coral polyps (*Actiniaria*, fam. *cnidaria*). In their natural environment, they band together to form a plant-like presence, allowing the entire colony of polyps to be fed by nutrients in the water surrounding them. Most coral is from the Mediterranean Sea or the Pacific; the jewelers of Hawaii for instance have a very strong presence in the coral jewelry market.

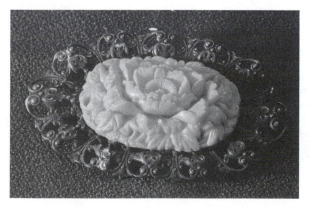

Victorian cloak pin made of silver and red coral. Copyright © 2007 by Anthony F. Chiffolo.

Coral jewelry is often red, pink, black, and, most recently, gold.[3] It was a favorite gem of the Victorian era, and it has a long history of religious significance. Tibetan lamas use coral rosaries and coral is one of the seven treasures listed in Buddhist writings. Coral necklaces, rings, and bracelets were thought to be a powerful talisman against evil spirits, bleeding, and hurricanes.

MOTHER-OF-PEARL

Mother-of-pearl is the interior shell coating of mollusks such as mussels and oysters. As a response to an irritant inside their shells, these mollusks deposit layers of calcium carbonate in a crystallized form, which is held together by a kind of glue-like compound called *conchiolin*. The combination of these elements results in what is called nacre, more commonly known as mother-of-pearl.

In ancient Egypt, mother-of-pearl was used as a decoration as long ago as 4000 B.C.E. It has since been used as inlay on furniture and guitars and on knife handles, floors, sinks, shirt buttons, watch dials, and the keys of musical instruments, such as trumpets and saxophones.

PEARLS

The only birthstone/gemstone that is not a stone, pearls are one of the most beautiful creations of nature. They are formed inside the shells of certain mollusks, such as mussels, abalone, and oysters. Treasured by all ancient civilizations,

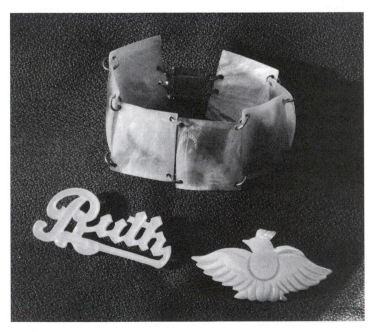

Mother-of-pearl bracelet and pins, early twentieth century. Copyright © 2007 by Anthony F. Chiffolo.

pearls are mentioned in the Bible and the Koran and figure prominently in ancient Hindu and Buddhist writings as well. The Romans in classical times were especially fond of pearls, and upper-crust Roman women of the day had pearls sewn onto their chaises and their clothing. Pearls are found in nearly every part of the world, in oyster beds of the Persian Gulf; along the coasts of India, Sri Lanka, Japan (*Biwa*), and Arabia; off the shores of Central and South America and among the islands of the Caribbean; among the countries of the South Seas and along the coast of California; and in freshwater beds of the Ohio, Mississippi, and Tennessee rivers. Until recently, most pearls were recovered through diving; in recent years, pearls have been farmed in shallow waters and are taken from their habitat more easily.

Because of their rarity and beauty, pearls were most often available only to the wealthy. However, the market changed greatly in the late nineteenth and early twentieth centuries thanks to the work and ingenuity of the Japanese inventors Tokichi Nishikawa (1874–1909), Tatsuhei Mise (1880–1924), and Kokichi Mikimoto (1858–1954). These gentlemen created a patented method of introducing foreign matter into an oyster and "culturing" the tissue to form a pearl sack; the sack then would secrete nacre (see above) to coat the nucleus of the sack, helping nature to do its work, resulting in the birth of a pearl. Today, Mikimoto produces some of the finest and most affordable pearls in the jewelry business, thanks to brilliant marketing, astute business acumen, and a great labor force.

Pearls come in eight basic shapes: round, semiround, button, drop, pear, oval, baroque (including *keshi*), and ringed. They are used in all kinds of jewelry but because of their size and luster are most often found strung as necklaces. In general, cultivated pearls are less expensive than natural pearls (thanks to Messrs. Mikimoto et al.); imitation pearls made of wax, coated glass, coral, conch, or

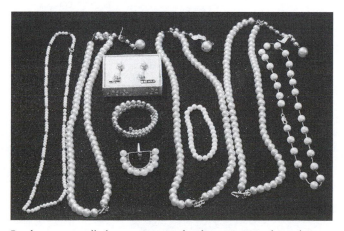

Pearls come in all shapes, sizes, and color variations, but whatever the format, they speak of elegance. Copyright © 2007 by Anthony F. Chiffolo.

mother-of-pearl are generally cheap, as the market goes.[4] The only way to assure that one owns a strand of genuine pearls is through an X-ray process.

In modern times, necklaces made of pearls have attained a unique linguistic status with vocabulary all their own "invented" to describe proportion and length. A choker is a pearl necklace that is 14"–16" long; a princess is 18" long; a matinee necklace is 22"–23" long; an opera length necklace is 30"–35" in length; and a rope is anything over 40".

Perhaps the most popular of high-quality imitation pearls, and certainly one of the most successful in terms of marketing appeal, have been those from Mallorca (sometimes spelled Majorca), Spain. Mallorcan pearls have been made for the last one hundred years or so by a process in which a dull glass nucleus is produced and covered with mother-of-pearl and fish scales, which is then lacquered and dry-heated on a rotating wheel to obtain uniformity. Mallorca now produces 50 million artificial pearls yearly. They won't say exactly how their successful coating formula is made (it is a closely guarded secret), but they do allow that it "involves a solution from the scales of a million fish."[5]

SCRIMSHAW

Scrimshaw is the art of etching a picture onto whale bone, ivory, shark's teeth, or some other durable substance, then highlighting the design in black. It is the hobby and craft of whalers who often have many long hours away from shore. Though no one knows just when it became popular, in the United States there is evidence going back at least to pre-Revolutionary times. In the past 40 years there has been a resurgence of interest in the craft, thanks in great part to President John F. Kennedy (1917–1963), who was an avid collector.

The tools of the scrimshander are knives, needles, dental picks, awls, and the like. Industrial producers use special scribes made of tungsten carbide, or high-

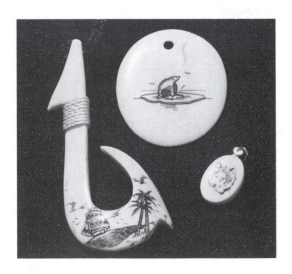

Scrimshaw, the carving and etching of ivory, was a favorite pasttime of sailors. Copyright © 2007 by Anthony F. Chiffolo.

speed drills, or lasers. The pieces are then set in silver, gold, brass, or some other casing or are strung on a chain, leather, silk, or another type of cord for wearing.

Today, with the prohibitions against using whalebone and ivory, scrimshaw is most often crafted from resin; recycled piano keys; fossilized ivory (such as wooly mammoth); tagua nut (*Phytelephas macrocarpa palmae*) or palm/vegetable ivory; antler and horn of deer, moose, wild boar, caribou, or elk; and hippopotamus teeth.

SEA GLASS

Sea glass (or beach glass) is part of the "gathered-along-the-shore" subcategory of jewelrymaking materials, but it is quite a popular one. It all begins with bottles that have been tossed into the ocean long before (and unfortunately, some after) recycling became the norm. As the ocean churned, the bottles broke into small pieces and eventually ended up at the shore, all sharp edges worn down and now with a frosted appearance. Some say it's nature's way of actuating her own "no deposit-no return" policy!

Many crafters along the coastlines collect and trade sea glass and have made the pieces into some fascinating examples of cottage-industry jewelry using gold and silver wire findings. With the advent of plastic, sea glass is getting more difficult to find, so it's always a treasure when one sees a piece that the waves have left behind.

TORTOISESHELL

Tortoiseshell is the yellowish-reddish-brown grained hard-plate shell from the back of the tortoise. It was very popular in jewelrymaking during the Victorian period (among others) and often used for women's toilette accessories, such as hair combs and dresser sets. Like ivory, tortoiseshell is a strictly regulated commodity and can no longer be used in jewelrycrafting. And like amber and horn, it is greatly forged, so older, authentic pieces are much prized. Most tortoiseshell

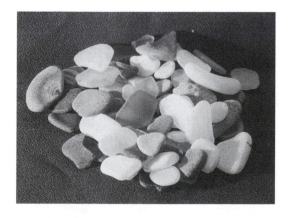

A child's collection of sea glass, its rough edges smoothed by the tides. Copyright © 2007 by Anthony F. Chiffolo.

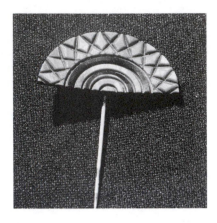

A carved tortoiseshell hat/stick pin, circa 1910. Copyright © 2007 by Anthony F. Chiffolo.

on the market today is plastic or Tortoisene, a product of the Sadler Brothers Company of South Attleboro, MA.

☞ DID YOU KNOW?

In modern times, when nearly any valuable item can be forged, it should be no surprise that as readily as it occurs in nature, mother-of-pearl is often produced in imitation. Pyralin, a type of plasticized celluloid that masquerades as mother-of-pearl on the keys of many musical instruments, is one of several m.o.p. unnatural substitutes, earning it the name among musicians of "mother-of-toilet seat"!

NOTES

1. It was recently discovered that early humans strung together mollusk shells to make jewelry as early as 75,000 years ago. This jewelry discovery was a major find, hinting that our earliest ancestors had much more advanced concepts of symbolism and language than had been previously realized. See Muir, Hazel, "Ancient shell jewelry hints at language," NewScientist.com news service, April 16, 2004, http:www.newscientist.com/article.ns?id=dn4892

2. Jewelry that is based on sea life, sea shells, or rocks is sometimes referred to in the trade as *rocaille* (from rococo).

3. Gold coral was discovered in 1971 in the Hawaiian waters; due to both federal and state laws, it can only be harvested at a rate of about 3 percent per year. It is extremely rare and has a special characteristic called *chatoyance*, a kind of "cat's eye" inner movement that shows up under certain lights.

4. Pearls farmed in freshwater are known as cultured freshwater pearls, or CFW.

5. See "I'll Never Tell: Mallorca Pearl Story" at http://illnevertelljewelry.com/generic19.html

Settings

The shape of a stone matters most when buying a ring;
but it's *the setting* that sets the tone for a gem of beauty. (Memory Lane Antiques)

A setting is the way by which a jeweler or craftsperson secures a stone in a piece of jewelry; it is also a crucial factor in presenting a gemstone's clarity, color, and cut. There are many types of settings; some have been used for hundreds of years, while others are newly invented. A few of the most common settings seen today are:

Arcade setting: The arcade setting (sometimes called a coronet or châton setting) features a stone that is secured by a series of metal claws set around a metal ring.

Bezel setting: A bezel setting places the stone inside a metal band that is cut to fit precisely around its edge. It is one of the oldest-known settings and has been preferred by jewelers for centuries due to its ability to protect both the middle and the base of a gemstone from chips and scratches. Bezel settings are perfect for fragile stones, such as opals, and are often used in men's jewelry to highlight height, dimension, and the "modern look."

Channel setting: Used primarily for round or baguette-shaped gemstones, a channel setting places the jewels inside a metal channel with a slight rim that runs along the edges. The rim and the cut of the stone help to keep it in place. The modern tennis bracelet (see **Bracelets**) and eternity bands are good examples of pieces that have been channel set. A variation on this theme is the bar setting, with each stone docked in its own channel but further separated by two thin metal bars for an intricate and innovative design.

Claw setting: One of the most frequently used settings of the nineteenth century, the claw setting employs a series of four to six metal prongs (claws) to grip the stone just above the girdle around its edges, and with no metal beneath (an open setting). This method allows light under the stone and is used to greatest effect with faceted, transparent gems; it is therefore a frequent choice for solitaire engagement rings and in bridal rings, as well as in earrings, necklaces, and bracelets. Also known as a prong setting, it is fairly simple and inexpensive to create. Prong settings with six claws are known as a Tiffany setting, as Tiffany & Company introduced the style in 1886; it remains the most popular ring setting of the twentieth and twenty-first centuries.

Closed setting: A closed setting (as opposed to an open setting [see above]) is one in which the metal has not been cut away beneath the stone. Since light is not shining through, closed settings are often used for doublets or triplets or in cases where foil is used as a reflector at the base of the gem.

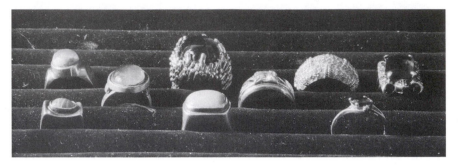

A ring's setting is what truly "sets" one style apart from another. Copyright © 2007 by Anthony F. Chiffolo.

Collet setting: A collet setting is one of the oldest recorded methods of setting stones. It features a round metal band that completely encircles the gemstone; one edge of the band is crimped over the stone and another is soldered to the shank of the ring or the base metal of the jewelry object to hold it securely. Prior to the fourteenth century C.E., some collets had prongs to provide more support for the stone.

Cut-down setting: In a cut-down setting, the metal used to secure the stone is worked around its edge, and then reinforced with metal ridges for further strength and holding power.

Gipsy setting: A recessed setting whereby the stone is sunk into the base metal, "the gipsy" (or flush setting) is a style developed in the late 1800s. It is sometimes referred to as a "star setting" due to the star-like patterns that are often engraved around the stone.

Millegrain setting: In this very unique setting, the stone is secured in place by small grains of metal or a band that has been decorated with tiny metal beads.

Pavé setting: Pavé set stones are gems (often diamonds) that are set very close together, showing no metal between them.

Tension Setting: In this setting, pressure is used to make the gemstone appear as if it's floating between the opposite open ends of a metal mounting. Tension settings are often created in platinum for an elegant look.

☞ DID YOU KNOW

Speaking of settings, here's some interesting trivia about gemstones and their *stately* settings:

- Named (appropriately enough) "The Gem State," Idaho produces 72 types of precious and semiprecious stones, many of which are unique to Idaho!
- The state gem of Arkansas is the diamond. It was officially adopted as such in 1967 by the General Assembly. Arkansas is the sole diamond-producing site located in the United States.

- Alaska's state gem is jade. There are large deposits of jade in the state, including an entire mountain of it on the Seward Peninsula. Jade is also the official state gem of Wyoming.

- It seems as though agates reign supreme as state gems. Six U.S. states list some form of agate as their official gemstone, more than any other gem: Kentucky, Louisiana, Minnesota, Montana, Nebraska, and South Dakota. And Arizona lists the fire agate as its official state mineral!

- Wherever there's water, it's likely to be inhabited by some form of pearl-producing mollusk. Pearls are found in significant quantities in the waters of California, Delaware, Florida, Hawaii, Illinois, Indiana, Iowa, Kentucky, Maine, Maryland, Mississippi, Missouri, Nebraska, New Jersey, New York, Tennessee, Texas, Vermont, Washington, and Wisconsin.

- Some states have official gemstones unique to their setting, like Hawaii (black coral) or Florida (moonstone); some have official gemstones that one might have suspected, like New Mexico and Arizona (turquoise) or Washington (petrified wood); for others, one has to dig a bit deeper (no pun intended), as in the case of Colorado, which chose aquamarine because some of the finest samples come from that state; or Maine, which chose tourmaline, presumably for the same reason.

- One U.S. state not only has an official gemstone (blue topaz) but has an official gemstone cut to go with it. Yes, the House of Representatives of the State of Texas (the State Senate concurring) passed a resolution in 1977 claiming the Lone Star Cut, a unique shaping of stones into a five-point star (the symbol of Texas), as its own. The resolution even went so far as to give specific dimensions and instructions on how to make the cut, including the number of facets and the specified angle (in degrees) to make the grade.[1]

To date, no state has an official gemstone setting.

NOTE

1. See "Texas Symbols, Gemstone Cut: Lonestar Cut" at http://www.shgresources. com/tx/symbols/gemstonecut

Silver

Periodic table symbol: Ag

Atomic Number: 47

Origin of name: from the Anglo-Saxon word *seolfor*; periodic table symbol from the Latin, *argentum*

Important historical background information: known by ancient cultures since before the fourth millennium B.C.E.

Geographical location of element: now found chiefly in Mexico,[1] Canada, the United States, Peru, and Australia; often found in ores such as argentine, cerargyrite and stephanite, or as a by-product of lead, zinc, gold, and copper ores

Silver is an extremely ductile, malleable transition and precious metal that is soft and white in appearance. It has the highest thermal conductivity, the highest optical reflectivity, and the lowest contact resistance of any metal. These characteristics make it ideal for its primary usages, which include coinage, jewelry, tableware, dentistry and medicine, photography, and mirrors. Silver is one of just eight precious metals used for coinage. In trading or commerce, silver is measured in Troy ounces (1 pound = 14.58 Troy ounces).

Silver has been in use for thousands of years, and its precious qualities were well known to many ancient civilizations. The Egyptians were fond of silver (though it was second to gold), and the Greeks revered it; the Chinese were said to have refined silver as early as 2500 B.C.E.; it was one of the major trading commodities of the Chaldeans, and is mentioned in the Bible in the Book of Genesis, where Joseph is called a man "rich in silver . . . ."

In the pre–Common Era, most silver originated in the Anatolia region of Turkey until a large deposit was discovered in the Laurium mines near Athens on the mainland of Greece. From that time forward, and for nearly a thousand years (ending around the first century C.E.), most of the world's silver came from Greece. As the ancient Greek empire began to crumble, the Carthaginians were just beginning their exploitation of Spanish silver mines. These mines were the source for most silver in global trade from about the first century C.E. to the time of the Moorish invasion in the eighth century, after which alternative sources of silver were uncovered in Germany, Austria-Hungary, and elsewhere in Eastern Europe.

When the Spanish arrived in the Americas in the late fifteenth century C.E., they found three incredible silver sources: in the Potosí district of Bolivia, the Cerro de Pasco district of Peru, and the Aztec communities of Mexico. For more than 300 years, these three communities accounted for 85 percent of the world's production of silver (with the remaining 15 percent contributed by Germany, Hungary, Russia [and some other European countries], Chile, and Japan.) The discovery of the Comstock Lode in Virginia City, Nevada, in 1859 put the United States on the map as one of the world's major contributors to the silver market. This windfall and the mania it caused made prospecting for silver a full-time occupation for many, subsequently allowing for a concentrated effort at improving mining techniques through innovation and technology. Steam-assisted drilling, mine de-watering, fuming, and haulage improvements helped to create a silver industry. One might say that with the discovery of the precious metal at Comstock, the modern silver market was born.

Silver has had a great influence on history; yet in the spiritual world, it has a longstanding presence and exalted status as well. Since ancient times, silver has been associated with the moon, and it was thought that lunar influences were

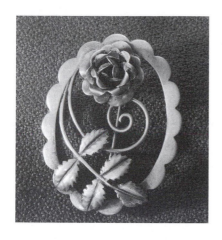

An elegant sterling pin circa 1930 in the style of master craftsman Georg Jensen. Copyright © 2007 by Anthony F. Chiffolo.

manifested in silver (hence the song, "By the Light of the Silvery Moon . . . "). The Egyptians connected it to Isis, and the Greeks to Artemis: Thus all things silver carried the properties of creativity, flexibility, and intuitive and intelligent emotion. In alchemy, silver was one of the seven sacred metals, and in the chakra system of the body's sacred energy centers, it is associated with the sixth chakra, known as the "third-eye," the center of self-reflection and analysis. The ancient Vedas believed that silver was a liver and spleen detoxifier.[2] In Islamic alchemy, silver was considered one of the seven sacred bodies.

Silver is such a fine metal that its workings have a terminology all their own. Crafters who work with the metal are called "silversmiths"; later, many of these same persons were called "jewelers," reflecting the high standard accorded their handiwork. Silver can be shaped by hammering, spinning, or drawing using wooden hammers, styli, dies, punches, presses, and the like. It is often decorated through etching, chasing, embossing, and engraving; there is even a process known as *repoussé*, by which a piece is hammered in relief from the inside out.[3]

In the twentieth century, the masters of silver jewelrycrafting can easily be divided into three groups: the Mexican school, headed up by William Spratling (1900–1967) (see **Mexican Silver Jewelry**); the Scandinavian school, exemplified by the work of Georg Jensen (1866–1935); and the Native American craftspeople of the U.S. Southwest (see **Native American Jewelry**).

Silver jewelry remains a cornerstone of the fine jewelry and costume jewelry markets. One of its main drawbacks, of course, is its tendency to tarnish. Tarnishing is caused by some of the impurities of silver that react to oxygen in the air. But a little silver polish and elbow grease can take care of nearly any silver problem, keeping silver looking its best and a step ahead of other pretenders to the jewelry throne.

☞ DID YOU KNOW?

- Silver can be hammered into sheets so thin that it would take 100,000 of them to stack an inch high.

- No word in the English language rhymes with "silver."
- Although the name Argentina means "land of silver," there is actually very little silver there.
- Both "Ferris wheel" and "cartwheel" are nicknames for silver dollars made in the United States.
- Silver is 1 of 10 of the 105 elements of the periodic table that were discovered and in use in prehistoric times (the others are lead, gold, iron, copper, zinc, tin, sulfur, carbon, and mercury).
- The U.S. government keeps its supply of silver at the U.S. Military Academy at West Point, New York.
- The Lone Ranger's horse was originally named "Dusty" (not "Silver," as in the television versions).

NOTES

1. Mexico is the world's largest silver producer, accounting for about 15 percent of all silver produced worldwide (see "Silver" at http://en.wikipedia.org/wiki/Silver).

2. See "A History of Silver: A Brief Esoteric Overview of Silver Use" at http://www.silvermedicine.org/history.html

3. *Repoussage* is actually the correct term for this technique. The most famous of repoussé pieces is undoubtedly the Statue of Liberty, which was formed in copper sections, then assembled using wooden structures to help shape the final product.

Silver Hallmarks

Definition: 1a: an official mark stamped on gold and silver articles in England to attest their purity; b: a mark or device placed or stamped on an article of trade to indicate origin, purity, or genuineness; *Etymology:* Goldsmiths' Hall, London, England, where gold and silver articles were assayed and stamped. (Merriam-Webster OnLine)

If one is lucky enough to own a piece of fine jewelry, one might notice that it has a stamp on it; if it is gold, there might be a karat mark (10k, 14k, 18k); if it is silver, it may have a numerical indication of the amount of silver content (.925, for instance), along with other marks that tell a story about when and where and by whom it was made. These marks, known as hallmarks,[1] can play a very important part in valuing a piece and in understanding its origins.

Nearly every country that has produced or is producing silver jewelry has its own hallmarking system. Some English and French hallmarks date back to the 1300s C.E. Other countries, like the United States, have been marking silver for just a little over 200 years. The intent of hallmarking was to legislate authenticity and purity of product; but for the uninitiated, hallmarks can be quite confusing and, unless "decoded" by a knowledgeable silver afficionado, totally unhelpful.

The word hallmark is derived from London Goldsmith's Hall of the Worship-ful Company of Goldsmiths, a guild of artisans, many with royal connections, who sought to protect the quality of their work and fend off impure imitations and forgeries by marking their creations with a series of symbols unique to their studio and profession. In England, this often presented itself in a pattern of five markings on each piece; the order of each symbol differs according to the maker, but the meaning is the same, regardless of placement in the series. A fine piece of English silver will have a lion passant (a heraldic term for "walking on all fours") facing left (nearly always): This is the British standard for sterling, or .925 of 1000 percent silver. A second marking is the city symbol: A crowned leopard's head indicates a London piece; three castles stands for Exeter or Newcastle, de-pending on the arrangement of castles; an anchor, Birmingham. A third marking (found on silver between 1785 and 1890) has an effigy of the reigning mon-arch, which is a duty mark, indicating that the proper tax was paid on the piece. A fourth marking—a letter of the alphabet, either in capitals or in lower case, and often in varying type fonts—is a date mark, noting the year of fabrication. The final marking is the maker's mark, using the initials of the maker's given name and surname. Sometimes a piece will have two initials on top of a second set to demonstrate that a partnership or firm was involved in the creation of the piece.

The standard hallmarks for other parts of the (current and former) British empire include the thistle (Edinburgh), the lion rampant (walking on two legs: Glasgow), and the harp (Dublin).

Other European countries that produce goods in silver have their own marks and purity standards. For instance, the silver standard for Austrian pieces is .835 (of 1000 percent), usually with a W (for Vienna); Danish silver is marked .830, frequently coupled with a three-towered Copenhagen assay mark; Russian silver is marked "84" or "13" and often has a crowned monarch, representing St. Peter (of St. Petersburg). Asian, African, and Middle Eastern countries, such as Egypt (the cat), Iran, Turkey, the People's Republic of China, and Japan have silver standards ranging from .800 to .970, each with accompanying country or city identifica-tion marks. The silver standard in Mexico today is .925 (as it is in Peru and other silver-producing Latin-American countries), although some pieces may be marked .875 or .980 or have a "spread eagle" mark as a guarantee of purity.

Silver made in the United States is often stamped ".925 Sterling," especially pieces made after 1906. Earlier pieces may say ".900," an indication that they are coin silver (melted silver coins reconstituted as a spoon or pin, for instance). Today, the rule of thumb on new pieces is that if it does not say "sterling," then it isn't. U.S. coin silver usually has the full name of the maker on the obverse.

PSEUDO-HALLMARKS

Probably because of the association of British sterling with quality, silvermakers in the United States, in an attempt to emulate English finery, added their own makers' marks to their products. Because U.S. silver was not

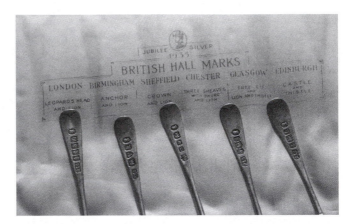

British hallmarks from five English cities, each a proud stamp designating quality of production. Copyright © 2007 by Anthony F. Chiffolo.

under regulation in the same way as that of other countries, the symbols used by U.S. silver manufacturers often intentionally imitated British hallmarks (some would claim deceptively so), though in effect they were nothing more than trademarks and often were in code. These marks on U.S. sterling, coin, and silverplated items, usually found in conjunction with the retailer's name, are referred to as pseudohallmarks, as they are not hallmarks per se; however, these markings do help to identify a piece and often the year in which it was made. For example, Gorham Silver Company of Providence, RI, used the symbol of a lion facing right, followed by a Gothic letter "G," concluding with an anchor. Quite often a smaller emblem was added somewhere else on the piece (a hatchet, a star, a heart) to indicate the year.

☞ DID YOU KNOW?

There's a lot to look for and consider when buying silver jewelry. Here are some other terms one might run across on U.S. pieces:

Alaska silver: In the late nineteenth and early twentieth centuries, nickel silverwares were sold under a variety of names, including Alaska Silver, Brazil Silver, Nevada Silver, Aluminum Silver, Japanese Silver, Indian Silver, Burmaroid, Argentine, and other names. Basically, they are the same as silverplated items prior to the plating process. They were touted as being a superior alternative to plated wares because they never "wore through."

Alpaca: a silver substitute alloy consisting of 55 percent copper, 20 percent nickel, 20 percent zinc, and 5 percent tin.

Base metal: Any combination of alloys of nonprecious metals of comparatively low value to which a coating or plating of silver is usually applied. Also known as pot metal or white metal.

Britannia metal: A composition of tin, copper, and antimony.

Commercial silver: A term applied to commercial grade silver, which is 99.9 percent pure.

Electroplating: The use of electricity to deposit a thin layer of precious metal on the base metal of a silver item. Invented by Luigi V. Brugnatelli (1761–1818) in 1805.

E. P. N. S.: Electroplated nickel silver. Other variations are E.P.C. (on copper), E. P. B. M. (on base metal), and E. P. W. M. (on white metal).

Filigree: A design made with thin wire intricately interlaced or bent into rosettes, spirals, or vines. The wire is typically gold or silver and may be plain, twisted, or plaited.

German silver: A composition of 10 percent nickel, 50 percent copper, and 40 percent zinc. It was first made in Germany in the early nineteenth century in imitation of the much older Chinese alloy known as paktong. German silver contains no silver.

Nickel silver: An alloy composed of 65 percent copper, 28 percent nickel, and 17 percent zinc. It does not contain any silver.

Patented (followed by a year date): This is the year in which the patent for a particular silver item or pattern was granted. It should be noted, however, that this is not the same as the year in which the piece was actually made. For instance, Rogers Bros. silverplate often carries the patent year 1847, although millions of these same pieces were made in the twentieth century.

Plate: An English term for sterling. Not to be confused with silverplate, which is entirely different.

Sheffield plate: Originally made by bonding sheet silver to copper, then rolling and manufacturing the bonded metals, Sheffield pieces sometimes are more expensive than sterling itself. Not to be confused with the city of Sheffield in England, which produces fine sterling.

Silver-on-copper: Just what it says.

Silverplated (or double-, triple-, or quadruple-plated): Silverplate is made by electroplating fine silver onto a base metal alloy, usually nickel or Britannia metal, or sometimes brass or copper. Silverplate is measured in microns and can vary greatly from one piece to the next. Top quality silverplating may contain two or three times the silver thickness of less expensive plating.

Vermeil: a substantial amount of real gold that has been chemically bonded to sterling silver. The finish looks so much like solid gold that, except for the price, it may be difficult to tell the difference.[2]

NOTES

1. Gold and platinum jewelry pieces often show hallmarks, especially those made in England; many of the same rules apply as with silver hallmarking, though metal quantity and quality will vary. Antique English pewter is also sometimes hallmarked.

2. Source: "Sterling Silver Terms" at http:www.jwmercantile.com/infosilver.html; "Jewelry Glossary of Semiprecious stone and Silver Terms" at http:www.zulumoon.

com/glossary/S-glossary.htm; "Silver Glossary, Terms and Definitions" at http://www.
abesilverman.com/Silver_Glossary_Terms_Definitions.html; and "Antiques and Collectibles
Questions and Answers" at www.mygrannysatticantiques.com/html/antique_and_
collectible_questi.html

Souvenir Jewelry

"Souvenir": a token of remembrance; a memento, from the Latin, "to
come to mind." (*The American Heritage Dictionary of the English Language,
Fourth Edition*)

Though not a universally accepted term, souvenir jewelry are pieces that were collected during one's travels and are usually "place-specific," often with the name of
the locale inscribed somewhere on the item. Souvenir pieces usually incorporate
a location's theme or some portion of its most memorable history: Gold nuggets
for those who visited California after the Gold Rush of 1849 or Murano glass
items for those who traveled to Venice are typical examples. Much souvenir jewelry is made specifically for the tourist market.

Although travelers have undoubtedly regaled their families and friends
with treasures from their journeys since before the beginning of recorded history, the term "souvenir jewelry" seems to have originated with participants on
the Grand Tour, a European travel itinerary, particularly for the wealthy and
upper class. It was seen as a rite-of-passage, whereby the individual would visit
all the important historical and architectural sites of Europe as a kind of aesthetic finishing school course. It was popular between 1660 and 1820. Many
who visited Italy, for instance, had their first look at cameos from Pompeii and
neighboring southern-Italian towns. The U.S. market for cameos in the nineteenth century was created by tourists from the United States returning home
with these beautiful handcrafted souvenirs. Clearly, few enterprising merchants
at any tourist destination would miss the opportunity to sell a remembrance to
visitors, and jewelry items themselves were among the most popular, not only
for their easy portability but often for their striking beauty. In jewelrycrafting
since 1750, perhaps some of the best-known and most representative samples of
souvenir jewelry are:

> *Mosaic jewelry:* Often called *pietra dura* ("hard rock"), mosaic jewelry found
> its most popular moment soon after the excavations of Pompeii and
> Herculaneum in the eighteenth century C.E. Pins constructed of small
> pieces of malachite, lapis lazuli, coral, opal, and other stones, set against
> a black background, usually of marble, were highly prized collectibles for
> those who traveled to southern Italy in the nineteenth century. Referred

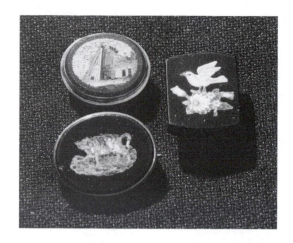

Mosaic jewelry, like these Victorian pieces, takes a steady hand to work small bits of stone; but the finished product makes a beautifully smooth presentation. Copyright © 2007 by Anthony F. Chiffolo.

to as archaeological jewelry, many pieces had a botanical theme and were so skillfully crafted that they were indeed miniature works of art. (Other mosaic works were created out of colored glass in place of stone and are equally beautiful.) High-end mosaic work was often framed in gold, pinchbeck, or sterling; pieces of lesser quality were set in brass or gold-filled mountings. Mosaic jewelry reached its zenith in popularity in early- to mid-Victorian England, although pietra dura is still a popular souvenir for anyone visiting Ravenna, Pompeii, or southern Italian cities today.

Vatican souvenir jewelry: One of the most sacred places on earth for Roman Catholic Christians, the Vatican manufactures and sells tens of millions of dollars worth of jewelry each year. From rosaries to medals of the saints, crosses, earrings, rings, pins, bracelets, and key rings, the shops in Vatican City and in Rome are full to the brim with souvenir jewelry of every description made of every conceivable material, including precious metals and rare gemstones. The majority of items sold could be broadly categorized as "coin jewelry" (see **Coin Jewelry**), since most of the souvenir jewelry from the Vatican (besides crosses) are medals that depict the saints and popes of the Church.

World's Fair jewelry: Beginning with the Grand Tour and the Philadelphia Exposition of 1876, and continuing to the present day, jewelry commemorating the World's Fairs was not only a favorite during the years the fairs ran, but is a popular collectible among hobbyists today. Each fair had a unique architectural structure or historical moment to celebrate, and these buildings and important events were reproduced on all kinds of jewelry as souvenirs for the millions who visited. For instance, if one were in Chicago in 1893, Gorham sterling rings recalling the 400th anniversary of Columbus' expedition to the Americas were on sale. Or had one visited the 1901 Pan American exhibition in Buffalo, New York, it would have been a treat to buy the very popular match safe (see **Necessaries**) and cigar cutter with the Manufactures and Liberal Arts Building emblazoned on its reverse side. At the 1904 World's Fair in St. Louis, visitors could purchase an Art Nouveau–style sterling and brass pin featuring the Palace of the

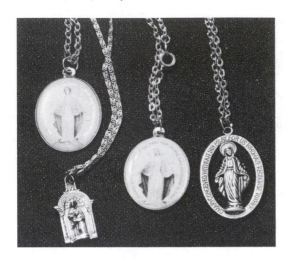

Vatican pendants, worn by the faithful, are often used as a talismans, as well as outward signs of religious devotion. Copyright © 2007 by Anthony F. Chiffolo.

Arts, or a watch fob commemorating the one-hundredth anniversary of the Louisiana Purchase. Travelers to the 1939 World's Fair in New York City would find for sale an adjustable ring, charm, or tie-tack with the Trylon and Perisphere emblazoned on them. At the fair of 1964, once again in New York (Queens), animated gemstone watches, "spinner" charm bracelets, and picture lockets were among the available must-have jewelry items; souvenir pendants featuring the pavilions of various countries were plentiful at Expo '67 in Montreal. Truly there has been no end to the marketing savvy of fair promoters. (The same could probably be said of Olympic Games promoters). They knew that no one wants to go home from such an important event empty-handed, and today, millions of World's Fair collectibles collected by past generations can be found in antique stores, attics, and pawn shops and on eBay.

There are many other kinds of "souvenir jewelry" being sold today. What is available and called souvenir, tourist, or local handicraft jewelry may be due to large stockpiles of a particular "gem" (for instance, larimar in the Dominican Republic

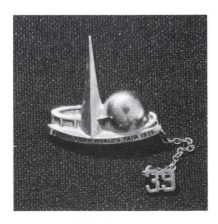

Nearly every World's Fair sold souvenir jewelry, like this pin from the 1939 World's Fair in New York City. Copyright © 2007 by Anthony F. Chiffolo.

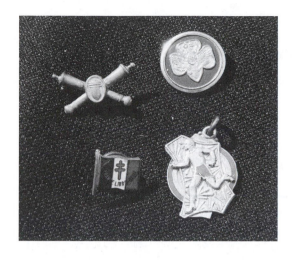

Fraternal organizations, from the armed forces to the Girl Scouts, have jewelry made to symbolize their basic tenets and beliefs. Copyright © 2007 by Anthony F. Chiffolo.

or amber in Russia), proximity to a universally known architectural landmark (Eiffel Tower pins are a major collectible), or exquisite natural settings (there are more Niagara Falls charms and bracelets than one might imagine)—not to mention historical events (Gettysburg Civil War Battlefield belt buckles made of pewter and white metal are manufactured in plentiful amounts). Advertising jewelry is also sometimes referred to as "souvenir."

☞ DID YOU KNOW?

Though not souvenir jewelry per se, organizational pieces are often sold as souvenir jewelry, since they many times trace their origins to an historic event or a commemoration of a particular experience in the life of the wearer. Organizational jewelry includes adornments worn by military and paramilitary groups (such as police and fire departments, Boy Scouts, Girl Scouts and Explorers), as well as clubs, fraternal organizations, schools and colleges, and company or workplace pieces. Many items of organizational jewelry have a high dollar value, but there is also sentimental and pride value that help to determine their worth. Recently a nineteenth-century Sigma Chi fraternity pin sold for $8,000 on eBay, and another from 1852 was posted at $14,000. Neither badge had a lot of gold or gemstones, but to members of their respective organizations, who believe that the pins belong rightly to them as descendants of the original issuers, keeping these insignias out of the hands of outsiders was evidently a top priority.

Titanium

Periodic table symbol: Ti
Atomic Number: 22

Origin of name: named for the Titans of Greek mythology

Important historical background information: "discovered" in 1791 by (The Rev.) William Gregor (1761–1817) at Creed in Cornwall, England[1]

Geographical location of element: Australia, Scandinavia, North America, Malaysia, Kenya; also found in meteorites and in rocks brought back from the Moon; additionally found in coal ash, plants, and humans

Titanium is a light but strong metal that is silvery-white in color; it occurs primarily in the minerals anatase, brookite, leucoxene, perovskite, rutile, and sphene. Though rare in pure form, titanium ores are very common. In fact, there is more titanium in the earth's crust than nickel, zinc, chromium, tin, lead, mercury, and manganese combined.[2] Titanium is corrosion resistant (it can stand up to the ravaging effects of seawater and chlorine) and is a common element found in everyday "white" products, such as typing-correction fluid, toothpaste, paints, plastics, sunscreen, cement, fireworks, copy paper, and jewelry.[3] It is easy to work, paramagnetic, and so strong that it is a major ingredient in the outer skin of aircraft, fire walls, landing gear, and hydraulic tubing.

As a metal alloy, titanium was not commonly used until after World War II. It is most often mixed with molybdenum, manganese, iron, or aluminum in manufacturing; due to its versatility, it has a wide range of practical applications. In fact, in recent years, scientists and manufacturers have seen great advantage to adding titanium to many products on the market. Because it is resistant to corrosion by salt water, it is very popular with shipbuilders and makers of submarines, particularly in parts of vessels that suffer wear in water, such as propellers and rigging (for oil platforms). Divers' knives are often made of titanium, as are spectacle frames and many surgical instruments and joint replacement implants (hip sockets, for instance). In the sports world, titanium is increasingly used in golf clubs and lacrosse sticks, in the manufacture of bicycles, and in outdoor camping and hiking equipment.

Because of its strength and light weight (titanium is 45 percent lighter than steel with comparable strength, and twice as strong as aluminum, while being only 60 percent heavier), it has found a niche among jewelrycrafters, especially those who create men's wedding rings, watch casings, and artificial gemstones. It is available for purchase in many formats, including foil, granules, mesh, nano-sized activated powder, powder, rod, sheets, sponge, and wire. However, it is not an easy metal to craft; making titanium rings, for instance, necessitates a lathe or a mill with a superabundance of power, flexible shaft tools, and a good working knowledge of titanium's unique properties. Titanium, unlike gold and silver, cannot be soldered, and the labor costs of working with titanium tend to make it a more expensive alternative than traditional jewelry metals.

In recent years, titanium has become the metal of choice for body jewelry used in piercings (see **Body Piercing**). The Internet is replete with sites that sell titanium labrets, belly rings, captive bead rings, tongue barbells, nipple rings, nose rings, earrings, spikes, pinchers, plugs, and a host of other innovative items that

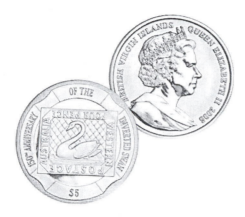

The British Virgin Islands' 150th Anniversary $5 Titanium Coin. (It's blue!)

have quickly become a multimillion dollar phenomenon in the jewelry industry. The time was that sterling silver and gold were the only safe and acceptable materials for body piercings; but because it is hypoallergenic, titanium is being used by most body jewelrycrafters. And why not? It is relatively inexpensive, it doesn't weigh much, and in an industry always looking for something new, titanium is cutting-edge fashion grey (color-neutral), sleek, and durable (hard to scratch or dent)—just what most jewelry buyers are looking for in purchasing a quality heirloom or body adornment.

☞ DID YOU KNOW?

Ever wondered how they got that star in star sapphires? It's the presence of titanium dioxide that causes the white, shiny star reflection, known as an asterism, a reflection that appears when two or more intersecting bands of light cut across the surface of the sapphire, which has been cut in a cabochon (domed) shape. But it's not just sapphires that can exhibit this rare quality. Rubies, garnets, topazes, and various quartzes also export their asterisms when viewed under a single strong light source. Perhaps the most famous example of a spectacular asterism is the one found in the *Rajaratna,* the world's largest ruby (2,475 carats), owned by G. Vidyaraj (1930–), a retired lawyer in India, the descendant of a long line of Vijayanagar rulers that died out in the sixteenth century C.E. Rumor has it that Mr. Vidyaraj is currently looking to sell the ruby, purportedly because he has no way to safeguard it and the many other precious stones he has inherited. The price tag? A mere US$500 million.

NOTES

1. Gregor called it menachite. About the same time as his discovery, Franz-Joseph Müller von Reichenstein (1742–1845) also was able to produce the same substance, but he could not identify what it was. Several years later, German chemist Martin Heinrich Klaproth (1743–1817) "rediscovered" it and recognized that it was a new element. He was the one who named it titanium.

2. Hummel, Richard C., "Titanium" at http://www.csa.com/discoveryguides/titanium/overview.php

3. Titanium, in the form of titanium oxide, is the white food coloring used to print the Ms on M&M chocolate candies.

Tungsten

Periodic table symbol: W

Atomic Number: 74

Origin of name: originally called wolfram (Latin *wolfranium,* hence the periodic table symbol); *tung sten,* in Scandinavian languages, means "heavy stone"

Important historical background information: first speculated by Peter Woulfe (1727–1803/5) in 1779; Carl Wilhelm Scheele (1742–1786) in 1781 and Torbern Bergman (1735–1784) did further speculative work; however, "discovery" of the element as we know it today is credited to Juan José (1754–1796) and Fausto (1755–1833) Elhuyar of Spain in 1783

Geographical location of element: found in wolframite, scheelite, ferberite, and hübnerite ores, whose greatest mineral deposits are located in Portugal, Russia, Bolivia, the People's Republic of China, South Vietnam, and the United States (California and Colorado)

Tungsten is a very hard and heavy transition metal with unique properties: It has the highest melting point, the lowest vapor pressure, and the highest tensile strength of any nonalloyed metal. Tungsten is primarily used in electrical manufacturing, particularly in filaments for lightbulbs and as a component in cell phones and pagers; it is also used in radiation shielding and in the sports world for golf balls and shot. In color, tungsten is steel-gray to white, which makes it ideal when alloyed or pure-crafted for use in jewelry if a platinum-like luster is desired. It is also nearly corrosion-proof as well as hypoallergenic, making it one of the new "hot" alternative materials in jewelrycrafting.

In recent years, tungsten has made a mark in the jewelry world, especially among watchmakers; when formulated into tungsten carbide, it creates a metal so hard (nearly "8"–"9" on the Mohs hardness scale) that it is virtually scratch-proof, making it ideal for watch casings. In men's jewelry, it has become very desirable, especially in wedding bands, as it is lightweight when worked, takes a high polish, and is scratch resistant (it is nearly 10 times harder than gold, 4 times stronger than titanium, and twice as hard as steel). Hence, jewelry made from tungsten nearly always looks new, and its durability often encourages the maker to offer a lifetime-repair warranty.

There are a few drawbacks with tungsten jewelry, however. Due to its hardness, rings cannot be resized; also, it is nearly impossible to engrave on tungsten

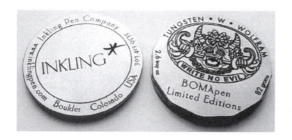

A tungsten coin, produced by the Inkling Pen Company for its BOMA line of products. Used by permission. ® 2003 Micke Scherer, Inkling Inc.

surfaces; if it can be accomplished at all, the results are very faint. Yet tungsten jewelry, because it is both unusual and unusually resistant to the forces of nature, has become very trendy, leading one tungsten jewelry manufacturer to proclaim in its promotions that their product is "high tech . . . , wearable, never rusts, and shows the apotheosis of modern urbanism: freedom, romance, fashion, individuality."[1] According to another manufacturer, tungsten carbide jewelry (along with titanium jewelry) is the fastest-growing segment of the jewelry industry in the last five years.[2]

Like titanium, tungsten is popular in the making of body jewelry, especially for piercings. Modern jewelrycrafters can purchase tungsten in many formats, including foil, mesh, nanosized-activated powder, powder, rod, sheets, and wire. Some tungsten crafters use a process called "vacuum metalizing" to make jewelry and other products from the versatile metal.[3]

☞   DID YOU KNOW?

Many people had a hand in the discovery of tungsten (see above). But in 2003, another layer to the story was added when a farmer in Cornwall, England, discovered a 150-year-old, 42 lb., pineapple-sized hunk of tungsten in a field he was clearing. Known today as the Trewhiddle ingot, its presence was not that surprising on the one hand, as wolfram mines are found all over Cornwall. What made this discovery so unusual was its age and its size. Was it merely a heap of discarded metal that was dumped from a smelting vat centuries ago? A plausible theory, but doubtful. And here's where the story starts to get interesting. It seems that in 1783, the German scientist Rudolph Eric Rapse (1737–1794), author of the fanciful Baron von Munchausen stories, made a surprise and unannounced visit to the mines near Trewhiddle.[4] It was well known at the time that Rapse was interested in the uses of tungsten. Soon after his arrival, there was a terrible fire at the home of one of the site managers of the mines. The speculation is that Rapse had convinced the miner to help him isolate tungsten from the ores in which it is found. This would have required incredible smelting power, at heat reaching more than 3000 degrees Fahrenheit; the process, if poorly managed and with improper equipment, would undoubtedly result in a fire explosion of great magnitude. That is, to be sure, the documented fate of the mines around Trewhiddle. But was the fire a result of an attempt to produce tungsten metal? The discovery of the Trewhiddle ingot, the only one of its kind to date, makes the

Rapse-fire-tungsten metal-theory more than just a flight of fancy; it rewrites the history of who exactly discovered tungsten as we know it today, with a mysterious tale of scientific intrigue that quite literally explodes on the scene.[5]

NOTES

1. "Tungsten Jewelry" at http://www.made-in-china.com/china-products/product viewsaLQxdRgqmZt/Tungsten-Jewelry.html (adapted).

2. See "Tungsten Carbide Rings" at http://www.metalcollections.com

3. See the *Midwest Tungsten Service* site at http://www.tungsten.com

4. The same year that the Elhuyar brothers discovered tungsten.

5. Source: "A Mysterious Metal" at *BBC Inside Out,* http://www.bbc.co.uk/insideout/southwest/series6/tungsten.shtml

Victorian Jewelry

Period: 1837–1901

Birthplace: England

Origins: British goldsmiths and silversmiths

Influences: Queen Victoria (1819–1901), death of Prince Albert (1819–1861), loyalty of British aristocracy, invention of the steam engine, archaeological expeditions to Egypt, Italy, and Greece

Cameos, silver repoussé, mourning jewelry, rolled gold plate, jet, seed pearls, and orange and red corals—when one thinks of Victorian jewelry, it is usually these materials that come to mind. The period of Queen Victoria's reign was one of the most complex and fastest-changing eras of jewelrycrafting in history. Marked by the whims and fancies and ups and downs of Victoria's personal life, the fashion of the times either prospered or suffered depending upon the "royal mood." Once Prince Albert, Victoria's consort (and the love of her life), died in 1861, the mood was decidedly somber, and the queen's moribund and dour self-presentation nearly bankrupted the jewelers of her day.

But there were good days to offset some of the more dismal ones, and the smithies of gold and silver learned to be creative, and above all, they learned to adapt. Accordingly, some would argue that there is no distinct Victorian style, though several design themes were prominent. An emphasis on natural origins, such as flowers, trees, and birds, can been seen in jewelry of this period, especially in the early years of Victoria's reign. Light, delicate designs in silver and gold, with elaborate engraving, were the order of the day. In the latter years of Victoria's reign, repoussé (literally, "pushed out") work in silver was all the rage. Many beautiful pins and hair ornaments, bracelets, and rings featured raised and hollow-backed images of young maidens or lovers at play, reminders of the

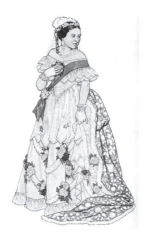

Queen Victoria of England (1819–1901). Notice her girandole earrings, which were royal "hand-me-downs." Used by permission of Tom Tierney from his book *Great Empresses and Queens Paper Dolls,* published by Dover Publications, 1982.

happy days of youth and carefree living. *Cannatille* jewelry was another innovation of the Victorian age. It utilized twisted strands of gold wire wound into elaborate designs.

Almost all jewelry of the early part of the Victorian epoch was either silver or gold. The sterling standard had long been in place at 925/1000 (at the minimum); gold pieces were 18k to 22k. Following the Stamp Act of 1854, the content of gold jewelry was reconstituted and was required to be hallmarked and stamped as either 9k, 12k, or 15k (though some pieces were still created using 18k or higher amounts of gold). At times, jewelers used gold alternatives such as pinchbeck or Prince's metal to keep costs down.

When Victoria came to the throne (at age 18), jewelry was "romantic and nationalistic."[1] Jewelrymaking during the next sixty years went through change upon change, and the Victorian period did, therefore, introduce a few unique innovations in jewelry themes. The most popular designs were those that featured bows, doves, hearts, crowns (of course), crosses, angels, monograms, feathers, knots, arabesques, hands, grapes, thistles, wheat, garlands, arches, arrows, peacocks, ribbons, eyes, scrollwork, tassels, and Celtic images. Cabachon-cut stones, turquoise, amber, bog oak, tortoiseshell, gutta percha, French jet, black pearls, and carnelian also made their first regular appearance during Victoria's reign. This era was also the epoch of the chatelaine, lorgnettes, sweetheart badges (in America), coral pacifiers, and mosaic souvenir jewelry (see **Souvenir Jewelry**) from Italy. The discovery of diamonds in South Africa (then a British colony) in 1867 opened up many new avenues for the jewelrycrafter to employ these most precious of stones in fine pins, bracelets, earrings, and most especially, rings.

The opening of the first department store, Bon Marché, in Paris in 1838 had a profound effect on how the Victorian consumer shopped and purchased jewelry. For the first time, many different types and styles were available to the public at one shopping stop. It was also during the Victorian period that catalog shopping made its premiere, which meant that even folks far away from urban areas could own what everyone in the city had—not to mention that is was delivered and brand new! Therefore, jewelrycrafters soon made their deals with the department and catalog stores, and all too quickly little-known craft studios were being transformed into major manufacturers, thanks in great part to these new windows on the world. In a very similar fashion, the 1851 Crystal Palace Exhibition in London and the 1853 Crystal Palace Exhibition in the United States were major showcases for the works of Victorian craftspersons, introducing their works to masses of potential customers in ways hitherto impossible.

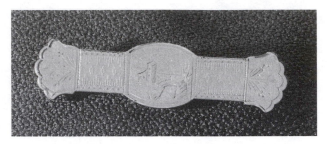

A nineteenth-century chased and engraved pinchbeck pin.
Copyright © 2007 by Anthony F. Chiffolo.

Because the Victorian period overlaps so many other important art movements in jewelry design (Arts and Crafts and Art Nouveau, for instance [see **Arts and Crafts Jewelry** and **Art Nouveau Jewelry**]), it is hard to single out any particular jeweler or craftsperson that is not a standout in a related field. However, one of the most significant moments in the history of Victorian jewelry was the establishment of the House of Cartier. In 1847, Louis-Françoise Cartier (1819–1904), a jeweler's assistant to the great French craftsman Adolphe Picard (d. 1847), took over his mentor's workshop at 29 rue Montorgueil in Paris. Within just a few years he was doing so well that he began to cater to a private and upscale clientele, and he soon opened a second shop. By 1899, the House of Cartier had gone international, with stores in Paris, London, and New York. The work of Louis-Françoise and his grandsons, Jacques (1885–1942), Louis (1875–1942), and Pierre (1878–1964), was so distinctive, so finely crafted, and so classy, that it became the definition of elegance itself. From diamonds (Pierre set the Hope Diamond) to platinum to wristwatches (invented by Louis), the House of Cartier became such a name and so important to fashion and jewelrycrafting that it was not long after Victoria's death that her son, Edward (1841–1910), named the House of Cartier "Jeweler of Kings and King of Jewelers."

Victoria's personal jewelry habits are well documented. The record shows that even after Albert died, she still wore jewelry, including rings on every finger. Among her favorite pieces was the Prince Albert Brooch, a huge sapphire that was given to Queen Victoria by the Prince the day before their wedding. In 1870, finding the official state crown too heavy, she designed and commissioned a smaller crown, which she wore on top of a widow's cap. It was said that Victoria asked to be buried holding a lock of John Brown's (1826–1883) hair (her companion of later years), a custom that was emulated in the mourning and burial jewelry of the well-to-do for years to come (see **Mourning Jewelry**).

☞   DID YOU KNOW?

Pinchbeck, a form of brass, was a very popular metal used in jewelrymaking during Victorian times. An alloy of copper and zinc mixed in proportions so that it resembles gold in appearance, it was easily worked and molded and was much cheaper in cost. Many Victorian pins were made of pinchbeck. Pinchbeck was invented in the 1700s by Christopher Pinchbeck (1670–1732), a London clock-maker. It is sometimes confused with Prince's metal, which is a type of alpha-brass, somewhat yellow in color. Prince's metal was named in honor of Prince Rupert of the Rhine (1619–82), who among his other accomplishments was a well-known seventeenth-century inventor.

NOTE

1. Thomas, Pauline Weston, "Jewellery in Costume and Fashion History" at http://www.fashion-era.com/jewellery.htm

Watches

> Never seem more learned than the people you are with. Wear your learning like a pocket watch and keep it hidden. Do not pull it out to count the hours, but give the time when you are asked. (Lord Chesterfield, 1693–1774)

A watch is a spring-driven timekeeper, and unlike its "parent," the clock, it is a jewelry item that is small enough to be carried on the person. Though clocks have been around for more than 5,000 years in the form of sundials or instruments that measure time with water, watches are a rather recent development in the timekeeping business. This is due to the fact that the driving power behind early clocks was weights, which were heavy and therefore impractical to transport. So it would not be untrue to posit, at least in this instance, that necessity became the mother of invention. Determined to solve the problem, a Nuremberg locksmith named Peter Henlein (1480?–1542) in 1510 (or thereabouts) created a timepiece (within a gilt musk apple, interestingly enough) using a movement made of steel but driven by a balance spring (versus a linear verge that required weights or some other force to make the spring wheel turn). It was a major innovation: His "mini-clock" chimed on the hour and was small enough to be worn on a necklace or chain. But it was expensive and not very accurate. Besides, it had only an hour marker, and every piece had to be handcrafted.

It was not long after that other watchmakers began to experiment in the time-keeping field. Some German and a few watches of French origin are reported as early as 1548, and the Swiss and English products make their first appearance around 1575. Watchmakers spent years trying to perfect the process of increased accuracy. The stackfreed, a spring with a small wheel that attempted to equalize the action of the clock movement, was the German solution; the English and French developed the fusee, a conical-shaped, grooved mechanism that balanced the unwinding of the mainspring; but despite these improvements, watches were years away from being "useful": at best, they were whimsical, attractive pieces of ticking amusement with exotic parts made of brass, catgut, and even stiff hog bristle.

Toward the end of the sixteenth century, astronomical data and dates were beginning to appear on watches, as were Roman numerals, often on porcelain faces, to mark the hours. Other embellishments, such as elegant, enameled casings and unusual shapes, added to the appeal of the watch as a fashion statement. The first glass crystals appear on watches circa 1620, but the glass was opaque and did not allow the user to see through to the face; therefore, watches could only be wound or regulated by opening their covers, either front or back. To this end, every part of the watch casing was decorated, from the intricate steel hands to the hinges to the numbers, which now appeared in Arabic form (1, 2, 3 versus I, II, III). And there were a lot of numbers to look at: Most German and all Italian watches used a 24-hour clock, with numerals 1–12 on an outer circle, numerals 13–24 on an inner ring.

In 1675, a major improvement in watchmaking came to the fore with the invention of the spiral balance spring. This invention (or some say, new usage)[1] allowed watchmakers to create instruments that could mark time with an accuracy of fractions of a minute, occasioning the addition of a minute hand to watches, along with a dial that was subdivided into 60 portions. During this time a fourth wheel was added to a watch's inner mechanism so that it could be wound once a day instead of every 12 hours.

Whether it was coincidental or merely incidental, in 1666 King Charles II of England (1630–1685), who himself was very fond of watches, announced his intention to introduce the waistcoat as the proper mode of dress for every gentleman. This new style in fashion allowed for watches to be worn in the pockets of the coat versus pendant-style from around the neck. Hence, the pocket watch was born.

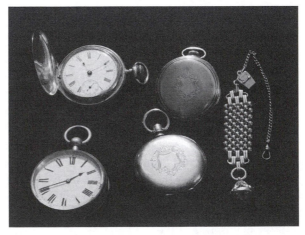

Late nineteenth- and early twentieth-century pocket watches, laid out next to a gold watch fob chain. Copyright © 2007 by Anthony F. Chiffolo.

The eighteenth century in watchmaking showed steady progress toward improvements and incorporation of new ideas. In 1704, watchmakers Nicolas Facio de Duillier (1664–1753), Peter (1689–1720) and Jacob Debaufre developed methods that allowed jewels to be used as bearings (which is why some watches today are listed as 15 jewels or 17 jewels). The Swiss-born Parisian watchmaker Jean-Antoine Lepine (1720–1814) introduced innovations that enabled watches to be thinner as well as assembled and repaired much more easily; he also created a template for watchmaking using individual cocks (the pivots that are between inner plates of the mechanism) that is still in use today. Makers' names appeared on watch faces sometime after 1750. In 1770, a Swiss watchmaker known as Abraham-Louis Perrelet (1729–1825) invented the self-winding watch, and one of the great masters, Abraham-Louis Breguet (1747–1823) was producing them by 1780 in his shop. In 1775, better-class watches had blued hands. All in all, the eighteenth century was an era more concerned with watch decoration than with mechanical updating. Gold and silver, brass and pinchbeck, hallmarked and dust-capped, enameled and bejewelled, engraved and embossed, watchmaking was fast becoming a major jewelry and design industry.

By 1800, a pocket watch that kept accurate time was generally available to the public. After 1800, watches in four-color gold became popular, and by 1830 or so, technology had evolved to a place whereby watches could be wound without a key and time could be set by hand from the outside of the case. Hence, a snap-on bezel was developed, and the hinged back could now be firmly shut, with a small lip to assist in opening the back for cleaning or any other adjustments.

The Swiss were the first to introduce interchangeable watch parts, thanks to the work of Georges-Auguste Leschot (1800–1884); and Frederic-Jalpy (1749–1812) devised machine tools that laid the groundwork for mass production. U.S. companies began volume production, with Waltham (1850), Elgin (1864), and Hamilton (1892) leading the way. The Swiss were not far behind, and by 1880, they too were in the volume business.

The twentieth century has its own share of important enhancements in watchmaking. The wristwatch was invented by Patek Philippe at the end of the nineteenth century, but it was seen as a woman's accessory.[2] Louis Cartier (1875–1942) was responsible for the men's version, having first made one for the Brazilian inventor Alberto Santos-Dumont (1873–1932), who needed a watch he could use more easily while flying. Cartier was able to market the idea in Paris to other gentlemen, and by the end of World War I, the popularity of the wristwatch was well in place. This of course had an effect on the production of pocket watches: Following World War II, their production was minimal. Interestingly enough, the same fashion trend that made pocket watches so popular was also their ultimate undoing: The waistcoat went out of fashion after 1945.

The battery-powered watch came on the market in 1952, and electronic watches, with movements that beat up to 2.5 million times per second (!), were being mass-produced, especially in Asia, by the 1970s. Perhaps one of the most important advancements in watch production during the twentieth century was the invention of the quartz analog watch. This electronic watch uses a piezoelectric quartz crystal as its timing element and as the mechanical movement that drives the hands. The first of these were made in a Swiss laboratory in 1962, but Seiko of Japan was ahead of all competitors in producing a quartz watch for public consumption by 1969. Today there are all types of quartz watches that are kinetically powered, battery powered (silver oxide or lithium), temperature powered, and even solar powered.

Perhaps the most popular watch of the twentieth century was the Timex wristwatch. With its catchy advertising, which focused on "the everyman"—commercials like "Takes a licking and keeps on ticking"—Timex (formerly the Waterbury Watch Company) ticked its way into millions of homes. In the 1950s, one out of every three watches purchased in the United States was a Timex.[3]

In the twenty-first century, the production of watches is a $100 billion fashion and jewelry industry. According to one Internet source that tracks brand name watches through comparison selling, the top ten most popular watches of 2006 were Rolex, Movado, Omega, Tag Heuer, Seiko, Citizen, Breitling, Swatch, Cartier, and Fossil (in that order);[4] but collectors fancy early models of all the major brands, along with some of the old-timers like Gruen, Hamilton, Longines, Piaget, Lucien Picard, and the like.

The most recent innovation in watches is perhaps the cellular telephone, which today has become the "new pocket watch."

☞   DID YOU KNOW?

At the end of the twentieth century, Swiss watchmakers attempted to revive their sagging market share by reinventing themselves. Their analog watches were considered out of fashion, so they joined forces with designers from all over the world and formed a new watch company that could make parts so cheaply that it was more reasonable to throw the watch away than to repair it. Hence the Swiss Watch Company was born (SWATCH for short), and every year, graphic designers are still called together to create a new collection. Today, the SWATCH watch is one of the biggest-selling watches in the industry.

NOTES

1. Just who was responsible for this major turn of events is a matter of dispute. It may have been Dutch mathematician Christiaan Huygens (1629–1695), English physicist Robert Hooke (1635–1703), or English clockmaker Thomas Tompion (1639–1713), all of whom had been experimenting in this arena.

2. Partners Antoine Norbert de Patek (1811–1877) and Jean Adrien Philippe (1815–1894), inventors of the stem-winding watch, named their energy company Patek-Philippe.

3. See "Timex Watches" at http://www.watch-universe.com/timex_watches.htm.

4. See http://www.splise.com/Watches/category_23.html?ref=144&d-7302178-p=1 According to the same source, some other well-known names were in the Top 20: Timex (14), Tissot (15), Tourneau (16), and Bulova (18).

Wood Jewelry

> Who would ever believe that some of the most unusual and striking jewelry in the world comes from plants? . . . In terms of aesthetic beauty and intrinsic value, plant jewelry may rank as high as any gemstone. (U.S. author W. P. Armstrong, *Terra*)

Jewelry throughout the ages has always made use of available materials, so it should come as no surprise that various types of both "exotic" and more common woods have been used by jewelrycrafters to create unique pieces for the buying and wearing public. Though the wood from nearly any tree or bush can be fashioned into a "gem" worthy of admiration, it seems that there are particular plants that lend themselves more easily to fashion design. What follows is a sampling of some of the most-used woods and their jewelry by-products.

BOG OAK

Bog oak (*Quercus petraea,* fam. *Fagaceae*) is a type of ancient wood that has been blackened and preserved by several millennia of submersion in the peat bogs of Scotland and Ireland. It was first used as structural timber for local dwellings as well as for fuel, thatched roofing, rope, and fishing spears. During the Victorian era it was "mined" by local artisans and carved into decorative objects, such as bowls, daggers, chests, and knife handles as well as inexpensive jewelry, particularly mourning pieces.

The process of hunting for bog oak was carried out by neighboring townsfolk who would explore the wet terrain for areas where the dew, frost, or snow would disappear first, suggesting the presence of buried wood. Using a long metal probe to confirm that timber was buried beneath them, the explorers would set about extracting the oak for use by carvers, builders, blacksmiths, fishermen, and others for use in their trades. Bog oak is still being used today to make jewelry and is especially popular among those who treasure the Celtic tradition of living off the land in the ways of their ancestors.

CINNABAR

A wood of the cinnabar tree, cinnabar is very soft and widely used because it is easily carved and molded. However, cinnabar is not the base wood for cinnabar-lacquered items (which is usually bamboo, white pine, or some other wood). What most people relate to as cinnabar is actually derived from a mineral of the same name, a kind of mercuric sulfide; its red color is the mercury extracted from the stone, which is highly toxic. Mineral cinnabar is found in large quantities near hot springs and volcanic sites in Spain, Serbia, Peru, the Hunan province of the People's Republic of China, California, Oregon, Texas, and Arkansas. Despite the dangers inherent in its mining and production, it has been in use for thousands of years and is the main ingredient, along with lacquer (a sap from the Chinese "lac" tree), in cinnabar lacquerware. Among Hindus, cinnabar is the pigment used for the red dot followers put between their eyebrows, and women sometimes put the pigment down the parting of their hair as a mark of devotion.

Cinnabar lacquerware was extremely popular in the entire Victorian era, especially once the trade routes with Asia were reopened in the late 1860s. Many beaded necklaces, earrings, rings, pins, and hair ornaments were fashioned of this product, generally with nature motifs (cranes, flowers, dragons, sylvan scenes) intended to illustrate the spiritual connection between the piece itself and its function.[1] Currently, most good pieces on the market are vintage, although many, many new jewelry items are being fashioned by and exported from Chinese and Japanese artisans today.

EBONY

Ebony is a wood of the Ebony tree (*Diospyros ebenum*), sometimes called Indian Ebony or Ceylon Ebony. The tree is native to southern India and Sri Lanka but is found in Kenya, Tanzania, Mozambique, and other warm-climate lands as well. The heartwood of these trees is highly valued as an ornamental gem, since it has a high density and fine texture and can be polished to a smooth luster. It has been used for many millennia, as is evidenced by its presence in ancient Egyptian tombs. During the sixteenth century in Europe, ebony was used in picture-frame construction and other carvings in Antwerp and gradually found its way to the artisan workshops of Paris, where it was used in cabinetmaking. Piano makers have used ebony as a material for the black keys for centuries.

During the Victorian period, ebony was very popular in jewelry, particularly in mourning wear. It was also an often-used wood in Art Deco jewelry creations. Today, ebony is a typical component in body-jewelry piercings (often for plugs), as it appears to be fairly hypoallergenic (see **Body Piercing**).

KUKUI NUT LUMBANG SEEDS

Kukui Nut Lumbang seeds are seeds of the candlenut tree (*Aleurites moluccana*), the state tree of Hawaii, so called because Polynesian people would ignite the oil inside the nuts for nighttime lighting. Their most common jewelry usage, which is wildly popular in Hawaii and southern California, is a necklace made of highly polished nuts that have been drilled and strung on knotted, black-silk ribbon. (The nuts are hulled during processing, so it is actually the husks that are polished and dyed for most jewelry pieces.) Though lei necklaces are the usual form of presentation, bracelets and chokers are also common. (Another popular wood from Hawaii that is often made into jewelry comes from the koa tree.)

OLIVE WOOD

Nearly every pilgrim to the Holy Land has been impressed by the multiplicity of opportunities to purchase jewelry, particularly crosses and Stars of David, made of olive wood. In fact, olive woodcrafting is one of the largest souvenir industries in the Middle East and North Africa. And it's no wonder: The wood from olive (*Olea europeaea*) trees (which are ubiquitous in the landscape) has a handsomely wavy, natural-red grain that is ideal for carving, and it makes a superb presentation. Many beads for rosaries are also carved from the heartwood branches of the trees, which darken and harden with age after pruning during the yearly harvest. Palmwood, sandalwood, and rosewood are also harvested and carved into jewelry and beads and are common sights in Middle Eastern markets and roadside stands.

PETRIFIED WOOD

Often listed as a gemstone, particularly in the Southwest United States, petrified wood (sometimes called "jasperized wood") is not wood that has turned to stone (a common misconception) but rather a replacement of the original wood by quartzes or other minerals (usually chalcedony or jasper) located in the area where a tree has fallen and has begun to fossilize. The most significant formation of petrified wood is located in Holbrook, AZ, home to the famous Petrified Forest.

Petrified wood is often used in Native American jewelry. According to mystical lore, it is said to be an aid in developing the patience to endure a slow inner transformation and to help develop both physical and emotional strength in terms of self-will.[2]

OTHER NOTABLE WOOD JEWELRY

During the 1930s in the United States, there was a proliferation of colored wood pins, bracelets, earrings, and necklaces that were marked "Made in Czechoslovakia." These, and pieces made by the designer Miriam Haskell (1899–1981), some signed and many unsigned, are popular with collectors of the Art Deco period.

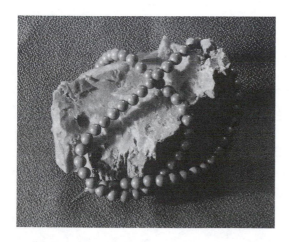

Petrified wood beads displayed on an ancient crosscut of petrified bark. Copyright © 2007 by Anthony F. Chiffolo.

☞ **DID YOU KNOW?**

For more than 200 years, Russian artists have been painting "troika" and other Russian folk scenes (the round dance, or Russian fair, for instance) on wooden and papier-mâché brooches as a kind of cottage industry, especially for the tourist market. It is said that the tradition began with a Russian merchant by the name of Korobov on the outskirts of the village of Fedoskino. He realized that there was money to be made in mass-producing cheap articles of simple materials using durable products like papier-mâché and lacquer—as many as four coats, applied and hand-dried on the wooden surfaces. Sometimes for a fancier look, mother-of-pearl or gold leaf was applied, or powdered silver dusted on—and all were detailed between coatings.

Today, the village of Zhostovo is especially well known for its floral wooden and papier-mâché pins. Most brooches available on the current market are 3" x 2" ovals or 3" rounds, with a simple safety-pin type clasp that has been glued on the back; all are hand-painted or hand-finished, sometimes by well-known artisans who sign their work. The prices range anywhere between US$4 and $300, so if one is an astute shopper, great bargains are to be had.

NOTES

1. See Springer, Carrie, "Cinnabar Lacquerware" at http://www.go-star.com/antiquing/lacquerware.htm

2. "Metaphysical Properties of Petrified Wood" at www.heavenandearthjewelry.com/articles/petrified_wood.html

Bibliography

Aber, Susan Ward. "Imitations and Identification of Amber" at http://www.emporia.edu/earthsci/amber/ident.htm

About.com. "Diamond Carat Weight" at http://jewelry.about.com/cs/thefourcs/a/carat_weight.htm

————."Diamond Cut—Pictures and Facts about Diamond Cuts" at http://jewelry.about.com/od/diamondshapes/ss/cutting_styles.htm

————. "It's about (German Time)" at http://german.about.com/library/weekly/aa031300a.htm

al-Khansa, Safia. "Mistress Safia's Middle Eastern Garb Do's and Don'ts" at http://www.willofyre.com/OriginalSite/Clothing/periodmideastgarb.html

Al Qasem, Fadwa. "Anklets Ahoy!" at http://www.contentmart.com/ContentMart/content.asp?LinkID=24856&CatID=13&content=1

Amazing Adornments. "Glossary of Jewelry Terms" at http://www.amazingadornments.com/

Amazon.com. "Cut Steel Salamander Antique Brooch" at http://www.amazon.com/Cut-Steel-Salamander-Antique-Brooch/dp/B000I30IGU

American Bible Society. *Holy Bible, Contemporary English Version (CEV).* New York: American Bible Society, 1995.

————. *Holy Bible, King James Version (KJV).* New York: American Bible Society, 1911.

American Federation of Mineralogical Societies. "Mohs Scale of Mineral Hardness" at http://www.amfed.org/t_mohs.htm

American Heritage Dictionary of the English Language (4th ed.). New York: Houghton Mifflin Company, 2006.

American Iron and Steel Institute. "Steel in Your Life" at http://www.steel.org/AM/Template.cfm?Section=Steel_in_Your_Life

Ancient Rome History Resource. "Roman Jewellery" at http://www.hadrians.com/rome/romans/fun/roman_jewellery.html

Anderson, Lee. "The History of American Indian Jewelry" at http://www.americana.net/jewelry_history_article.html

Answers.com. "Jewelry" at http://www.answers.com/topic/jewelry

————. "Strontium titanate" at http://www.answers.com/topic/strontium-titanate

Antique Jewelry Online. "Art Nouveau" at http://www.antiquejewelryonline.com/learn/art nouveau.htm

————. "Retro" at http://www.antiquejewelryonline.com/learn/retro.htm

Antiques Roadshow. "Collecting Cameos: Ancient Beauties" at http://www.pbs.org/wgbh/pages/roadshow/tips/cameo.html

Antwerp Blanka Diamonds. "Blanka diamonds, diamond glossary" at http://www.blankadiamonds.be/diamonds/index.htm

Armstrong, Wayne P. "Botanical Jewelry: Necklaces & Bracelets Made From Plants" at http://waynesword.palomar.edu/ww0901.htm#intro

Aufschneider, Michael. "Cut-Coin Jewelry" at http://www.cutcoin.com/

Bachman, Mary. "Collecting Combs As Decorations for the Hair" at http://www.oldandsold.com/articles/article042.shtml

Baker, Lillian. *Fifty Years of Collectible Fashion Jewelry: 1925–1975*. Paducah, KY: Collector Books, 1992.

————. *Hatpins and Hatpin Holders: An Illustrated Value Guide*. Paducah, KY: Collector Books, 1983.

Ball, Joanne Dubbs. *Costume Jewelers: The Golden Age of Design*. West Chester, PA: Schiffer Publishing Co., 1990.

Bates, Carol. "History of the POW-MIA Bracelets" at http://www.miafacts.org/bracelets.htm

BaxtersJewellers.com. "History of the Celts & Inspirations for Celtic Jewelry" at http://www.baxtersjewellers.com/celtic.html

Bawa, Mary P. "Nettie Rosenstein" at http://www.designerhistory.com/historyoffashion/rosenstein.html

Beads and Baubles Café. "Common Types of Chain Used in Jewelry Making" at http://www.beadsandbaublesny.com/wordpress/?p=38

Bellis, Mary. "The History of Plastics" at http://inventors.about.com/od/pstartinventions/a/plastics.htm

————. "Monopoly Monopoly" at http://inventors.about.com/library/weekly/aa121997.htm

Bernardine Fine Art Jewelry. "Zodiac Birthstones: Sun Signs II" at www.bernardine.com/birthstone/zodiac-birthstones.htm

Black, J. Anderson. *A History of Jewelry: Five Thousand Years*. New York: Park Lane, 1981.

Blueheronwoods.com. "Hair Comb History" at http://www.blueheronwoods.com/History Haircombs.htm

BME Enycyclopedia. "Ebony" at http://wiki.bmezine.com/index.php/Ebony

Bond, Constance. "Fabergé's labor of love: a case of cherchez la femme" at http://smithsonianmag.com/issues/1996/march/faberge.php

Bookrags.com. "Hattie Carnegie Biography" at http://www.bookrags.com/biography-hattie-carnegie/

Boullianne, Michelle M. "Gothic Period Jewelry" at http://www.ostgardr.org/costume/mouche.gothic.jewelry.html

Boyle, Beth Maxwell. "Pewter History" at http://www.ramshornstudio.com/pewter.htm

Brepohl, Erhard. "The Theory and Practice of Goldsmithing" at http://www.ganoksin.com/borisat/nenam/nillo-work-10-1.htm

British Broadcasting Corporation. "Inside Out: A Mysterious Metal" at http://www.bbc.co.uk/insideout/southwest/series6/tungsten.shtml

Bulmer, G. "The Battle on the Styles of Victorian Architecture" at http://everything2.com/index.pl?node_id=1511999

Burrows, J. R., and Company. "Founders of the Arts and Crafts Movement 1870–1900" at http://www.burrows.com/found.html

Busetto, Giorgio. "American Silverplate Marks" at http://www.silvercollection.it/americansilverplatemarksTZ.html

————. "Basic Hallmarks Identification" at http://www.silvercollection.it/basichallmarks.htm

Bytheseajewelry.com. "What Is Sea Glass or Beach Glass" at http://www.bytheseajewelry.com/theglass/what.php

Calgary Coin.com. "Ancient Chinese Cast Coins" at http://www.calgarycoin.com/cast1.htm

Cameo Collection. "The History of Cameos" at http://www.thecameocollection.com/html/history.html

Camera, Lucille. "The History and Aesthetics of African Jewelry" at http://www.yale.edu/ynhti/curriculum/units/1993/4/93.04.02.x.html

Cano-Murillo. "Shrinkable plastic jewelry" at http://www.azcentral.com/home/crafty/articles/0419craftyideas19.html

Cherry, John. *Medieval Crafts: A Book of Days.* New York: Thames and Hudson, 1993.

Chevallier, Jim. "Sundries: An Eighteenth century newsletter" at http://www.chezjim.com/sundries/s23.html

ChinaPage.com. "Ancient Archaeological Sites Newly Discovered" at http://www.chinapage.com/archeology/ancient-site.html

ChinatownConnection.com. "Ancient Chinese Jewelry" at http://www.chinatownconnection.com/ancient-chinese-jewelry.htm

China View Magazine. "Ancient Chinese may have worn necklaces 20,000 years ago" at http://www.stonepages.com/news/archives/001639.html

Coakley, F. "Costume" at http://www.isle-of-man.com/manxnotebook/history/dress/dress.htm

Col, Jeananda. "Etui" at http://www.allaboutjewels.com/jewel/glossary/indexe.shtml

Cooljools.com. "Fabulous Facets Manufacturers Hall of Fame" at http://www.cooljools.com/Hall_of_Fame.htm

———. "Trifari Jelly Belly Sterling Vermeil Angelfish Fur Clip" at http://www.cooljools.com/images/TrifariJellyBellyAngelFish.htm

Costa, Alan. "The History of Watches" at http://www.atmos-man.com/historyo.html

Craig, W. J. *The Oxford Shakespeare: The Complete Works of William Shakespeare.* Oxford: Clarendon Press, 1905.

Cummings, Celeste. "Arts and Crafts Movement" at http://anc.gray-cells.com/Intro.html

Dalí, Salvador. *The Secret Life of Salvador Dalí.* Mineola, NY: Dover Publications, 1993.

DanforthDiamond.com. "DiamondHistory" at http://www.danforthdiamond.com/education/diamonds/4cs/diamond_history.htm

Delany, Joseph F. "Use and Abuse of Amulets" in *Catholic Encyclopedia* at http://www.newadvent.org/cathen/01443b.htm

The Delineator. "Hair Ornaments." *The Delineator Magazine.* New York: Butterick Publishing Company, March 1911.

Demiguel, Melissa. "The House of Cartier" at http:www.bellaonline.com/articles/art40598.asp

Dettmers, Christina. "Rococo" at http://www.nehelenia-designs.com/Ye_Olde_Online_Shoppe/Rococo/rococo.html

Department of Medieval Studies at Central European University, Budapest. "Types of Jewelry and their Function" at http://www.ceu.hu/medstud/manual/SRM/types.htm

deSignet International. "History of the Celtic deSigns" at http://www.celticfolklore.com/history.htm

Diamond Bug Blogspot.com. "Bling, Tennis and Wimbledon" at http://diamondbug.blogspot.com/2005/06/bling-tennis-and-wimbledon.html

DiamondRegistry.com. "Grading Diamonds" at www.DiamondRegistry.com

Dickinson, Emily. *The Complete Poems of Emily Dickinson, with an Introduction by her Niece, Martha Dickinson Bianchi.* Boston: Little, Brown, and Company, 1924.

DiscoverIndia.com. "Mauryan and Sunga Periods [321–72 B.C.]—Ancient Indian Costume" at http://www.4to40.com/discoverindia/index.asp?article=discoverindia_mauryansungaperiod

Dollwet, Helmar. *The Copper Bracelet and Arthritis.* New York: Vantage, 1981.

Drewry, Richard D., Jr. "What Man Devised That He Might See" at http://www.teagleopto metry.com/history.htm

Earrings-Earrings-Earrings.com. "A Brief History of Earrings" at http://www.earrings-earrings-earrings.com/history.htm

Edersheim, Albert. "Sketches in Jewish Social Life" [Chapter 13–] at http://www.godrules.net/library/edersheim/edersketch13b.htm

Element Contemporary Jewellery. "Jewellery Culture" at http://www.elementjewellery.com/information-53-jewellery_culture.aspx

Erickson, Carolly. *Her Little Majesty: The Life of Queen Victoria.* New York: Simon & Schuster, 2002.

FengshuiBestBuy.com. "How Cloisonné Belongs to the Art of Royalty?" at http://www.fengshuibestbuy.com/SL10107-wulou.html

Filipponio, Frank. "Car piercing: You've got to be kidding" at http://www.autoblog.com/2006/10/03/car-piercing-youve-got-to-be-kidding

Fishman, Josh. "Carat Weight Measuring Chart" at www.afishman.com

Fowler, Monica Beth. "In Praise of Cameos" in *Antiques and Art Around Florida,* Winter/Spring 1998 at http://aarf.com/fecame98.htm

Franklin, Benjamin. *Poor Richard Improved: Being an Almanack and Ephemeris of the Motions of the Sun and Moon, etc.* Philadelphia: Franklin and Hall, 1753.

Freeman, Jerry W. "Sterling Silver Terms" at http://www.jwmercantile.com/infosilver.html

Gaston, Mary Frank. *The Collector's Encyclopedia of Limoges Porcelain.* Paducah, KY: Collector Books, 1992.

Gemologica.com. "Gold" at http://www.gemologica.com/gold.php

Gemsheaven.com. "Gems Heaven: The Heaven of Rough and Faceted Gemstones" at www.gemsheaven.com/birthgems.htm

"Gilty Pleasures: News of baubles, rings and other glittering prizes." *Mirabella* (October 1992).

G. M. L. Publishing. "Charles Horner hatpins" at http://www.charleshorner.co.uk/p1_hat.htm

Goines, David Lance. "Button Button" at http://www.goines.net/Writing/button_button.html

Goldenmine.com. "Gold Karats" at http://gold.goldenmine.com/goldkarats.htm

Gold Palace Jewelers, Inc. "Coral Jewelry" at http://www.goldpalace.com/coral.htm

Goldpoint Jewelers.com. "Advice on Diamonds: The 5 C's" at http://www.goldpointjewellers.com/index.html

Grant, Lucille. "Fabulous Fakes." *Antiques & Collecting Magazine* (February 1999).

Guyot Brothers Company, Inc. "Jewelry Findings Glossary" at http://www.guyotbrothers.com/jewelry-findings-glossary.htm

Haab, Sherri. *The Art of Resin Jewelry: Layering, Casting, and Mixed Media Techniques for Creating Vintage to Contemporary Designs.* New York: Watson-Guptill Publications, 2006.

Harold Weinstein Ltd.com. "Diamond Grading and the 4 C's" at http://www.hwgem.com/diascale.htm

Harpanddragon.com. "Welsh Lovespoons" at http://www.harpanddragon.com/lovespoo.htm

Hatch, Eric. *The Year of the Horse.* New York: Crown Publishers, Inc., 1965.

Hatpin Society of Great Britain. "History of Hat Pins" at http://www.hatpinsociety.org.uk/history.htm

Hawkes, Jacquetta. *The First Great Civilizations: Life in Mesopotamia, the Indus Valley, and Egypt.* New York: Alfred A. Knopf, 1973.

HeavenandEarthJewelry.com. "Metaphysical Properties of Petrified Wood" at http://www.heavenandearthjewelry.com/articles/petrified_wood.html

Hefti, Diana L. "The World's Most Popular Collectible Secret!" at http://www.worldcollectorsnet.com/buttons/buttonsarticle.html

Holy Bible: New King James Version (NKJV). Nashville: Thomas Nelson Publishers, 1982.

Hothem, Lar. *Indian Trade Relics*. Paducah, KY: Collector Books, 2003.

Hougart, Bille. *The Little Book of Mexican Silver Trade and Hallmarks*. TBR International, Inc.: Distributed by Cicatrix, Washington, DC, 2001.

Hummel, Richard C. "Titanium" at http://www.csa.com/discoveryguides/titanium/overview.php

Hunt, Leigh. "Hair" as found in *Godey's* magazine, May 1855.

Huntfor.com. "Art Deco" at http://www.huntfor.com/arthistory/C20th/artdeco.htm

I'llNeverTellJewelry.com. "Mallorca Pearl Story" at http://illnevertelljewelry.com/generic19.html

J'antiques.com. "Arts & Crafts Era" at http://www.jantiques.com/jewelryhistory/lessons8.html

———. "Assyrian Revival Jewelry" at http://www.jantiques.com/jewelryhistory/revival.html

———. "Georgian Era" at http://www.jantiques.com/jewelryhistory/lesson2.html

Jeffers, Grace. "Plastics" at http://www.wilsonart.com

Jewellery Catalogue co. uk. "Evolution of Jewellery" at http://www.jewellerycatalogue.co.uk/antq/evolution-of-jewellery.php

———. "Edwardian Jewellery" at http://www.jewellerycatalogue.co.uk/antq/evolution-of-jewellery.php

Jewelrymall.com. "Understanding Gold Markings" at http://www.jewelrymall.com/news letters/050426.html

———. "US State Gems, Gemstones, Minerals, Rocks and Stones" at http://www.jewelrymall.com/stategems.html

Johnson, David. "2000 Years of the Necktie" at http://www.infoplease.com/spot/tie1.html

Jonas, Joyce. "Appraising Antique Jewelry: Glossary." (Class work at the New School for Social Research, New York)

Jones, David Three Feathers. "About the Pewtercraft" at http://www.threefeatherspewter.com/pewtercraft.htm

J. Robin Gems. "What Are the 4 C's?" at http://www.jrobingems.com/the4cs.htm

Justine Mehlman Antiques. "Antique and 20th Century Paste Jewelry" at http://www.justinemehlmanantiques.com/Paste%20Jewelry%20Collection%20Page.htm

Kandampully, Victor. "Karats" http://www.oedilf.com/db/Lim.php?Word=carat

Kantouris, Costas. "Greek Hiker Finds 6,500-Year-Old Pendant" at http://abcnews.go.com/International/wireStory?id=1628346

Kent, J. J. "History about Buttons Made from Precious Stones" at http://www.jjkent.com/articles/buttons-stones-history.htm

Kiplinger, Joan. "Vintage Fabrics—In Search of Warp Ends" at http://www.fabrics.net/joan902.asp

———. "Hooked on Buttons" at http://www.fabrics.net/joan902.asp

Komrad, Audrey. "Champlevé with Ferric Chloride" at http://www.ganoksin.com/borisat/nenam/ferric-chloride-champleve.htm

Koon, Larry. *Roycroft Furniture & Collectibles: Identification & Value Guide*. Paducah, KY: Collector Books, 2004.

Kovel, Ralph, and Terry Kovel. *Kovels American Antiques: 1750–1900*. New York: Random House Reference, 2004.

———. "Mexican Silver." *Kovels on Antiques and Collectibles* (June 2006).

Kuntzsch, Ingrid. *A History of Jewels and Jewelry*. New York: St. Martin's Press, 1981.

LaborLawTalk. "Fuller Brooch" at http://dictionary.laborlawtalk.com/Fuller_brooch

Landsberg, Norman. "Diamond Grading" at http://www.normanlandsberg.com/2001/nld2001gia.htm

Lanllier, Jean, and Marie-Anne Pini. *Five Centuries of Jewelry in the West*. New York: Leon Amiel Publisher, 1983.

Ledesma Enterprises. "Pierce Your Ride: Rebel against Conformity" at http://www.pierce yourride.com

Levine, David. "Ancient Coin Jewelry" at http://www.shopnbc.com/product/?familyid= C19516&storeid=1&track=1&taxid=1&propid=974

Luce, Edward. *In Spite of the Gods.* New York: Doubleday, 2007.

Mackmurdo, Arthur. *Wren's City Churches.* Orpington: Kent, England: G. Allen, 1883.

MadeinChina.com. "Tungsten Jewelry" at http://www.made-in-china.com/china-products/ productviewsaLQxdRgqmZt/Tungsten-Jewelry.html

Maginnis, Tara. "18th Century Jewelry" at http://www.costumes.org/History/100pages/ 18THJEWL.HTM

———. "Turn-of-the-Century Detachable Collars" at http://www.costumes.org/HISTORY/ 100pages/collarsmen.htm

Mahajan, Nupam. "India's First Coinage" at http://www.med.unc.edu/~nupam/welcome.html

Martin, Steve W. "Glass Facts: History of Glass" at http://www.texasglass.com/glass_facts/ history_of_Glass.htm

Mason, Anita and Diane Packer. *An Illustrated Dictionary of Jewellery.* New York: Harper and Row, 1973.

Matlins, Antoinette L., and A. C. Bonanno. *Jewelry & Gems: The Buying Guide.* South Woodstock, VT: GemStone Press, 1987.

Maui Divers Jewelry. "Precious Coral" at http://www.mauidivers.com/overview_1.asp

McGrew, John R. *Manufacturer's Marks on American Coin Silver.* Hanover, PA: Argyros Publications, 2004.

McManus, Barbara F. "Roman Clothing: Women" at http://www.vroma.org/~bmcmanus/ clothing2.html

McNamara, John B. "Ancient Christian Jewelry" at http://www.johnbmcnamara.com/index.html

Medalye, Jacqueline. "Coco Chanel's Costume Jewelry" at http://www.medalyedesigns.com/ article_coco-htm

Mephistopheles. "Birthstones" at http://www.oedilf.com/db/Lim.php?Quote=61184&Popup=1

Merriam-Webster OnLine. "Hallmark" at http://www.m-w.com/dictionary/hallmark

Mertz, Barbara. *Red Land, Black Land: Daily Life in Egypt.* New York: Dodd, Mead and Company, 1978.

Mesoamerican Gallery at the University of Pennsylvania Museum of Archaeology and Anthropology. "Adornment and Concepts of Beauty" at http://www.museum.upenn.edu/ new/exhibits/galleries/mesoamericaframedoc1.html

MetalCollections.com. "Tungsten Carbide Rings" at http://www.metalcollections.com

MetricConversions.org. "Carat conversions" at http://www.metric-conversions.org/weight/ carat-conversion.htm

Metropolitan Museum of Art.com. "Southeast Asia, 1000 B.C.–1 A.D." at http://www.met museum.org/toah/ht/04/sse/ht04sse.htm

Michaels, Chris Franchetti. "Kukui Nut Lumbang Seed Jewelry" at http://www.bellaonline. com/articles/art34145.asp

———. "Lucite Jewelry—An Ideal Accessory for the Sunny Months Ahead" at http://www. bellaonline.com/articles/art19939.asp

Midwest Tungsten Service. General Information at http://www.tungsten.com

Milner, Catherine, and Victoria Gurvich. "Bling-bling for dogs," *The Age* (December 9, 2003) at http://www.theage.com.au/articles/2003/12/08/1070732142445.html

Minerals-n-More.com. "The Mineral Cinnabar" at http://www.minerals-n-more.com/Cinna bar_info.html

Moller, Kate. "Arts and Crafts Jewelry Design" at http://www.victorianweb.org/art/design/ jewelry/moller10.html

Morrill, Penny C. *Silver Masters of Mexico: Hector Aguilar and the Taller Borda.* Atglen, PA: Schiffer Publishing, 1996.

Morrill, Penny Chittim, and Carole A. Berk. *Mexican Silver: 20th Century Handwrought Jewelry & Metalwork.* Atglen, PA: Schiffer Publishing, 1998.

Moro, Ginger. "Dutch Arts & Crafts Jewelry—The Amsterdam School 1900–1940" at http://www.modernsilver.com/Dutchartsandcrafts.htm

Muir, Hazel. "Ancient shell jewelry hints at language" at http://www.newscientist.com/article.ns?id=dn4892

Mundy, Oliver. "English Silver Hallmarks 1736–1975" at http://www.horologia.co.uk/hallmarks1.html

Museum of American Financial History. "Mbole Anklet" at http://www.financialhistory.org/EXHIBITS/africa/af_selec.htm

MyAntiqueMall.com. "Collectable Compacts: Style, Fun and Function" at http://www.myantiquemall.com/AQstories/compacts/Compacts.html

My Granny's Attic. "Antiques and Collectibles Questions and Answers: Brazil Silver" at http://www.mygrannysatticantiques.com/html/antique_and_collectible.questi.html

Net-Pearls.com. "History of Pearls" at http://www.jewelry-paideia.com/reference/ref-pearl-jewelry-3.php

Nilestone.com. "Egyptian Jewelry" at http://www.nilestone.com/jewelry-history.htm

Oldford, Kathleen. "A History of Charms and Charm Bracelets" at http://www.mymotherscharms.com/history.htm

Old and Sold Antiques Market and Auctionplace. "German Clocks" at http://www.oldandsold.com/articles01/article580.shtml

Online Encyclopedia of Silver Marks, Hallmarks & Maker's Marks. "British Hallmarks" at http://www.925-1000.com/british_marks.html

———. "Hallmarks of Other Countries" at http://www.925-1000.com/foreign_marks.html

"Online Etymology Dictionary" at http://www.etymonline.com/

Overstockjeweler.com. "Trade Crosses" at http://www.overstockjeweler.com/history.html

Padataditakam. "Anklets" at http://209.85.165.104/search?q=cache:tamDENdasT0J:mgrcentral.com/articles.aspx%3Ftopic%3DTop/Arts/Performing_Arts/Dance/Classical_Indian%26o%3Dxml+Padataditakam&hl=en&ct=clnk&cd=13&gl=us

PalaceGallery.net. "Coptic Crosses" at http://home.sprynet.com/~gipsyped/brooches.htm

Parry, Karima. "Plastic Fantastic" at http://www.plasticfantastic.com/about.html

Pearl-Necklace.info. "Mother of Pearl" at http://www.pearl-necklace.info/mother-of-pearl.htm

Philatheles. *Metamorphosis of Metals* at http://www.levity.com/alchemy/philal1.html

Piercing Pleasures LLC. "Body Piercing History" at http://www.painfulpleasures.com/piercing_history.htm

Platt, Garry. "Amber—Frozen Moments in Time" at http://www.ganoskin.com/borisat/nenam/amber.htm

PreciousPlatinum.com. "About Platinum" at http://www.preciousplatinum.com/output/Page26.asp

"Pre-history Africa & the Badarian Culture" at http://www.homestead.com/wysinger/badarians.html

Pugin, Augustus W. N. *Contrasts: or, A Parallel between the Noble Edifices of the 14th and 15th Centuries and Similar Buildings of the Present Day, Showing the Present Decay of Taste.* London: C. W. Dolman, 1841.

Reeve, Arthur B. *The War Terror: Further Adventures with Craig Kennedy, Scientific Detective.* New York: Hearst's International Library, 1915.

Reif, Rita. "Antiques: The Jeweler's Eye Reflects a Passion for Collection" at http://topics.nytimes.com/top/reference/timestopics/subjects/a/antiques/index.html?offset=20&query=JEWELS%20AND%20JEWELRY&field=des&match=exact

R. F. Moeller Jeweler: "Art Deco Jewelry" at http://www.rfmoeller.com/estate/artdeco.htm

————. "Art Nouveau Jewelry" at http://www.rfmoeller.com/estate/artnouve.htm

————. "Edwardian Jewelry" at http://www.rfmoeller.com/estate/edwardia.htm

————. "Retro Jewelry" at http://www.rfmoeller.com/estate/retro.htm

————. "Victorian Jewelry" at http://www.rfmoeller.com/estate/victoria.htm

Riley, M. E., and Kass McGann. "The Evolution of the Kilt" at http://72.14.209.104/search?q = cache:YSF1DZL_PKoJ:www.reconstructinghistory.com/scottish/medievalscot.html+HISTORY+OF+BROOCHES&hl=en&gl=us&ct=clnk&cd=6

Roberts, Lucy P. "The History of Body Piercings—Ancient and Fascinating around the World" at http://ezinearticles.com/?The-History-of-Body-Piercings—Ancient-and-Fascinating-Around-the-World&id = 2948

Roberts, Luke. "East Asia Cash Coins" at http://www.history.ucsb.edu/faculty/roberts/coins/index.html

Romero, Christie. "Basic Hallmarks Identification" at http://www.modernsilver.com/basichallmarks.htm

RosaryWorkshop.com. "The History of the Rosary" at http://www.rosaryworkshop.com/HISTORYjournalingBead.htm

Rosen, Barbara. "Late Georgian Period Jewelry 1780–1830" at http://www.barbararosen.com/Pages/Georgian.html

Rosenberg, Jennifer. "The History of the Swastika" at http://history1900s.about.com/cs/swastika/a/swastikahistory.htm

Royal Magazin. "Lover's Knot Tiara" at http://www.royal-magazin.de/lovers-knots/loversknots.htm

Rushmore, Louis. "The Crucifix" at http://www.gospelgazette.com/gazette/2002/aug/page2.htm

Scherer, Mike. "Tungsten BOMA Coin" at http://inklinginc.com/

Scrimshaw.com. "Frequently Asked Questions about Scrimshaw and Ivory" at http://www.scrimshaw.com/id2.html

Seiyaku.com. "The Swastika and the Swavastika Crosses" at http://www.seiyaku.com/customs/crosses/swastika.html

Shane Co. "The Four Cs—Carat Weight" at http://www.shaneco.com/jewelry/carat_weight.asp

Sherrow, Victoria. *Encyclopedia of Hair: A Cultural History.* Westport, CT: Greenwood Press, 2006.

Shoppingsense.ca. "About Gold & Gold Jewelry" at http://www.shoppingsense.ca/about_gold_jewelry.htm

Silverman, Abe. "Silver Glossary, Terms and Definitions" at http://www.abesilverman.com/Silver_Glossary_Terms_Definitions.html

SilverMedicine.org. "A History of Silver: A Brief Esoteric Overview of Silver Use" at http://www.silvermedicine.org/history.html

SimplyIrish.com. "The History of Celtic Jewelry Making" at http://www.simplyirish.com/celtic_jewelry_history.asp

Sisters Vintage Button Accessories. "Button, Button, Who's Got the Button?" at http://www.kk-design.com/scti/in103/students/buttons/button_project/home/home.htm

Sly, Peter. "Pewter History" at http://www.pec.on.ca/pewter/history.htm

Smith, Carolyn Steinhoff. "Antique Glass Beads." *The Appraisers Standard* (July/September), 2004.

Smith, Sandra I. "Carats and Karats" at http://ww.ganoskin.com/borisat/nenam/sandra02.htm

Solis-Cohen, Lita. "The Jackie O. Sale: A Marketing Triumph." *Maine Antique Digest* (June 1996), at http://www.maineantiquedigest.com/articles/jack0696.htm

Sommer, Elyse. *Contemporary Costume Jewelry: A Multimedia Approach.* New York: Crown Publishers, Inc., 1974.

Southwestern Native American Trading Post. "Southwestern Silver Jewelry Silversmithing" at http://www.adobeclassic.com/category49/index.html

Splise.com. "Most Popular Watches" at http://www.splise.com/Watches/category_23.html?ref =144&d-7302178-p=1

Springer, Carrie. "Cinnabar Lacquerware" at http://www.go-star.com/antiquing/lacquerware.htm

StateHistoryGuideResources.com. "Texas Symbols, Gemstone Cut: Lonestar Cut" at http:// www.shgresources.com/tx/symbols/gemstonecut

Steingräber, E. *Antique Jewelry.* New York: Frederick A. Praeger, 1957.

Stiver, Stanley L., and David J. Stiver. "Enkolpion" at http://www.crosscrucifix.com/glo ssaryhome.htm

StraightDope.com. "What's the significance of Monopoly game pieces?" at http://www. straightdope.com/mailbag/mmonopoly.html

Strangeblades and More. "Chainmail & More" at http://www.sblades.com/collars.php

SwordsofHonor.com. "Medieval Jewelry" at http://www.swordsofhonor.com/celcrospenwn.html

TACE.com. "Periods & Motifs: Art Nouveau—1880–1914" at http://www.tace.com/ref erence/periods/artnouv.html

———. "Periods & Motifs: Edwardian—1901–1910" at http://www.tace.com/reference/ periods/edward.html

Tait, Hugh, ed. *Jewelry: 7000 Years: An International and Illustrated Survey from the Collections of the British Museum.* New York: Harry N. Abrams, Inc., 1986.

Technische Falkutät der Christian-Albrechts-Universität zu Kiel. "Damascene Technique in Metal Working" at http://www.tf.uni-kiel.de/matwis/amat/def_en/kap_5/advanced/t5_1_ 1.html

ThomasMichaels.com. "Gold" at http://www.thomasmichaels.com/thomasmichaels/gold.html

Thomas, Pauline Weston. "Jewellery in Costume and Fashion History" at http://www.fashion-era.com/jewellery.htm

Thompson, Ryan. "Faq's, Myths and Rumors" at http://famousdiamonds.tripod.com/faq.html

Thompson, Ryan. "The World's Most Famous Diamonds" at http://famousdiamonds.tripod. com/famousdiamonds.html

Thomsom, Gale. "Tiara." *How Products Are Made* at http://www.madehow.com/Volume-7/ Tiara.html

Three Graces. "Glossary of Terms" at http://www.georgianjewelry.com/reference/helpful_terms

TiaraTown.com. "History of Tiaras" at http://www.tiaratown.com/history.htm

Tierney, Tom. *Great Empresses and Queens Paper Dolls.* Mineola, NY: Dover Publications, 1982.

Tolkowsky, Marcel. "Diamond Design" at http://folds.net/diamond_design/

Topazery.com. "Antique Jewelry Periods" at http://www.topazery.com/jewelry-periods.htm

———. "Modern Diamonds" and "Antique Diamond Cuts" at http://www.topazery.com/ antique-diamonds.htm

TourArmenia.com. "Metsamor" at http://www.tacentral.com/history/metsamor.htm

Troute, Elaine. "Fabergé: The Perfect Gift" at http://www.fabergetheperfectgift.com/objets deluxe.html

Truett, William L. "Significance of Cuff Designs of Maya Lords" at http://www.fluffycat.com/ maya/maya.html

Trinidad Trading Company. "Abalone Shell Jewelry" at http://www.trinidadtrading.com/ abalone_shells.html

Tyler-Adam Corp. "The Most Expensive Watch in the World" at http://www.tyler-adam.com/97.html

United States Census Bureau. "Facts for Features: The Opening of the National Museum of the American Indian" at http://www.census.gov/Press-Release/www/releases/archives/facts_for_features_special_editions/002776.html

United States Patent Server. "White gold compositions without nickel and palladium" at http://www.uspatentserver.com/686/6863746.html

Verstandig, Bruce Diller. "What is Estate Jewelry?" at http://www.jeweler.com/estate_and_antique_jewelry.htm

Victorian Bazaar. "The History of Cameos" at http://www.victorianbazaar.com/cameos.html

Victorian Station. "Cameo: Portrait on a Shell" at http://www.victorianstation.com/cameos.html

Von Hase-Schmundt, Ulrike, Christianne Weber, and Ingeborg Becker. *Theodor Fahrner Jewelry: Between Avant-Garde and Tradition: Art Nouveau, Art Deco, the 1950s.* Lancaster, PA: Schiffer Publishing, 1991.

Watch-Universe. "Timex Watches" at http://www.watch-universe.com/timex_watches.htm

Webster, David. "Setting Types & Functions" at http://www.asia-gems.com/jewelry/settings-type-function.php

Weinstein, Harold. "Clarity, Color, and Cut Grading Scales" at http://www.hwgem.com/hwabout.htm

Whitehouse, Richard. "A History of 20th Century Jewelry" at http://www.mschon.com/jewelry history.html

Wiesmann, Shirley. "New and Vintage Costume Jewelry Designers & Manufacturers Reference Information and History" at http://www.jacksonjewels.com

Williams, Robert O. "The History of the Cross" at http://www.cumberlandinn.com/cross/history1.htm

Wilner, Tony. "The Evolution of Art Deco Style Jewelry" at http://www.adsw.org/perspective/2003/Jewelery/

Wikipedia.org. "Abalone" at http://en.wikipedia.org/wiki/Abalone

———. "Art Nouveau" at http://en.wikipedia.org/wiki/Art_Nouveau

———. "Body piercing" at http://en.wikipedia.org/wiki/Body_piercing

———. "Brooch" at http://en.wikipedia.org/wiki/Brooch

———. "Cameo" at http://en.wikipedia.org/wiki/Cameo

———. "Carat (mass)" at http://en.wikipedia.org/wiki/Carat_(mass)

———. "Celluloid" at http://en.wikipedia.org/wiki/Celluloid

———. "Christian cross" at http://en.wikipedia.org/wiki/Christian_cross

———. "Cinnabar" at http://en.wikipedia.org/wiki/Cinnabar

———. "Cullinan Diamond" at http://en.wikipedia.org/wiki/Cullinan_Diamond

———. "Diamond" at http://en.wikipedia.org/wiki/Diamond

———. "Ebony" at http://en.wikipedia.org/wiki/Ebony

———. "Elsa Schiaparelli" at http://en.wikipedia.org/wiki/Elsa_Schiaparelli

———. "Gold" at http://en.wikipedia.org/wiki/Gold

———. "Matthew Boulton" at http://en.wikipedia.org/wiki/Matthew_Boulton

———. "Mercury" at http://en.wikipedia.org/wiki/Mercury_(element)

———. "Nacre" at http://en.wikipedia.org/wiki/Nacre

———. "Pearl" at http://en.wikipedia.org/wiki/Pearl

———. "Pewter" at http://en.wikipedia.org/wiki/Pewter

———. "Platinum" at http://en.wikipedia.org/wiki/Platinum

———. "Rhodium" at http://en.wikipedia.org/wiki/Rhodium

———. "Silver" at http://en.wikipedia.org/wiki/Silver

———. "Titanium" at http://en.wikipedia.org/wiki/Titanium

Winder, Mimi. "What Is a Pow Wow?" at http://www.unh.edu/naca/history.html

Winter, Mark. "Mercury" at http://www.webelements.com/webelements/elements/text/Hg/key.html

Wooley, Richard W. "A Short History of Identification Tags" at http://www.qmfound.com/short_history_of_identification_tags.htm

Wolver Hampton Museum of History. "Japanning: What It Is and How It Developed" at http://www.localhistory.scit.wlv.ac.uk/Museum/metalware/japtech.htm

Wortley Montagu, Lady Mary. "Dining with the Sultana." In Eva Marsh Tappan (ed.), *The World's Story: A History of the World in Story, Song, and Art, Vol. VI: Russia, Austria-Hungary, the Balkan States, and Turkey.* Boston: Houghton Mifflin, 1914.

www.thelongestlistofthelongeststuffatthelongestdomainnameatlonglast.com. "The World's Longest Gold Chain" at http://thelongestlistofthelongeststuffatthelongestdomainnameatlonglast.com/long283.html

www.24carat.co.uk. "Diamonique" at www.24carat.co.uk/diamoniqueframe.html

Wyrdology.com. "Diamonds—A Girl's Best Friend" at http://www.wyrdology.com/stones/natural/diamond.html

Xinhua. "Ancient Chinese May Have Worn Necklaces 20,000 Years Ago" at http://english.people.com.cn/200512/15/eng20051215_228143.html

ZuluMoon.com. "Jewelry Glossary of Semiprecious Stone and Silver Terms" at http:www.zulumoon.com/glossary/S-glossary.htm

Zwerdling, Dan. "Electronic Anklets Track Asylum Seekers in U.S." at http://www.npr.org/templates/story/story.php?storyId=4519090

Index

Page numbers in **bold** indicate encyclopedia entries.

About the Author

RAYNER W. HESSE, JR. (THE REV. DR.), is the author, with Anthony F. Chiffolo, of *We Thank You God, for These: Blessings and Prayers for Family Pets* and *Cooking with the Bible: Biblical Feasts, Food and Lore.* A graduate of Union Theological Seminary and the General Theological Seminary in New York, he completed his doctoral work at New York Theological Seminary in 2005. Dr. Hesse is also an appraiser, auctioneer, and owner of Memory Lane: Antiques and Collectibles in Hartsdale, New York. He is a frequent lecturer and columnist on the antiques circuit and has hosted a cable television show as well as a radio call-in show on antiques and collectibles. At present he is working on a fourth book to be published in 2008. Dr. Hesse is an ordained Episcopal priest serving a parish in New Rochelle, New York.

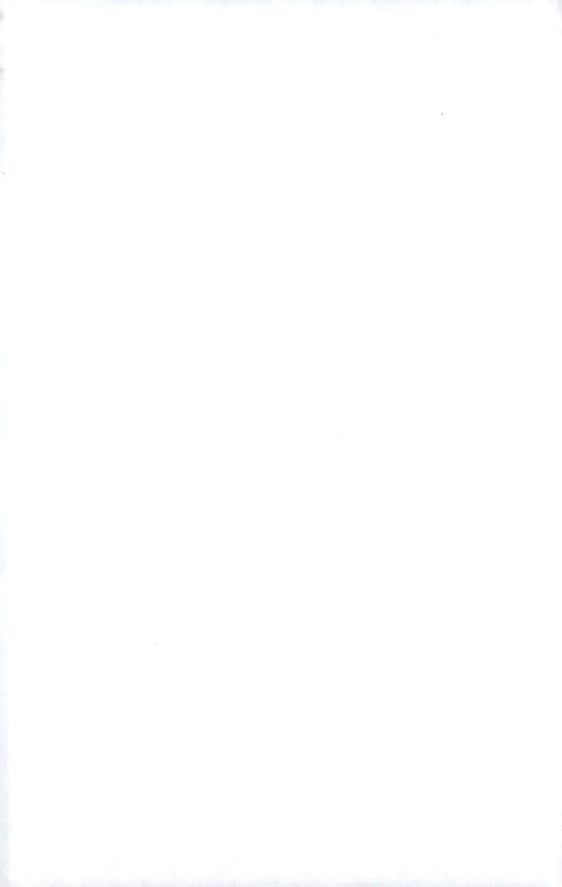